TIME PRISON

THE LOST BOOKS OF JESUS AND JOHN

ELIJAH HASCOM

ARCHWAY PUBLISHING

Archway Publishing books may be ordered through booksellers or by contacting:

Archway Publishing
1663 Liberty Drive
Bloomington, IN 47403
www.archwaypublishing.com
1 (888) 242-5904

ISBN: 978-1-4808-5488-8 (sc)
ISBN: 978-1-4808-5489-5 (e)

Library of Congress Control Number: 2017918466

Print information available on the last page.

Archway Publishing rev. date: 12/26/2017

Dedication

In dedication to those who came before me and those who will come after. Strong is the voice of many when we are the voice of one that is righteous and fair. To my only begotten son, love conquers all.

"I'm taking down notes from the voices inside
The windows are open that trap all the flies
In the innocent life, innocent life, innocent life"

Acknowledgements

A special thanks to Reuben Perez. A man who took a book many would not dare touch.

Ruben Perez
Author/Ghostwriter/Screenwriter
https://www.amazon.com/author/rubenperez

rubenous12000@gmail.com

I also want to thank my mom for believing in me when many did not and her financial support through very rough times.

Contents

Prologue

In birth by God we are never forgotten. We rise from the dust and we fall to the dust. Great minds rise and fall, and great spirits live on to tell their tale. This is the story of Jesus & John who were legendary among men.

Time BC-AD

Turn out the lights don't fall asleep
Let me take you back to a place called memory
Read the words of a master's hands and decide for yourself
Time was like a waiting book sleeping on my shelf
Tick tock tick tock, forward backward through the plains of time
I'm still looking at the cross, that none can deny
Tick tock tick tock, forward backwards around I spin
Here I am today just waiting on a friend
Tick tock tick tock, I'll open your mind to see
Time was like a waiting book, time is BC-AD
Read the words of a master's hands and decide for yourself
Time was like a waiting book sleeping on my shelf

I

OUR FOREFATHERS

Ecclesiastes 1:9-11 *What has been will be again, what has been done will be done again; there is nothing new under the sun.* **10** *Is there anything of which one can say, "Look! This is something new?" It was here already, long ago; it was here before our time.* **11** *No one remembers the former generations, and even those yet to come will not be remembered by those who follow them.*

The greatest enigma of this globe is its creation and who were our ancestors of long ago. We have many questions today, which none of them can't be answered with great certainty. When we bring God into the picture, the mystery gets more complex and becomes the topic of many arguments. We, as humans, must question good and evil and what are the intentions of God. If evil did not exist, there would be no need for God nor would there be a need for His son, Jesus Christ, which is spoken about in the biblical scriptures. Today, we have law enforcement, military, and intelligence powers that use their skills in gathering data to implement the law as it is written uniquely to each state and province. As it is on earth, so it is in the heavens. Many matters that we serve today as a society are symbols of our past or are at once linked to the former and have been re-attested in the universe we dwell in today. The laws that we have today were passed down through time and have lived among humans because we trust in the value of those laws for the most part. Of the first laws ever recorded and written were given to Moses on Mt. Sinai by the Lord of the Heavens. Those who live in the heavens, which are spoken about in Revelations, have their own set of laws. They are borne away in a comparable way, as here on dry land.

Revelations 12:7-8 *Then war broke out in heaven. Michael and his angels fought against the dragon, and the dragon and his angels fought back.* **8** *But he was not strong enough, and they lost their place in heaven.*

In the book, *20,000 Leagues under the Sea*, author Jules Verne, envisions and describes many effects that would soon come to be on earth, but had not yet been. There was also a man named Albert Einstein, who came up with theories on relativity and time travel. Benjamin Franklin, one of our founding forefathers, discovered electricity or so he may have thought.

There are people all throughout time who came up with inventions or ideas that brought advancement to humans. We are becoming aware that our early ancestors who used architecture were a lot more intelligent through history than we first realized. There is nothing new in this world, it has only been altered, reinvented, or made better. I will try to explain with great patience many things under this sun so you, as my people, understand who we are and the price we must pay on behalf of our forefathers. We, as humans, are finally ready to realize who and what we are. I, am but a common man born from the spirit of the ages. It is significant for me to enlighten humanity of certain events that happened through the ages. Not every creature that exists in this universe is of human origin; however, they have sent representatives to speak on their behalf many times. I am a voice of that representation of the power of the Holy Spirit. Some may say *this guy is crazy* or even *a fool* to me but that is ok, I will accept that. I know the price our ancestors have paid as well as my own price. Many were not ready to pay such an excessive cost.

The body of Christ and the forerunner of the Christ stand for a connection to the heavens. This is how it was set up long ago by powers that are greater than the mind of the common man can grasp. The power of Jesus Christ comes from the resurrection of the spirit. The wisest of souls have walked this earth many times. I must say this right off the bat so that you will know knowledge is based on time. Knowledge comes from many walks and many paths on this earth. "I have walked this world many times", so says the Holy Spirit, "because there is much suffering on this earth, my arrival suggests a countdown from the heavens." Will we change our ways for the better or will things continue to get worse?

The heavens intervened long ago to save us from ourselves and to protect others. Our ancestors, being greedy and reckless with technology, were forced from the heavens down to this earth. This was the great war of Michael the archangel, and the dragon that is mentioned in the book of Revelations. War is war, I am a prisoner to the Holy Spirit who dwells among men. Woe to the inhabitants of this earth.

Revelation 11:17-18 "*We give thanks to you, Lord God Almighty, the One who is and who was, because you have taken your great power and have begun to reign. **18** The* *nations were angry, and your wrath has come. The time has come for judging the dead, and for rewarding your servants the prophets and your people who revere your name, both great and small and for destroying those who destroy the earth."*

Revelation 12:7-8 *Then war broke out in heaven. Michael and his angels fought against the dragon, and the dragon and his angels fought back. **8** But he was not strong enough, <u>and they lost their place in heaven</u> {physically, among the stars}.*

These events have passed, I will reveal the timeline of the book of Revelations in a way that no other man has attempted. With that, you may judge me in the authenticity of the Holy Spirit. The war in heaven ends halfway in the Revelation of Jesus Christ. This is very important in setting up the thousand years as well as the second coming of the Lord's army. The battle of heaven has already been fought. We must adhere to a strict timeline to decide if the year 2000 is considered a part of the thousand years in the book of Revelations. Soon you will see that my interpretation is correct as I break down "time" with complete thoroughness. You will then know that Jesus is Lord and Savior by the power of unhuman hands. He is heavenly wisdom when we need it the most. I suffer in the flesh to give glory to the highest.

Greetings and salutations friends, colleagues, and scholars of science and truth. I will start this book by giving acknowledgment to those men seeking truth, not only in Scripture but in science itself. Certain Biblical scriptures were clearly intended for those who would view them later in time and can put the pieces of a puzzle together to make sense of it. I speak from the silence and I truly believe it is better this way. Life has given me many demons to battle but it is the truth of time I wish to reveal to all so that the mystery of God, as I know him, can be understood.

When I read books such as *Chariots of the Gods* written by Erich Von Daniken, I become excited that there are men who would seek out the origin and roots of humanity. We are now in a space age, race to seek out new life as well as new science to protect the planet and propagate the advancement of humanity. We must wonder was it ever like this for our ancestors whom we know very little about. I am an enthusiastic fan of *Ancient Aliens*, a show that is being broadcast on cable television, which shows many forms of evidence supporting the belief that our ancestors came from the sky. In this show, we are shown to be descendants and the offspring of these incredible people who built structures that are beyond our imagination and ability today. *Ancient Aliens* cast put together many forms of evidence to help us draw conclusions about our ancestors. They do a respectable job of bringing facts to the table and laying them out. Most people will never see things the way other people see them. Thus, the reason there are many debates about religion and spirituality in this world.

The greatest weapon of Jesus Christ is the truth of his words, not miracles. We will talk of miracles later in this book as it is highly important to do so. Therefore, I will write to you anonymously in this day. What I write is not something I wish to debate with anyone. It is my interpretation of many biblical events that have happened and will happen. The Holy Bible tells us we can bypass all this knowledge by truly believing the Holy Spirit of Christ is our redeemer. This is absolute truth when it comes to the believer. This is a book for those who are unsure who Jesus Christ was, is, and will be. As well, it is a book of time and recorded history by the power of the heavens.

Is it really that hard for us to think that our ancient ancestors built such complex structures when we see them every day in modern times? It would seem we are close to being just like them in many ways. Although certain architectural designs and technologies perished with the people that created them, we have great minds who follow them. Look at the Washington Monument, Mount Rushmore, and the Statue of Liberty. Look at our complex courthouses, libraries, and the capital building. The symbols on some of these massive architectural structures we have today can be traced back to Roman and Egyptian civilizations. These are tributes to our ancient ancestors who were very gifted in mathematics, stone carving, and building very complex structures. Any time a kingdom is built so large that it reaches the ends of the earth for all to hear, you become a target. You will always have others that say it should be mine.

Our earth is made up of many levels of sediment; time goes back billions of years. I can assure you there are many documents and many items that people have unearthed or discovered, and they have been sealed away in vaults where the eyes of most people will never get to see. We, as modern-day humans, in many parts of the world, are not too different from our Egyptian ancestors. Although, we talk, look, and dress differently. We are very similar.

If you look at an American culture you will see the similarities; for example, we have the Egyptian pyramid on the dollar bill for our modern currency and we build massive stone structures and idols just as they did. Oddly enough, we also treat our dead as the Egyptians did by embalming them and dressing them for view with trinkets and tokens of this life. In case anybody did not notice <u>we are mimicking our ancestors</u>. It is not a crime to mimic or copy our ancient ancestors which I'm aware of. It would only seem natural for us to follow them, being they were our descendants. When we follow in the footsteps of our ancestors, we must look very closely at the cause of their destruction. Every kingdom that was a superpower in the history of this earth has fallen victim to war, disease, or natural disaster. As quickly as a kingdom can be built, it can fall, and something or someone will take its place. Humans have been the superior power in this universe for ages, before Michael, the archangel forced our ancestors to the earth. When we speak of Michael, we're not talking about a human being but a spiritual being that inhabits a vessel for a very specific reason and is the work of the Holy Spirit.

I come not to remind the reader of our troubled past, but to be a reminder of how all kingdoms have failed. There's only one kingdom that will stand the test of time, the kingdom of Jesus Christ. This kingdom is not built on a whim nor extravagance. It is a kingdom built on time and righteousness, so that it can last forever. May His glory be to those who believe the message that I deliver. I've come in this life to speak to you as an author and tie many events together in the history of man. I would like to be thought of in this way so you may have a greater understanding of our past and our future. When we look at the architectural techniques of ancient Egypt from a scientific prospective, as a modern race, we are completely amazed. This tells us something very specific. Advanced technology existed prior to our voyages into space and the creation of the microchip. It may have looked different and worked in a different way; however, advanced technology did exist. As advanced and sophisticated as the Egyptians were as a race of humans, they were also very different. When I say different, what is it that I mean? The Egyptians were the first advanced race known to have certain ceremonies affiliated with the afterlife and death. This shows a distinction between an advanced race and an unevolved race, such as the linage of Adam in the book of Genesis.

The Egyptians were on their way to perfecting the art of completely preserving a dead corpse. This is not seen in any other civilization known here on earth until around the time of the first Pharaohs. This is one of the great mysteries left behind by our early ancient ancestors. I will talk about evolution further down the road, yet leave you with this until we get there. What type of evolving man or woman decides one day to remove the organs and brain matter of another human to preserve their flesh? I must admit that sounds rather strange. We would have to wonder where this evolution came from. That would be a very odd way for humans to evolve. Not only did the Egyptians build a pyramid so great in size that it could be seen easily for miles upon the earth, it also could be recognized from the heavens just as easily. Their pyramids had very specific alignments to the heavens per several different sources. Most people today do realize these cities with pyramids and other advanced structures all over the world, were built by superior men many centuries ago. Thus, the next great question would be why. Why great big sphinxes and tomb guardians? Why Anubis with the ceremonial death mask of a canid or wolf? Why did they have chambers and dark tunnels in these constructions? Where did they all come from? Why did they build elaborate structures for their dead Pharaohs? Who taught them this ancient wisdom? These are the questions that will need many answers. Let us start by talking about ceremonies and sacrifices that are mentioned in the Old Testament. I wish to start here specifically to show the value of correct interpretation of scripture as well as the result of misinterpretation. I will show you how religions have become corrupt or tainted at the hands of men who called themselves priests or high priests of religion. Therefore, Jesus issues a letter to the seven churches of Asia. They all had one thing in common, they emulated religious from those that came before them or those who are thought to have come from the sky, such as the 1st Pharaoh. Each time a ceremony was recorded it was either translated from the writings or copied by those it was passed down to. I will show you how this can be very dangerous and misleading for those who like to follow trends. Although this is the most boring chapter of the book, I must show you how easy it is for people to be deceived by religion. When you do something in the name of heaven and the Holy Spirit you must decide authenticity of origin. That is easy, if it is based on love. I will then discuss in depth the Revelation of Jesus Christ and the heavier aspects of good and evil, as seen by the eyes of the Holy Spirit.

All interpretations of scripture are based on my studies of history combined with biblical scriptures. Some information out there is like my own or certain cases already are widely known by devout students of scripture. I have never considered the book interpreted in the way I will try to answer. History is specific and so is the revelation of Jesus Christ. I must carefully put out all the facts to be sure the script is completely understandable to the usual reader. I believe I have walked this world many times before which gives me an exceptional ability to understand biblical and historical events. When it talks of the first resurrection in the book of Revelations, it is for those who were executed by the beast for their testimony of God. That's me! In that regard, I feel I own the right to interpret these books to you in the clearest way possible. This is my firsthand account and translation of the book of Genesis, Exodus, and the book of Revelations. When I speak of a character of the bible or the nature of the cosmos, it is in perspective of the Holy Spirit, and the power of resurrection. I cannot cite the source of information behind that, it would be impossible. I will use the term, per my past life theory to be given with citing sources and copyright issues. I must say from my point of view, it's hard to be in violation of copyright law when you believe you are the generator of those scripts.

You may take this whole book as theoretical, fact, or fiction. It is a story based on the seven spirits of God mentioned in the Holy Bible. All poetry is the personal work of *Elijah Hascom*. The life of Adam, Moses, Elijah, Jesus, John the Baptist, and John the Prophet are intertwined very intimately. You will soon see from my story that life is a revolving cycle. The Holy Spirit speaks for the seven sons of God in a unique manner. Sometimes within poetry, music, or bible verses. Sometimes through riddles and puzzles. Today is the day of blunt honesty and an exact depiction of time. This is my rendering of time as I have viewed it through my eyes. I have traveled an ocean of stars to give glory to my Risen King. As I mentioned, you need not accept my words as fact or fiction, but know there is great wisdom behind them.

These are the lost books about Jesus and John the Baptist.

II

BURNT OFFERINGS

A burnt offering in Judaism, is a sacrifice first described in the Hebrew Bible in the book of Noah. In the First and Second Temple period, the burnt offering was a twice-daily animal sacrifice. The offering of the animal was completely consumed by fire on the altar. However, the skin was not burnt and was preserved for the high priests and their priestly division. These skins were mentioned as one of the twenty-four priestly gifts in *Tosefta Hallah*. How do you completely consume an animal with fire and not burn the skin? You would have to remove the skin or skin it before fire consumed it? What type of god would need a twice-a-day animal sacrifice like that? Why did the priests receive the skins of the people's daily sacrifice? Could some priests have possibly taken the finest cuts after skinning the animal before consuming it by fire? Is this an early form of tithing to the priests of the temple? That's seems to be a waste of a lot of meat! When we talk about killing animals today, most of us do not like to see animals being killed whether for food or ritual. Today, if people had to watch animals slaughtered before their food was placed on the table every night, most people would not eat the meat. In the Book of Genesis, many believe God requested Adam and Eve to be vegetarians in the garden of paradise.

*Genesis 1:28-31 God blessed them; and God said to them, "Be fruitful and multiply, and fill the earth, and subdue it; and rule over the fish of the sea and over the birds of the sky and over every living thing that moves on the earth." **29** Then God said, "Behold, I have given you every plant yielding seed that is on the surface of all the earth, and every tree which has fruit yielding seed; it shall be food for you; **30** and to every beast of the earth and to every bird of the sky and to everything that moves on the earth which has life, I have given every green plant for food"; and it was so. **31** God saw all that He had made, and behold, it was very good. And there was evening and there was morning, the sixth day.*

These verses are debated; however, I'm sure that this is the case. I think most of us will agree after the flood there was a great demand for protein on this earth. Therefore, Noah built an ark at God's request. The ark was to preserve a linage of certain animals here on the earth for food, domestication as well as beauty. No, the earth was not completely flooded, only the regions in which many were living. So, the animals they took were necessity creatures. The book of Revelations is based on events in around the Mediterranean. Europe, Asia Minor, North Africa, and Babylon. I will prove this with great authority. You're not fitting a pair of elephants and giraffes on an ark, the stench would kill you after 40 days. How would Noah and his family catch two of every living animal on the planet? They would and could not. That would be a recipe for disaster putting a lion and tiger with domestics.

We must ask ourselves some very specific questions to understand the sacrifice that comes after the flood. Was the sacrifice at the first and second temple of Jerusalem exactly what the Lord told Noah, Isaac, and Moses to do? It is very strange that Abraham was willing to kill his son and give him as a sacrifice on the altar to the Lord and his angels. He seemed very confused. Today, we call that Satanism. We can say at the least and agree that it sounds very demented that he would do this. We must have a greater understanding of this sacrifice when used as a daily ritual in the first and second temple of Jerusalem. This is something we must give a lot of thought, so that we might have greater clarity of God of the Old Testament. Why would the God of all universes and creation want to see an animal slaughtered and burned into ash? We can see that Abraham loved God and his angels to heart. Whatever the meaning was behind this sacrifice, he was willing to do it instantly even if it required his son's life. What was Noah's intent when he sacrificed an animal to appease what seems to be God's strange fetish? Was this God a physical being or a spirit? Could this sacrifice in the Old Testament be some type of ceremony where they cooked meat and offered it to God and then was taken out of context later? I highly question the slaughter and burning of an animal into ash just to appease the holy spirit of heaven. I will use the terminology GOD many times in this book. When I use this terminology, I am referring to someone or those who came from the heavens. I will use it in place of a name and or names which I do not know in each time I am discussing. In the case of burnt offerings let us see what God told Moses. We must always be very careful about people's translation of scripture and practicing of sacred ceremonies until we understand what they really mean. Let us read what Moses was told at the Mount of Sinai by the Lord. If God is the same in the beginning as he is in the end, we can get a very clear understanding of burnt offerings in the time of Moses with this translation.

*Numbers 28:1-8 The Lord said to Moses, **2** "Give this command to the Israelites and say to them: 'Make sure that you present to me at the appointed time <u>my food offerings</u>, as an aroma pleasing to me.' **3** Say to them: 'This is the <u>food offering</u> you are to present to the Lord: two lambs a year old without defect, as a regular burnt offering each day. **4** Offer one lamb in the morning and the other at twilight, **5** together with a <u>grain offering</u> of a tenth of an ephah of the finest flour mixed with a quarter of a hin of oil from pressed olives. **6** This is the regular burnt offering instituted at Mount Sinai as a pleasing aroma, a food offering presented to the Lord. **7** <u>The accompanying drink offering is to be a quarter of a hin of fermented drink with each lamb.</u> Pour out the drink offering to the Lord at the sanctuary. **8** Offer the second lamb at twilight, <u>along with the same kind of grain offering and drink offering that you offer in the morning</u>. This is a <u>food offering</u>, an aroma pleasing to the Lord."*

You will notice God selects a perfect cut of a very tender type of meat. Lamb is an expensive butcher's cut for roasting or grilling. Lamb, hogget, and mutton are terms for the meat of domestic sheep at different ages. He, as well requests a fermented drink and a grain offering. This would be a very high-class meal in the biblical days. It also will tell us a lot about the God of Moses. In the case of Numbers 28:2, I believe all you have to do is read these verses correctly. Have you ever been out camping or in a place far way and enjoyed the smell of grilled or cooked meat? I go crazy when my neighbor brings out his barbecue grill, the smell is so phenomenal. I will show you why you must question translation so we don't get the wrong idea about these people of long ago.

When the Lord first meets Moses on Mt Sinai, he warns them not to bring their flocks up to the mount or they would surely die, with good reason. I will explain this when I have spoken of Moses in greater detail in a later chapter. Why would the Lord, who created all living things, save those flocks just so he could watch them be sacrificed? Sacrificed on an altar two times a day for the sheer pleasure of aroma and ash. Now that's heavy and hard to believe. I would find that a little bizarre. It would seem the interpretation of burnt offering was lost somewhere thereafter. It is very like when Aron turned the people's gold into a calf and they worshipped it out of ignorance, they didn't know any better. I completely disagree with any translation of ancient scripture or ceremony that says the Lord of Heaven was pleased to watch an animal carcass be consumed by fire into ash just for aroma. Although, there is a big difference between God of the Old Testament and Jesus Christ. I surely know: the way of the Father.

When God was up on the mountain, what did He and Moses ate? God had already told Moses for them not to bring livestock up on the mount. We know from scripture that Moses people were angered and frustrated because he was up on the mountain for so long. I think we might know exactly what Moses and the Lord ate: the offering of the Israelites. They sat up on the mountain and enjoyed the finest cuts of meat, wine, and grain that you could possibly have. They did this while the Lord of Mt. Sinai, a master stone mason, carved out the 10 commandments. I imagine the Lord did not have a barbecue grill in the vessel that he descended in from the heavens. The Lord almighty arrived in something clearly described as a ball of fire that shakes the mountain as it is engulfed in smoke. It is quite possible he did not have ice or a refrigerator either. Cooked meat and smoked meat last much longer than someone bringing a carcass up the mountain. I hope you can understand what I'm trying to explain. We now know God and his angels had to eat just as Jesus Christ had to eat. And we know Jesus is the image of the Father. We know the Lord is a physical being because he handed a carved stone to Moses with the Ten Commandments, twice. If anybody today asked you to slaughter and burn two animals daily in the name of Jesus Christ or God you would tell them go jump in a lake, rightfully so. If it doesn't make sense, why would we believe it? Now if people arrived in a vessel from the heavens, teaching mankind, I'm sure most people would accommodate their offering in whatever way they could. Why would God have his people waste two animals a day and take away food from these people who were very unsure of their future after a great exodus? I can assure you on behalf of the Holy Spirit, no one needed to burn or slaughter animals to atone for their sins. This is what God requested for being their spiritual teacher. The only atonement that is being recognized is the error of the father who lived luxuriously off his people. If you read on in the verses after Numbers 28:8, you will see the Lord of Mt. Sinai loved his wine and food. It was given as continual offering at his request. In the people's eyes, there was no doubt the Lord of Sinai held great power and Moses was an extension of that power.

I am astonished and amazed the burnt offering was ever made into such a brutal act. Maybe they were hoping it would bring the return of the God who smote the Egyptians with great power. The angels and God did not return and the people were filled with sorrow because of their enemies. I do not blame them for trying, the Holy Spirit is forgiving in such matters. We still have people today in this world that sacrifice animals and pray before Gods of stone.

If I'm writing a book to help you with translation in the modern day, we can be sure many people are lost in God's word. Scripture tells us Jesus Christ is the Holy Spirit and the word of God. Let it be so that he is the only thing we need to redeem us from the bondage of sin. Let us not be misguided about ancient ceremonies and those who worshiped stone idols and slaughtered animals and humans to appease gods. This is the way of our forefathers and therefore, we need the Holy Spirit to give us further knowledge and instruction of those who reside in the heavens. Any time you have people who worship an object that was left behind by the ancients you are committing a sin of our forefathers. Any time you sacrifice an animal or human in the name of God you are committing a serious sin. There is a big difference between sacrifice and giving thanks. Let us study these last set of verses before we move on, to get some greater clarity before we abandon this subject.

The Offering of Isaac *Genesis 22:1-14 Now it came about after these things, that God tested Abraham, and said to him, "Abraham!" And he said, "Here I am."* **2** *He said, "Take now your son, your only son, whom you love, Isaac, and go to the land of Moriah, and offer him there as a burnt offering on one of the mountains of which I will tell you."* **3** *So Abraham rose early in the morning and saddled his donkey, and took two of his young men with him and Isaac his son; and he split wood for the burnt offering, and arose and went to the place of which God had told him.* **4** *On the third day Abraham raised his eyes and saw the place from a distance.* **5** *Abraham said to his young men, "Stay here with the donkey, and I and the lad will go over there; and we will worship and return to you."* **6** *Abraham took the wood of the burnt offering and laid it on Isaac his son, and he took in his hand the fire and the knife. So, the two of them walked on together.* **7** *Isaac spoke to Abraham his father and said, "My father!" And he said, "Here I am, my son." And he said, "Behold, the fire and the wood, but where is the lamb for the burnt offering?"* **8** *Abraham said, "God will provide for Himself the lamb for the burnt offering, my son." So, the two of them walked on together.* **9** *Then they came to the place of which God had told him; and Abraham built the altar there and arranged the wood, and bound his son Isaac and laid him on the altar, on top of the wood.* **10** *Abraham stretched out his hand and took the knife to slay his son.* **11** *But the angel of the LORD called to him from heaven and said,*

*"Abraham, Abraham!" And he said, "Here I am." **12** He said, <u>"Do not stretch out your</u>* <u>*hand against the lad, and do nothing to him; for now I know that you fear God, since you*</u> <u>*have not withheld your son, your only son, from Me."*</u> *__13__ Then Abraham raised his eyes* *and looked, and behold, behind him a ram caught in the thicket by his horns; and Abraham* *went and took the ram and offered him up for a burnt offering in the place of his son.* __14__ *Abraham called the name of that place The LORD Will Provide, as it is said to this day,* *"In the mount of the LORD it will be provided."*

This is a very strange set of verses when we look at them closely. Let us figure out the meaning by considering the story of Moses <u>on the mountain</u> which I have had given. In Genesis, the spirit tests Abraham when it comes to the offering of the Lord and his angels <u>on the mountain</u>. Because Abraham had no lambs or other animals to serve as a burnt offering, Abraham was willing to kill his son and offer him up to the Lord and his angels as an offering. Quickly the angel tells him not to dare lay a hand on the child. It is then Abraham notices an animal stuck in the bushes and he quickly kills it. This tells me one thing very specifically: The Lord and the angels relied heavily on the natives of the land to give them food, protein after the flood. Oh yes, there were people who ate other people all the time, it was common when starving to death. The Lord and the angels were not hunters nor shepherds by nature. In return, the people of the earth were receiving knowledge and wisdom. This is the work of the Holy Spirit bringing two different races together for a common cause.

When we speak of God as a deity, these men were only vessels of that higher existence which the Holy Spirit knew of. I know that these men, coming from the sky, did not get their pleasure watching animal carcasses burning in the wind, that's senseless. The Holy Spirit brought Abraham to that mountain because the Lord and his angels were starving, they had traveled a long distance to help the people of the earth. Why would the spirit call for a sacrifice when Isaac didn't have one? It was here that the Holy Spirit blessed them both by an animal being stuck in the bushes. What was Abraham supposed to sacrifice the next day and the next day when he had no livestock? This is where we get the term "the Lord shall provide". God was pleased with Abraham, and Abraham was pleased he could serve God. I'm not sure Isaac was as happy as Abraham, knowing he was almost slaughtered. We can see this as some type of early parable that teaches us with faith all things will be provided.

Does anybody truly know where the fire came from to build these burnt offerings? Early and Cro-Magnon men could either build endless fires from lightning or eventually somebody gave them knowledge. This is where burnt offerings originally came from. When mankind was evolving as a creation, they offered cooked meat to the Lord of heaven in appreciation of teaching them knowledge. This is something that had existed for many ages. This is the reason war came to the earth. In the fall, the ability to travel the universe in great distance was removed from humans.

So, a war began over territory, food, and water rights.

III

THE SEVEN SEALS

John's first portion of prophecy

Jesus resurrects *Revelation 1:17-20 When I saw him, I fell at his feet as though dead. Then he placed his right hand on me and said: "Do not be afraid. I am the First and the Last.* <u>**18**</u> *I am the Living One; I was dead, and now look, I am alive for ever and ever! And I hold the keys of death and Hades.* <u>**19**</u> *Write, therefore, what you have seen, what is now, and what will take place later.*

<u>**20**</u> *The mystery of the seven stars that you saw in my right hand and of the seven golden lampstands is this: The seven stars are the angels of the seven churches, and the seven lampstands are the seven churches."*

This is a very significant set of verses because of the nature in which they are expressed. The angel told John to write a revelation concerning three parts which contained the <u>past, present, and future.</u> It is very clear where these shifts are in the time line of the Book of Revelation and is the first clue in cracking the code of the same. The second clue is the timeline surrounding Jesus' death. We can tell much of this has already passed due to the language that is used in describing events that took place. I am here to develop down the word of Jesus Christ like no other human being. By this revelation, you will or might judge my intent. Please take short notifications of historical dates, and you will realize the timeline is discrete.

Per ancient Hindu mythology, there are 10 avatars of the Vishnu. Kalki is believed to be the destroyer of the Yuga that's full of filth. Per many in Hindu belief, we have arrived at that point and exactly as many Christians theorize we are in the period called: the end of times. I think both sides are correct in that setting. Kalki would be the equivalent of an archangel holding Satan, the destroyer, in an age of long ago.

In Hindu art, the avatar comes riding on a white horse. Why do I see this in a Christian book? Because there are many similarities in religious belief. I think the intent of the Lord was many ways, at many times, and in all nations before becoming the ultimate sacrifice for mankind. I will tie the forerunner of the Messiah to many similarities by the end of this book. He is a spiritual and physical conqueror in the name of Christ. He is known to me as Elijah, the herald, and the Archangel of the Christ. I will clearly prove this fact with scripture.

The First Seal: Rider on a White Horse.

Revelation 6:1-2 *I watched as the Lamb opened the first of the seven seals. Then I heard one of the four living creatures say in a voice like thunder, "Come!"* *2* *I looked, and there before me was a white horse! Its rider held a bow, and he was given a crown, and he rode out as a conqueror bent on conquest.*

Per ancient historians, the Egyptian Empire was the superpower of the Mediterranean until its conquest by Alexander the Great around 332 B.C. King Hammurabi was the sixth baron of the Babylonian dynasty. Under his rule from 1792-1750, they greatly increased their borders with military conflicts. He is known to have written the code of Hammurabi, a well-preserved Babylonian code of law written in cuneiform. The Assyrian army took the Israelites into captivity some-where around 740-732 B.C. They also occupied Egypt some were around 656-639 B.C. They were conquerors in the region we know today as ancient Babylon or Mesopotamia. More specifically in the area believed to be the Garden of Eden. The country was captured by King Nebuchadnezzar in 605 B.C. The one common bond these nations and rulers shared is the slavery of the Israelites.

Egyptian riding horse (glyph)

The Second Seal: War.

Revelation 6:3-4 *When the Lamb opened the second seal, I heard the second living creature say, "Come!" 4 Then another horse came out, a fiery red one {Greek soldier}. Its rider was given power to take peace from the earth and to make people kill each other. To him, he was given a large sword.*

Per ancient historians, the term Ancient Greece generally refers to the period between 800 to 150 B.C. It was a time of government, city, and country. Alexander III of Macedon, conquered the lands of Persia, Syria, Asia Minor, and Egypt before expanding his empire into India and modern day Pakistan.

The Third Seal: Famine

Revelation 6:5-6 *When the Lamb opened the third seal, I heard the third living creature say, "Come!" I looked, and there before me was a black horse! Its rider was holding a pair of scales in his hand. 6 Then I heard what sounded like a voice among the four* *living creatures, {consuls of the roman republic} saying, "Two pounds of wheat for a day's wage and six pounds of barley for a day's wage and do not damage the oil and the wine!"*

According to ancient historians, Romulus and his twin brother, Remus, founded Rome somewhere around 753 B.C. Rome records one of its first famines in 441 B.C., according to an internet article by Christopher Creagan, who posted a transcript copy of *The Famine*. In the English standard version of the bible, as well as others, it refers to the verses of the third seal in this way: *"A quart of wheat for a denarius, and three quarts of barley for a denarius, and do not harm the oil and the wine!"* This refers to a roman silver coin minted in 211 B.C. A clever way for John to lead us to Rome. However, there are many more clues in this puzzle.

The Fourth Seal: Death

Revelation 6:7-8 *When the Lamb broke the fourth seal, I heard the voice of the fourth living creature saying, "Come." **8** looked, and behold, an ashen horse; and he who sat on it had the name Death; and Hades was following with him. <u>Authority was given to them over a fourth of the earth, to kill with sword and with famine</u> and with pestilence and by the wild beasts of the earth.*

Per ancient historians, Cyrus the Great, was the founder of the Persian Empire under the Achaemenid dynasty. He was considerably known for conquering the Babylonian empire. The Cyrus Cylinder, was found in the ancient ruins of Babylon and Ur. It is another book of law which sets up declaration of human rights. This tells us that the inhabitants of Babylon were highly sophisticated and educated if they could produce something like the Ten Commandments that God gave to Moses. Cyrus was also known for ending the captivity of the Jews and letting them rebuild their temple in Jerusalem. This is important information when I talk of brotherhoods and peace later in this chapter. Where politicians stand, I hope you would hear my words.

The Fifth Seal: Martyrs

Revelation 6:9-11 *When the Lamb broke the fifth seal, I saw underneath the altar the souls of those who had been slain because of the word of God, and because of the testimony which they had maintained; **10** and they cried out with a loud voice, saying,*

"How long, O Lord, holy and true, will You refrain from judging and avenging our blood on those who dwell on the earth?" **11** *And there was given to each of them a white robe; and they were told that they should rest for a little while longer, until the number of their fellow servants and their brethren who were to be killed even as they had been, would be completed also.*

The Sixth Seal: Terror

Revelation 6:12-17 *I watched as he opened the sixth seal. There was a great earthquake. The sun turned black like sackcloth made of goat hair, the whole moon turned blood red {sun blocked out by volcanic ash and smoke},* **13** *and the stars in the sky fell to earth, as figs drop from a fig tree when shaken by a strong wind {meteor showers}.* **14** *The heavens receded like a scroll being rolled up, and every mountain and island was removed from its place {earth knocked off its axis}.* **15** *Then the kings of the earth, the princes, the generals, the rich, the mighty, and everyone else, both slave and free, hid in caves and among the rocks of the mountains.* **16** *They called to the mountains and the rocks, "Fall on us and hide us from the face of him who sits on the throne and from the wrath of the Lamb!* **17** *For the great day of their wrath has come, and who can withstand it?"*

You will acknowledge the first four seals stand for four powerful kingdoms which precede the life and demise of Jesus. This delivers a very similar substance to the statue in the dream of King Nebuchadnezzar in the Book of Daniel. How do we know who these kingdoms and figures are? The rest of revelation will reveal that information clearly. Each presents the coming of the wolf or the anti-Christ and his kingdom which is given authority to seize. In this age, earthquakes started to get so violent that continents shifted as the world was knocked off its axis. A precursor, to what was to come, just as it will be in modern day age. This leads us into the seventh seal and the first four trumpets.

This is considered the first judgment of man.

There is a very good reason for these events, they are natural events. It is unfortunate we do not have ships to flee away from this ground when it suffers violent phases, or do we? We will notice John clearly says *caves* in his vision. We must assume 'caves' is not a symbolism at the time John wrote this. John clearly knew what modern structures were. *Xenophon's Anabasis is a story published in seven books which tells a narrative of people who lived and dwelled in underground cities at Kaymakli and Derinkuyu.* Many of these caves have been discovered and gives us a sign that underground cities existed, possibly as early as 4th century B.C. The book *Xenophon's Anabasis* provides a detailed account of events in the region of Turkey by a professional soldier who was on an expedition. Many sought refuges in these unoccupied cave dwellings when meteor showers plagued the world. The Petra caves, which reside in Jordan, are a quite a sight.

Ancient cave dwelling, Petra

The Seventh Seal

Revelation 8:1-6 *When the Lamb broke the seventh seal, there was silence in heaven for about half an hour {symbolic, cease of celestial events}. **2** And I saw the seven angels who stand before God, and seven trumpets were given to them. **3** Another angel came and stood at the altar, holding a golden censer; and much incense was given to him, so that he might add it to the prayers of all the saints on the golden altar which was before the throne.*

_**4**_ _And the smoke of the incense, with the prayers of the saints, went up before God out of the angel's hand._ _**5**_ _Then the angel took the censer and filled it with the fire of the altar, and threw it to the earth; and there followed peals of thunder and sounds and flashes of lightning and an earthquake._ _**6**_ _And the seven angels who had the seven trumpets prepared themselves to sound them._

IV

THE FIRST JUDGMENT

The First Four Trumpets

Revelation 8:1-13 *The first sounded, and there came hail and fire, mixed with blood {volcanic super storm, hail mixed with lava and ash}, and they were thrown to the earth; and a third of the earth was burned up, and a third of the trees were burned up, and all the green grass was burned up.* **8** *The second angel sounded, and something like a great mountain burning with fire was thrown into the sea; and a third of the sea became blood {volcanic eruption},* **9** *and a third of the creatures which were in the sea and had life, died; and a third of the ships were destroyed {ocean temperature's rising, global warming}.* **10** *The third angel sounded, and a great star fell from heaven, burning like a torch, and it fell on a third of the rivers and on the springs of waters.* **11** *The name of the star is called Wormwood; and a third of the waters became wormwood, and many men died from the waters, because they were made bitter {large falling star, poisoned waters.}* **12** *The fourth angel sounded, and a third of the sun and a third of the moon and a third of the stars were struck, so that a third of them would be darkened and the day would not shine for a third of it, and the night in the same way {volcanic black out}.* **13** *Then I looked, and I heard an eagle flying in mid-heaven {upper atmosphere, observers of earth}, saying with a loud voice,* <u>*"Woe, woe, woe to those who dwell on the earth, because of the remaining blasts of the trumpet of the three angels are about to sound!"*</u>

The first four trumpets signify different full-blown eruptions and meteor showers over the region we once called Eurasia. The trumpets sound just prior to the time of the crucifixion of Jesus Christ. This is the time and era when the Mediterranean lost a third of their naval fleets. Let us think of John's Revelation when it concerns about a very specific subject in the world, not the whole globe. Let us not be blind to the fact that John uses fractions a lot when making his numbers. A third of the angels, a third of the earth, and a third of the creatures. We can take this number as a very general estimate and not higher than that. If we have not established people coming from the sky, surely, we will. Jesus and John both came to warn the inhabitants in that region of certain doom and they were verbally shot down for that. Those in heaven have come many times and in many ways, they usually were tortured and killed. I am nothing but a voice telling you what is coming and that it's inevitable. My love is with this world and its people as we are all the same in nature, no matter the outcome.

What this world really needs to know is what happened to our ancestors or the angels that brought Jesus and John into the world. What happened to Elijah, Moses, and the Lord of Mt. Sinai? All these men I mentioned to you were hunted men. They wanted to change the system of power that has been corrupted. When all things went to hell, many left the earth in fear. When they came back, the world was in utter chaos. These are the elders spoken about in Johns' prophecy. <u>They are your ride off this planet.</u> However, there are many things that will happen first, to insure the safety of the SECOND COMING. How do I know that? Per my theory, the spirit of the Father was a commanding officer in heaven till a huge mistake was made. This will be addressed in full. In other words, the greatest of sinners can become the greatest of saints. Therefore, I must endure in this lifetime, to see life as it is for the grace of my people. In the following chapters, you will realize things are not always what they seem to be. When a lion is in a cage, the cage may have features that look like home but it's not. It is a creation of an atmosphere for us to observe or watch their behaviors. As it is on earth, so it is in the heavens. That would be a reasonably simple concept for most humans to understand. With star exploration, there are certain dangerous risks and we shall embrace them all equally. Welcome to the twilight zone, welcome to planet Earth.

The Fifth Trumpet

Revelation 9:1-12 *The fifth angel sounded his trumpet, and I saw a star that had fallen from the sky to the earth. The star was given the key to the shaft of the Abyss.* **2** *When he opened the Abyss, smoke rose from it like the smoke from a gigantic furnace {large volcanic ash plume}. The sun and sky were darkened by the smoke from the Abyss.* **3** *And out of the smoke locusts came down on the earth and were given power like that of scorpions of the earth.* **4** <u>*They were told not to harm the grass of the earth or any plant or tree,*</u> *but only those people who did not have the seal of God on their foreheads.* **5** <u>*They were not allowed to kill them but only to torture them for five months. And the agony they suffered*</u>

was like that of the sting of a scorpion when it strikes. **6** *During those days people will seek death but will not find it; they will long to die, but death will elude them.* **7** *The locusts looked like horses prepared for battle. On their heads, they wore something like crowns of gold, and their faces resembled human faces.* **8** *Their hair was like women's hair, and their teeth were like lions' teeth.* **9** *They had breastplates like breastplates of iron, and the sound of their wings was like the thundering of many horses and chariots rushing into battle.* **10** *They had tails with stingers, like scorpions, and in their tails, they had power to torment people for five months.* **11** *They had as king over them the angel of the Abyss, whose name in Hebrew is Abaddon and in Greek is Apollyon (the Destroyer).* **12** *The first woe is past; two other woes are yet to come.*

In most hieroglyphs, Annunaki and Babylonians appear to bear long hair and generally, a crown of gold, which is a lot different than an Egyptian crown. The vessels of these advanced races and their antecedents are unknown to us in modern day (Annunaki were Sumerian Gods who many believe came from the sky by their many stone glyphs and statues that they left behind). Some could have been like our own in modern times. The description sounds about like ancient saucers. At some point in history, we found glyph's in the temple of Osiris at Abydos that appeared to have strange looking vessels that are close-looking to modern day war machines (Pharaoh's saucer, a submarine, etc.).

We must remember we don't still have accurate dates of the pyramid as many would immediately believe the pyramids could have been here as early 10,000 B.C. For certain, mankind was roaming the earth during that time. Why did they come here?

The angels fell for daughters of men, who had become very beautiful and pleasing to our Lord. That's a mistake any one of us could have made. With that said, there were many lessons for the sons of god who had fallen for the daughters of men. You cannot wage war against your brother and steal his women and children for your own desires. This period seems to be just prior to Michael, the archangel, claiming victory in war against Satan and his angels. They were cast down to the earth and cannot travel back into the heavens. We know this is an accurate description of events due to the fact we are very limited in how far we can travel in space. We have lost much technology in the fall from heaven. What you saw in the past is technology resurfacing, not evolution. Then it is being stomped out by wars on the earth. We can determine that these beings are in flying machines or machines that fly on the account John describes them as locusts prepared for battle. We can make no conclusion other than it sounds like an ancient weapon that was practiced on men and it did not obliterate them. This very well could be the first explanation we hold of chemical agents being deployed on mankind. This would be an order among the Annunaki who waged war on the sons of God. They waged war when the sons of God fell for daughters of men, which is biblically noted. This has a lot to do with the Babylonian empire and why it was the first kingdom to come into judgment. Therefore, heaven showed its strength and might at the abuse of unevolved men and women. Thus, it is not Jesus you must care about expressing his anger, he is but a lamb hoping to redeem all as He is a Prince of Peace. Yet, you must be worried at how many tears he shed on your behalf. All of heaven has declared him King of this universe for his steadfast patience and endurance in establishing law for humans. The Earth has become increasingly wicked over the centuries after Jesus' departure.

We will note that the seals have not snapped off all in one time and era, rather sequentially through time. Each seal represents a time or an era when one of the seven sons of God walked the earth by the power of the Holy Spirit. This as well is attributed to the trumpets, plagues, and bowls of wrath. Note the words bow and sword mentioned in the first 4 seals. This tells us specifically these were ancient wars not wars of the future. To show you that the spirit is a master at deciphering its own work, there are a couple of book arrangement errors, historically speaking. It is so evident to understand; however, it needs a detailed time line to see this out. It also would require someone who has extensive knowledge in the book of Daniel and the Book of Revelation written by John. This may sound odd, but I believe I have had my hands on this story for ages. I will bring this historical timeline to the attention of scholars so they may judge my spirit and the authenticity of Christ's return. After all, it is not a competition of knowledge, it is the mystery of iniquity most would wish to work. No vision can be made perfect when written in pieces and pieced together by man. Especially documents this old. Only time can make that vision whole. There is no doubt this is a book of many pieces with different thoughts and topics. It is composed in a very awkward way, matching no known style or source in the history of time. The exception is Daniel, the prophet. Although, I am very familiar with my colleague's material, I will not have the time to solve it in its entirety. Why the Holy Spirit works in this particular way it is not necessarily known to me. It does have something to do with the seven spirits, and what is pleasing to the spirit in the quest of life. It likes to leave puzzles and clues for the resurrection, that way the host is well informed. Therefore, there are seven spirits, continual presence on earth and in heaven.

The first crucial piece of the book which takes us out of a consistent timeline is the fall of Babylon being out of place in the Holy Scripture. We recognize from history the fall of Babylon came before Christ. Babylon was a great city in the Babylonian empire. Two different times, under two different kings, the kingdom flourished. This is what established the head of gold in the dream of Nebuchadnezzar in the book of Daniel. The second crucial timeline error we have, is the sixth and seventh trumpet. The sixth and the seventh trumpet must follow the destruction of Christ and cannot come ahead. There are a few reasons why and we will discuss them thoroughly. I will put the verses in the correct timeline, but I will not change the verse number or heading. It will be marked as <u>revised position</u>. If you read the description, the sixth trumpet is clearly describing artillery fire and modern war. Therefore, John does not have a name for the weapon as in the case of a bow and sword, so he uses fire and brimstone and a third of mankind was killed by the same. A cannon or gun were not invented until the thirteenth century. That is exactly what comes out of the mouth of a cannon or gun, fire, and brimstone.

Better known as sulfur, one of the key components in gunpowder, it has taken countless lives on earth. This gets us out of the consistent timeframe that has been proven. A quick introduction to these verses will help you understand the timeline more clearly.

The British Empires original household, Calvary, wore a very distinct helmet and uniform. Wearing the colors of red, dark blue, with golden-silver armor and yellow trim. They were fierce soldiers. They also wore a plume of horse hair like the Romans and Greeks. Of these feathers look like a lion's mane atop of the helmet, matching John's vision. Napoleon also experienced very similar colors on their Calvary. These colors will match John's description as well. The single thing that will be consistent and link these armies is that they struggled under the flags of red, white, and blue.

It is important, information wise, to discover the armies we are talking about in the sixth trumpet. In the verses of the sixth trumpet it also mentions the number of mounted troops is calculated at 200 million. Because the record of Apocalypse is very exact in almost all instances, we must care for it as such. This would clearly be after the time of Christ in Revelation 12:1, and falls into the development of modern nations. This must occur afterwards in time based on the numbers of soldiers and population alone. Once more, the description of a cannon or guns jumps us completely out of the timeline being it precedes the birth, death, and resurrection of Christ in Revelation 12:1. The death of Christ must fall in line with the rise of the Roman Empire and the mark of the beast. This will precede us into the second season of prophecy: modern day war, as considerably as the sixth and seventh trumpet. Jesus does not become worthy to dominate with the Holy Spirit until his demise. The seventh trumpet cannot come until after his demise and resurrection. It would have been easy for the revelations of the trumpets to be grouped together just as the seals, not knowing about the next 2000 years.

It takes someone like me to put the pieces together and give it clarity. It should give you a clear understanding of this complex, coded book. I tell you as sure as my son has risen, I have come to give you an accurate account of events. Modern-day war is the only time in history we can account for 200 million mounted troops. The time period from <u>World War I and into World War II gets us into these numbers.</u> In an article posted by *Statistics Brain*, 65 million troops reported to battle in World War I. They were of all faiths, religions and creeds. They came from a host of nations.

Clearly, you will see something is very out of order in the chronology of biblical scripture in the Book of Revelation. That's ok, it's still very solvable. Hopefully, I will make it very clear and less confusing. It is best to follow the last book of the bible by clues of history rather than verse number and heading. That is my major clue to help you decipher any info on the prophetic books of John and Daniel. When you follow a timeline of history and events, it becomes astonishingly clear just how accurate John the prophet was. Essentially, John the prophet, Jesus' best friend, was a continuation of the Christ spirit after his life was cut so devastatingly short.

V

THE FALL OF BABYLON

The Three Angels and Babylon's Fall *Revelation 14:6-13* (revised position) *The Three Angels.* **6** *Then I saw another angel flying in midair, and he had the eternal gospel to proclaim to those who live on the earth—to every nation, tribe, language and people.* **7** *He said in a loud voice, "Fear God and give him glory, because the hour of his judgment has come. Worship him who made the heavens, the earth, the sea and the springs of water."* **8** *A second angel followed and said, "Fallen! Fallen is Babylon the Great,' which made all the nations drink the maddening wine of her adulteries."* **9** *A third angel followed them and said in a loud voice: "If anyone worships the beast and its image and receives its mark on their forehead or on their hand (Roman empire),* **10** *they, too, will drink the wine of God's fury, which has been poured full strength into the cup of his wrath. They will be tormented with burning sulfur in the presence of the holy angels and of the Lamb {Guns, cannon fire, etc}.* **11** *And the smoke of their torment will rise for ever and ever. There will be no rest day or night for those who worship the beast and its image, or for anyone who receives the mark of its name."* **12** *This calls for patient endurance on the part of the people of God who keep his commands and remain faithful to Jesus.* **13** *Then I heard a voice from heaven say, "Write this: Blessed are the dead who die in the Lord from now on." "Yes," says the Spirit, "they will rest from their labor, for their deeds will follow them {first death, under the Assyrian and Babylonian Kings}*

The Seven Bowls of God's Wrath *Revelation 16:1-21* (revised position) *Then I heard a loud voice from the temple saying to the seven angels, "Go, and pour out the seven bowls of God's wrath on the earth."* **2** *The first angel went and poured out his bowl on the land, and ugly, festering sores broke out on the people who had the mark of the beast and worshiped its image.* **3** *The second angel poured out his bowl on the sea, and it turned into blood like that of a dead person, and every living thing in the sea died {lava, eruption, ocean temperature change, etc.}.* **4** *The third angel poured out his bowl on the rivers and springs of water, and they became blood {surface water and wells poisoned}.* **5** *Then I heard the angel in charge of the waters say: "You are just in these judgments, O Holy One, you who are and who were;* **6** *for they have shed the blood of your holy people and your prophets,* and you have given them blood to drink as they deserve." **7** And I heard the altar respond: "Yes, Lord God Almighty, true and just are your judgments." **8** The fourth angel poured out his bowl on the sun, and the sun could scorch people with fire {heat waves, similar to what we are experiencing in modern day}. **9** They were seared by the intense heat and they cursed the name of God, who had control over these plagues, but they refused to repent and glorify him. **10** The fifth angel poured out his bowl on the throne of the beast, and its kingdom was plunged into darkness. People gnawed their tongues in agony **11** and cursed the God of heaven because of their pains and their sores, but they refused to repent of what they had done. **12** The sixth angel poured out his bowl on the great river Euphrates, and its water was dried up to prepare the way for the kings from the East. **13** Then I saw three impure spirits that looked like frogs; they came out of the mouth of the dragon, out of the mouth of the beast and out of the mouth of the false prophet. **14** They are demonic spirits that perform signs, and they go out to the kings of the world, to gather them for the battle on the momentous day of God Almighty. **15** "Look, I come like a thief! Blessed is the one who stays awake and remains clothed, so as not to go naked and be shamefully exposed." **16** Then they gathered the kings together to the place that in Hebrew is called Armageddon {figurative, Tel Megiddo, the hill of many battles, Israel}. **17** The seventh angel poured out his bowl into the air, and out of the temple came a loud voice from the throne, saying, "It is done!" **18** Then there came flashes of lightning, rumblings, peals of thunder and a severe earthquake. No earthquake like it has ever occurred since mankind has been on earth, so tremendous was the quake. **19** The great city split into three parts, and the cities of the nations collapsed, God remembered Babylon the Great and gave her the cup filled with the wine of the fury of his wrath. **20** Every island fled away and the mountains could not be found. **21** From the sky huge hailstones, each weighing about a hundred pounds, fell on people {inflicted by heaven}. And they cursed God on account of the plague of hail, because the plague was so terrible.

The Woman on the Beast **Revelation 17:1-18** (revised position) One of the seven angels who had the seven bowls came and said to me, "Come, I will show you the punishment of the great prostitute, who sits by many waters {Black Sea, Red Sea, Persian Gulf, Caspian Sea, Mediterranean Sea}. **2** With her the kings of the earth committed adultery, and the inhabitants of the earth were intoxicated with the wine of her adulteries." **3** Then the angel carried me away in the spirit into a wilderness. There I saw a woman sitting on a scarlet beast that was covered with blasphemous names and had seven heads and ten horns. **4** The woman was dressed in purple and scarlet, and was glittering with gold, precious stones *and pearls {great royalty}. She held a golden cup in her hand, filled with abominable things and the filth of her adulteries.* **5** *The name written on her forehead was a mystery: Babylon the great the mother of prostitutes and of the abominations of the earth.* **6** *I saw that the woman was drunk with the blood of God's holy people, the blood of those who bore testimony to Jesus. When I saw her, I was greatly astonished.* **7** *Then the angel said to me: "Why are you astonished? I will explain to you the mystery of the woman and of the beast she rides, which has the* seven heads and ten horns. **8** *The beast, which you saw,* once was, now is not, and yet will come up out of the Abyss and go to its destruction. *The inhabitants of the earth whose names have not been written in the book of life from the creation of the world will be astonished when they see the beast, because it once was, now is not,* and yet will come. **9** *"This calls for a mind with wisdom {a call to decipher}. The seven heads are seven hills on which the woman sits {formerly Babylonian empire, seven hills of Constantinople, modern day Istanbul Turkey}.* **10** *They are also seven kings. Five have fallen, one is, the other has not yet come; but when he does come, he must remain for only a little while.* **11** *The beast who once was, and now is not,* is an eighth king. *He belongs to the seven and is going to his destruction {Constantine, ruler of the Byzantine empire, conquered by Mohamed the conqueror 1453}."* **12** *"The ten horns you saw are ten kings who have not yet received a kingdom {ten nations of the anti-Christ, conquered regions of Rome} but who for one hour will receive authority as kings along with the beast.* **13** *They have one purpose and will give their power and authority to the beast.* **14** They will wage war against the Lamb but the Lamb will triumph over them because he is Lord of lords and King of kings–and with him will be his called, chosen and faithful followers *{Muslim, Jewish defense of Jerusalem, crusades}."* **15** *Then the angel said to me, "The waters you saw, where the prostitute sits,* are peoples, multitudes, nations and languages. **16** *The beast {Roman Empire}, and the ten horns {nations formed} you saw will hate the prostitute {Babylon}. They will bring her to ruin and leave her naked; they will eat her flesh and burn her with fire {war}.* **17** *For God has put it into their hearts to accomplish his purpose by agreeing to hand over to the beast their royal authority, until God's words are fulfilled.* **18** *The woman you saw is the great city that rules over the kings of the earth."*

In Revelation 14:8 through 18:1 we find verses that refer to the desolation of the ancient Babylonian empire. Per ancient historians, Babylon was the capital of a small city state of Mesopotamia, named Babylonia. It is in what is now Iraq. Babylon reached its height of power two times. Once under Babylonian King Hammurabi, 1792-1750 BC. The city again came to height of power in 7th century

BC. This was the reign of Nebuchadnezzar II, right before the Persian conquest. Today, when we speak of Iraq and Syria many places that have had become desolate and torn apart from many wars. We will remember the name Aleppo and the mass genocide of human life. This sets the stage for where we are in this specific time in biblical scripture to what it is now and what it will become. Two separate times the angels spoke, "*Babylon has fallen.*" Revelation 14:8 as well as Revelation 18:1. Two times Babylon was great, and twice she has fallen. We will find these visions were grouped in a way that will help us identify the four beasts of Daniel's prophecy.

VI

THE BIRTH OF CHRIST

The second season. John's Second Portion of Prophecy

Secrets and Trust

You are my reflection
I am your mirror
King crowned by Glory
Wear the seal of gold upon thy finger
Wear my ring, wear my ring

Yesterday they sold the world our story
Made a profit off the prophets, that's what they made
I don't care if you take me down in the Glory
I'm just going to watch them all fade away
It's more than love, luck, time, confusion, secrets, and trust
It's more than love, luck, time, confusion, secrets, and trust
That's for sure

The Angel and the Small Scroll Revelation 10:1-11 *Then I saw another mighty angel coming down from heaven. He was robed in a cloud, with a rainbow above his head; his face was like the sun, and his legs were like fiery pillars.* **2** *He was holding a little scroll, which lay open in his hand. He planted his right foot on the sea and his left foot on the land,* **3** *and he gave a loud shout like the roar of a lion. When he shouted, the voices of the seven thunders spoke.* **4** *And when the seven thunders spoke, I was about to write; but I heard a voice from heaven say, "Seal up what the seven thunders have said and do not write it down {hold it for a future time}."* **5** *Then the angel I had seen standing on the sea and on the land raised his right hand to heaven.* **6** *And he swore by him who lives for ever and ever, who created the heavens and all that is in them, the earth and all that is in it, and* the sea and all that is in it, and said, "There will be no more delay! **7** But in the days when the seventh angel is about to sound his trumpet, the mystery of God will be accomplished, just as he announced to his servants the prophets." **8** Then the voice that I had heard from heaven spoke to me once more: "Go, take the scroll that lies open in the hand of the angel who is standing on the sea and on the land." **9** So I went to the angel and asked him to give me the little scroll. He said to me, "Take it and eat it. It will turn your stomach sour, but 'in your mouth it will be as sweet as honey" **10** I took the little scroll from the angel's hand and ate it. It tasted as sweet as honey in my mouth, but when I had eaten it, my stomach turned sour. **11** Then I was told, "You must prophesy again about many peoples, nations, languages and kings {judge the nations}."

<u>**Cross References**</u> **Ezekiel 3:1-15** And he said to me, "Son of man, eat what is before you, eat this scroll; then go and speak to the people of Israel {prophesize again}." **2** So I opened my mouth, and he gave me the scroll to eat. **3** Then he said to me, "Son of man, eat this scroll I am giving you and fill your stomach with it." So I ate it, and it tasted as sweet as honey in my mouth. **4** He then said to me: <u>"Son of man, go now to the people of Israel and speak my words to them.</u> **5** You are not being sent to a people of obscure speech and strange language, but to the people of Israel **6** not too many people of obscure speech and strange language, whose words you cannot understand. Surely if I had sent you to them, they would have listened to you. **7** <u>But the people of Israel are not willing to listen to you because they are not willing to listen to me, for all the Israelites are hardened and obstinate.</u> **8** But I will make you as unyielding and hardened as they are. **9** I will make your forehead like the hardest stone, harder than flint. Do not be afraid of them or terrified by them, though they are a rebellious people." **10** And he said to me, "Son of man, listen carefully and take to heart all the words I speak to you. **11** <u>Go now to your people in exile and speak to them.</u> Say to them, 'This is what the Sovereign Lord says,' whether they listen or fail to listen." **12** Then the Spirit lifted me up, and I heard behind me a loud rumbling sound as the glory of the Lord rose from the place where it was standing. **13** It was the sound of the wings of the living creatures brushing against each other and the sound of the wheels beside them, a loud rumbling sound {encounter with heavenly beings who came in a vessel}. **14** The Spirit then lifted me up and took me away, and I went in bitterness and in the anger of my spirit, with the strong hand of the Lord on me. **15** I came to the exiles who lived at Tel Aviv near the Kebar River. And there, where they were living, I sat among them for seven days—deeply distressed.

We now can be more certain how John the seer can give us prophecies prior to the time of Christ. We might determine this is the spirit of Ezekiel, one of the seven angels, by the context and which the cross reference is written. Also, we must look at the fact John prophesied three times: from the past, to the present, and into the future. By these two sets of scripture we can see the Lord is angered and tells John and Ezekiel they must prophet again. He sends Ezekiel to the place of his people's exile, Tel Aviv. The Lord brings John, the prophet, back into the holy land in the days of Christ and King Herod. King Herod conquered Jerusalem and the 2nd temple was eventually, destroyed by the romans. We can see the anger that the Lord had towards Israel in the passages of Ezekiel. He called them stubborn and obstinate. Although angered with Israel in the Old Testament, Jesus, the Son of God, came to Jerusalem to be crucified and after being rejected by Israel and its people.

The second woe *Revelation 11:7-14 Now when they have finished their testimony{the two witnesses}, the beast that comes up from the Abyss will attack them, and overpower and kill them. **8** Their bodies will lie in the public square of the great city—which figuratively called Sodom and Egypt-where also their Lord was crucified {Jerusalem} **9** For three and a half days some from every people, tribe, language and nation will gaze on their bodies and refuse them burial. **10** The inhabitants of the earth will gloat over them and will celebrate by sending each other gifts, because these two prophets had tormented those who live on the earth. **11** But after the three and a half days the breath of life from God entered them, and they stood on their feet, and terror struck those who saw them {figurative, resurrection of spirit, same as Jesus}. **12** Then they heard a loud voice from heaven saying to them, "Come up here." And they went up to heaven in a cloud, while their enemies looked on {heavenly ascension}. **13** At that very hour there was a severe earthquake and a tenth of the city collapsed. Seven thousand people were killed in the earthquake, and the survivors were terrified and gave glory to the God of heaven. **14** The second woe has passed; the third woe is coming soon.*

The earthquake mentioned in these verses very well could be the earthquake mentioned in the Gospels. We will note it says figuratively where Jesus Christ was crucified. That does not take place until the adjacent of verses, Revelation 12:5. Per an internet article by *Jennifer Vegas of Discover News*, geologists used waves to determine the timeline of significant quakes in the region of Jerusalem. Verves are annual layers of deposition in the sediments or sedimentary rock. This scientific method revealed that at least two major earthquakes affected the core. A widespread earthquake in 31 B.C. and a seismic event that happened sometime between the years 26 and 36 A.D.

The Woman, Israel *Revelation 12:1-2 A great sign appeared in heaven: <u>a woman clothed with the sun, and the moon under her feet, and on her head a crown of twelve stars; 2 and she was with child</u>; and she cried out, being in labor and in pain to give birth.*

The Red Dragon, Satan *Revelation 12:3-4 Then another sign appeared in heaven: and behold, a great red dragon having <u>seven heads</u> and <u>ten horns</u>, and on his head were <u>seven diadems</u>. 4 And his tail swept away a third of the stars of heaven and threw them to the earth {our ancestors from heaven}. And the dragon {demonic spirit} stood before the woman who was about to give birth, so that when she gave birth he might devour {murder} her child.*

The Male Child, Christ *Revelation 12:5-6 And she gave birth to a son, a male child, who is to rule all the nations with a rod of iron; and her child was caught up to God and to His throne. {the city of God, his vessel} 6 Then the woman fled into the wilderness where she had a place {Egypt} prepared by God, so that there she would be nourished for one thousand two hundred and sixty days.*

Most people studying scriptures can conclude easily that John tied himself to Israel by the <u>twelve stars</u> representing the <u>twelve tribes of Israel</u> and the <u>twelve disciples</u>. Understandably, this is the birth of Christ, the mid-book of the Revelations. Why is that significant? Not only the Christ is the alpha and omega (the beginning and the end), he's everything in between as well. When we go on to attend at the timeline of history along with the biblical cases, we can easily solve the enigma of these disclosures. We can see in these visions, that the heads upon the brute are in acknowledgment to the nations. They have horns (nations), crowns (kings), and diadems upon their heads. If there is any doubt these are nations, I will convince you differently with detailed scripture. John's vision covers an enormous measure of time. It was crazy times because of the force of government. They were wiping out people for their outspokenness on religion. Therefore, events were encoded by the spirit so the ability of the church would not lay their workforce on the revelation of Jesus Christ. John foretold their demise of power and the division of their kingdom. Had the Roman Empire known John was describing their descent by the hands of Germanics, Muslims and other kin groups and nations, they would have had him executed and confiscated his manuscripts.

Why was the Roman Empire so sadistic and vicious against those who spoke against them? When we read about King Herod killing innocent kids in Bethlehem that were under two years of age, it is nigh identical to the narration of Moses and the Pharaoh. It was an intention to slaughter the Christ child as we all knew from the scriptures. What was it about this child that made him such a threat to the Egyptian and Roman kingdoms? Let me rephrase that question. What made him a threat to the power of the dragon? By the end of the book you will know the Christ spirit is the same spirit that was with Moses. Per my theory of time, the spirit threw itself down into our affairs to redeem us from a great evil that has tortured, murdered, genetically altered, and modified humans since their appearance on this earth. Therefore, we have evidence of prehistoric man thousands of years ago, living on the earth before biblical history. This is when a period of great evolution took place for lesser men.

Adam and Eve are the root of biblical history. There is no possible way they were the first humans. They are a representation of the ancestry of Israel and why God selected them. If we are to stick with the consistent timeline in John's revelation leading up to the death of Jesus and after, we will have the complete mystery of John's revelation resolved.

The dragon who prepared to devour the child as he was born in Revelation 12:4, can only be <u>King Herod and the power of Rome.</u> Herod was king of Judea, a roman providence. This is one of the ten crowns of the seven heads of the dragon. This is a major clue and an event in the book of Revelations. It establishes New Testament from Old Testament in the timeline of the Roman Empire. It also establishes modern Israel from ancient Israel and the first and second temple. After years of Jewish conflict with King Herod, he captures Jerusalem. He is one of the dreaded horns with a crown on the beast. He captures Jerusalem and becomes King of the Jews. We will take note in the upcoming verses that the <u>42 months mentioned</u> in scripture matches almost perfectly with the historical amount of time the Jews were in conflict with King Herod before he captured the city. This is recognized as the "Jewish revolt", 66-70 A.D.

<u>The Fall from Heaven</u> Revelation 12:7-12 *Then war broke out in heaven. Michael and his angels fought against the dragon, and the dragon and his angels fought back.* **8** *But he was not strong enough, and they lost their place in heaven.* **9** *<u>The great dragon was hurled down—that ancient serpent called the devil, or Satan, who leads the whole world astray. He was hurled to the earth, and his angels with him.</u>* **10** *Then I heard a loud voice* in heaven say: "Now have come the salvation and the power and the kingdom of our God, and the authority of his Messiah. For the accuser of our brothers and sisters, who accuses them before our God day and night, has been hurled down. **11** They triumphed over him by the blood of the Lamb and by the word of their testimony; they did not love their lives so much as to shrink from death. **12** Therefore rejoice, you heavens and you who dwell in them! But woe to the earth and the sea, because the devil has gone down to you! He is filled with fury, because he knows that his time is short."

The Beast out of the Sea Revelation 13:1-10 The dragon stood on the shore of the sea {Mediterranean Sea}. And I saw a beast coming out of the sea. It had ten horns and seven heads, {the seven kings of ancient Rome, identical to the heads and horns of the dragon} with ten crowns on its horns {ten rulers of the roman providences} and on each head a blasphemous name {kings, above Christ}. **2** The beast I saw resembled a leopard, but had feet like those of a bear and a mouth like that of a lion (cross ref Daniel 7:1-8, Roman conquest of Babylon-195 B.C, Roman Conquest of Persia-54 B.C, Roman conquest Asia Minor 190 B.C.,). The dragon gave the beast his power and his throne and great authority. **3** One of the heads of the beast seemed to have had a fatal wound, but the fatal wound had been healed {fall of the roman republic 133-27 B.C, assassination of Julius Caesar 44 B.C., Octavian first roman emperor 27 B.C-14 A.D}. The whole world was filled with wonder and followed the beast {Roman Empire}. **4** People worshiped the dragon because he had given authority to the beast, and they also worshiped the beast and asked, "Who is like the beast? Who can wage war against it?" **5** The beast was given a mouth to utter proud words and blasphemies and to exercise its authority for forty-two months. **6** It opened its mouth to blaspheme God, and to slander his name and his dwelling place and those who live in heaven. **7** It was given power to wage war against God's holy people and to conquer them {Jerusalem, Judea, Israel}. And it was given authority over every tribe, people, language, and nation {conquering of Europe, Asia, North Africa and the middle east}. **8** All inhabitants of the earth will worship the beast—all whose names have not been written in the Lamb's book of life, the Lamb who was slain from the creation of the world **9** whoever has ears, let them hear. **10** "If anyone is to go into captivity, into captivity they will go. If anyone is to be killed with the sword, with the sword they will be killed "This calls for patient endurance and faithfulness on the part of God's people."

It very much seems the book of life was established at the crucifixion. This most definitely had set up a timeline of the kingdom of the dragon and its beasts with horns. To interpret each name of each ruler and kingdom is an enormous undertaking. I have put down a firm base for you, as well many others. I have provided you all that you need to understand in depth the final chapters of this book. I as well have tried to lay the Book of Revelations out chronologically correct for the ease of study. If I have given any identical or very similar information to any other author, it is out of coincidence of history and the comparison of scripture to ancient historians. I humbly will ask your forgiveness as I always try to maintain as much originality as possible in my work. The Book of Revelation is a small but important part of my story. It is all very historical, that's for certain.

When we express the dragon giving any beast power or preforming a miracle, it stems from an elite priestly order who gave spiritual life to the first Pharaoh on earth. A spiritual entity called Death, the god of war, which was given life from the *original* book of the dead. This is what many men preferred to worship knowingly and unwittingly. The Egyptians wore the serpent on their crest as a symbol of power and adoration to the creature, which we know as the dragon. The Egyptians believed in resurrection of body and soul, and that life was eternal. And if this is the case, you will now realize how I can tell you multiple stories of time about Moses and Jesus as well as many other biblical images. Moses was in the order of the dragon or serpent, a high-ranking magi and soldier with power of ressurection. These figures are a byproduct of the Holy Ghost. You will also know the price of being an elite Egyptian pharaoh was very high. To doubt what I am saying is to doubt the power of resurrection. It also means you doubt the words of God. Understandably, it talks about the first resurrection of those who were killed by the beast at the end of the Book of Revelation.

<u>I tell you these stories because my spirit has risen.</u>

The Egyptians had ceremonies to raise their people up from the dead and guide them in the afterlife. The problem was, many of them were cold blooded killers. These texts were from a book called the *Book of the Dead.* They blocked off using this practice just prior to the birth of Christ. What is the origin of the text in the book of the dead? Where did the Egyptians get such advanced skills to ramp up the pyramids and mold gold into such elaborate pieces? Why would such an advanced civilizations worship war, destruction, and the seizing of territories? Soon all those questions will be answered.

When I revealed the four kingdoms of the first four seals that sets the foundation <u>for all things to come biblically</u>. Babylon, Greece (Asia Minor), Rome (Europe), and Persia (Middle East, formerly Babylon). We must not confuse John's *revelation* with Daniel's Old Testament *revelation*. Daniels talks much about ancient Jerusalem when the first temple was brought down and the Jews were forced to live in exile in Babylonia. The book of Daniel clearly ties into the volume of revelations which gives us some clear answers to the dream of King Nebuchadnezzar. Equally there are many working theories and ideas on the Book of Revelation, mine is just another additional theory and source of information. The dragon symbolizes the resurrection power of the Pharaoh and the land of Egypt. The Pharaoh and the pyramids being the origin of a great spiritual force that swept the earth and still exists as we speak today. To quote this source of information to be true, we simply need to look at the *Book of the Dead*. Once more, if we stick to a rigid timeline, the upcoming verses will be about the ascension of the Byzantine Empire (mentioned earlier in the verses of the fall of Babylon are the seven hills). These events correspond to each other. It gives us a very strong clue to the rise of the Byzantine Empire when mentioned with the number of the beast. We can also track the kingdoms of the beast in Daniel's and John's prophecy by the rise of coins (currency). One of the earliest known silvers discovered is the Lydia lion coin. In accordance to an internet article by *Lunaticg coin*, the Lydia coin minted sometime around 600 B.C. in Lydia, Asia Minor, modern day Turkey. It's made of Electrum, an alloy of gold and silver called "white gold" in ancient times. This was once part of the Babylonian empire near what is thought to be the Garden of Eden.

When people had to buy land, food, and water that is not yours to sell, you have become a beast of the earth, per the scriptures Revelation 13:16-17. Acknowledging the beast of Daniels prophecy which each brought currency into form while Jews were in captivity. No longer is life free as God intended it to be in the beginning when he created Adam and Eve in the garden. You must take the number of the beast. This was the reason the God of Adam was angry. He instructed them to be alone and be self-sufficient, then somebody came and exploited what God had instructed them. <u>God asked his young children "who told you that you were naked"</u>. A spiritual creature does not clothe his naked children or throw them out of the garden. Nor does he help them deliver their children into the world. We were not all created equal. Whoever believes we were, must do some heavy soul searching. Many were created above other humans to be caretakers of knowledge and wisdom as humans evolved. This knowledge was clearly abused through time. We can get an actual timeline of Adam and Eve by tracing Pharaohs into the region of modern day Israel and Babylon. I say this because I attribute the serpent crown as the serpent who deceived Adam and Eve. Hence, we are decidedly not talking about the Neanderthals. Adam was a mix of a very low species of humanity, very hairy, with the above average genetics for that species because of the mixes. God had breathed life into Adam, Adam was very much a piece of himself. He taught him wisdom and knowledge, that knowledge was not evil.

I will give you some strong clues about the serpent who deceives humans in the chapter *Good and Evil* in this book. If we are to believe most scholars and students of the bible, the Garden of Eden was in what is now called the Middle East. The country was known as Babylon, a major city which was part of Mesopotamia, modern-day Iraq. Why would a pure-blooded Hebrew be in an area known for Islam? I assure you the early Hebrews and Muslims were treated like dirt by the fallen angels of Babylon. God showed great wrath upon that region; therefore, we have a religious war because each think that their way is more righteous. Let us remind ourselves that we are not in the Old Testament anymore. Barbaric punishment for broken laws of the Old Testament and Koran have no merit in the age of Christ.

The Byzantine Empire was the continuation of the Roman Empire. The Byzantine Empire survived the divide and fall of the Western Roman Empire in the 5th century. Its demise came in 1453 under the reign of Mehmed the Conqueror, per ancient historians. The attacks by Ottoman Turks, Seljuk Turks and the Crusaders continued to weaken the empire's power. The assault with newly invented large bronze cannons was devastating to the Roman Empire. The Roman Empire and those who worshipped the beast fell to the fire and brimstone as prophesized by John. The downfall of kingdoms happened in a very efficient and specific manner. Therefore, all power is rightfully for the glorification of Christ. Rome's city walls were violated in the year of 410 A.D by King Alaric, per ancient historians. It was the first-time Rome had been sacked in hundreds of years. Unfortunately, things continued to get worse for the great empire. The Roman Empire was divided into two parts, east and west. Corruption, overspending and weakened legions are few of the reasons that eventually led to the fall of the western empire. Could've been karma, the hand of God, I am not quite sure. One thing I do know, bullies never survive for long.

In European history, the Middle Ages, or Medieval period lasted from the 5ᵗʰ to the 15ᵗʰ century. This completes the fall of the Roman and Babylonian Empires. Some nations truly wanted peace or were genuinely good rulers. It is the power of a dragon that never lets it be due to too much hatred from the wars of the past. The demonic spirit known as the lord of the death, is proficient at what he does and with much determination and endurance. The Roman Empire had seized great power before its fall. When you're a giant and you turn a bully in the cosmos, one day you will get hacked down to size. All nations will come and take a piece of you and leave you for the vultures of death.

The Beast out of the Earth *Revelation 13:11-18 Then I saw a second beast, coming out of the earth. It had two horns like a lamb, but it spoke like a dragon {Constantine Christianized, Byzantine Empire}. 12 It exercised all the authority of the first beast on its behalf, and made the earth and its inhabitants worship the first beast, whose fatal wound had been healed {Roman republic, reemergence as the Roman or Byzantine Empire}. 13 And it performed great signs, even causing fire to come down from heaven to the earth in full view of the people {advanced weapons, vessels in the sky}. 14 Because of the signs it was given power to perform on behalf of the first beast, it deceived the inhabitants of the earth. It ordered them to set up an image in honor of the beast who was wounded by the sword and yet lived {roman republic}. 15 The second beast was given power to give breath to the image of the first beast, so that the image could speak and cause all who refused to worship the image to be killed. 16 It also forced all people, great and small, rich and poor, free and slave, to receive a mark on their right hands or on their foreheads, 17 so that they could not buy or sell unless they had the mark, which is the name of the beast or the number of its name. 18 This calls for wisdom. Let the person who has insight calculate the number of the beast, for it is the number of a man, that number is 666.*

It seems Rome and its people were never happy with one religion. The defeat of society caused people to seek out other faiths from the East, many of which were cults. According to sources, cults of Cybele, Isis, and Mithras, were suppressed and altered by the end of the fourth century A.D. *Christianity* became the dominant religion of the Roman world.

The Number of the beast is described in the passage of Revelation 13:18 and the actual number is only mentioned once in the verse. We must question why the mark or image of the beast, is placed with the fall of Babylon after the birth of Christ. This would be historically incorrect. I am speaking about the coming of the Byzantine Empire, many years after the downfall of Babylon. Prophecy is very tricky, but highly accurate. John had not seen the Byzantine Empire and then everything is very much coded. He uses 666 for a very specific reason, it lets us calculate the number of the beast and it's significant. We must remember ancient Babylon fell in the 5th century B.C to Persia. Many of its people through time became refugees and slaves to different empires including the Jews. If they did not take the name and number of the beast, they would be executed or imprisoned. Was there a system in for prisoners, slaves, and refugees of war to enable them to buy or sell on the day of ancient Babylonians' great empire? What about in the days of Rome's famine? What about the Byzantine Empire? Do these numbers or marks carry on into today or within the past? Of course! Nothing can change that, it is the prophecy being fulfilled. However, the language is very clear in the end of the Book of Revelations. Those who were struck down in the name of God and did not carry the name or number of the beast are the first into the resurrection. This mark or number is something more affiliated to ancient Empires rather than present day. Most scholars and scholars of biblical prophecy will agree and attribute the number 666 to the emperor Nero, who reigned about the time of John the Baptist's death, Jesus's death, and the exile of John the prophet. We do not have to associate Nero to the timeline, he is only a piece of the puzzle.

This is what is deciphered by most people studying internet articles and books on prophecy weather fact or fiction. If you add a numeric value to each letter in Caesar Nero's name in Hebrew, its value is 666. Without much thought or studying the numeric system used with that language, I would say that sounds very interesting. This would have been a very clever way for John to conceal the kingdom of the beast by using the emperor's name at the time he and Christ walked the earth. It shortly becomes clear the 10 horns of the wolf (10 kingdoms) and the seven heads, with crowns (seven business leaders) are nations and rulers who have used currency within their perimeters. Nero becomes emperor shortly after Christ death while John was incarcerated.

The Byzantine Empire was modeled after Rome and was its continuation. It also had seven hills just like Rome with seven head figures. So, it is very easy for us to see matching qualities in history to biblical scripture of the beast of the sea and the beast of the earth. This would be exactly what the number of the beast refers to in these verses and not necessarily a present-day mark or figure in the modern age. In other words, you could not buy or sell without the mark of the beast, the currency of the emperor or becoming a soldier or citizen. A helmet or some type of head covering with the Roman seal is a representation of the mark of the beast on the forehead. Most people who pass coins, pass coins with their right hand. This passing would represent the mark of the beast upon the hand. There would be severe consequences for the ones who did not bow before the Romans and their enormity. Some of those consequences include crucifixion, beheading, fight to the death at a gladiator arena, or eaten alive by wild animals in the Coliseum. You can become Rome and its people's entertainment. John leads us to the anti-Christ this way. These visions lead us to Rome in several different ways, which cannot be denied. There have been many anti-Christ's (beasts) in the ages of evil. However, there are some that were of a completely different caliber of evil than others. Men of the flesh seek wealth, territory, women to dominate, and whatever they seem to desire. The killing behind the treasure and territory was brutal and savage. We start to get the picture as these were really rough times for those who wanted peace or those under oppression.

Roman coins

Knights and Sages

I can tell you the dream of a thousand ages
I love to dream so turn my pages
I can tell you the tale of knights and their sages
And animals in cages
And you look at me and ask me what grace is?

Prophets and heroes all shackled in chains
Mothers that wept when they cried from the grave
I can tell you the dream of a thousand ages
I love to dream so turn my pages

I can tell you the tale of Kings and their taxes
Queens of the guillotine and double-edged axes
And you look to me to find out what the fact is?
<u>All the while I weep for the masses!</u>

Knight

Christianity is founded on many teachings that comes from all the way back to the Egyptian dynasty as well as Hinduism, Buddhism, Sumerian, and Muslims. These are some of the oldest civilizations on the planet. <u>They are of the old, I am about the innovative.</u> It's the Revelation of Jesus Christ that makes the bible a treasure and unlike any other textbook that has been penned. Hence, Christianity, as a faith, has endured the test of time by a prophetic truth which cannot be refused. Nations have been made great by their belief in Christ. Although, Christianity has strongly been ruled by deception and wealth; the believer in Christ is growing strong among many nations as the accuracy begins to be brought out. It shall rise even more as time passes by. The angels are not coming for one nation only, it is for all who believe in something greater than their own flesh and skin. Something greater than us as humans. We are all in this age with great reason and we are chosen in some fashion to live out a finality here on earth.

Many who performed false miracles and false teachings in days' past, were displayed by the seven spirits or seven angels who came forward when they themselves recognized the holy life of Christ. The false prophet in this sight is starting to be a spiritual leader who would perform miracles by the power of illusion and many people will follow such prophet. I was birthed and brought up in the Catholic Church. I embrace Catholics who love Christ.

Many prophets distort the truth and hide secrets that have brought this lashing of words. Pope Francis, on one hand, he seems like such a gentle soul and is loved globally by many. The Pope is a likable man, but I do not like those who pollute the catholic religion being that is a nationwide religion and Christ-centered. I trust He can shift the directions in the way things are running in their massive empire. I am a little skeptical of how quickly the archbishop of Naples claimed the Pope had performed a miracle. I get it, they want him to become a saint in a rapid manner as he is well-loved by the people. He's open-minded to many things and preaches peace and non-suffering. Alas, I cannot help to believe, in some ways he holds to be a puppet to the Vatican and its ability. Who would not have been? **Pope Francis Performs 'Miracle' In Naples; Turns Dry Blood to Liquid (2015).** This "miracle" was cited both by NBC news and the Huffington post. If the Pope's miracle is not an authentic miracle and a staged gimmick to help the vanishing Catholic Church flourish again, he would be a modern-day false prophet leading the masses astray. Even if it were the Vatican's or the archbishops of Naples idea. Let's face it, many things get down to the coin and paper. Even Jesus couldn't fight the force of that. At the point in time when currency became powerful, it seemed to carry much more weight among the poor than truth and wisdom. I shall give Pope Francis and the archbishop the benefit of the doubt, in hopes that all will hear my words. You don't need miracles to be a man standing for Christ or for people to follow you. Keep showing compassion and root the weeds out of your garden. This would be like doing fake healings, which is the world's biggest frauds and swindlers of all. You know who they are. Miracles being claimed by the Catholic Church should be looked at with great scrutiny and I say that with the utmost deference. Many scandals have rocked the Catholic Church, including sexual scandals with children. An internet article in 1994 by *Global Truth*, revealed allegations that show at least 231 children were abused at the Catholic boys' choir ran by Pope Benedict's brother. In February 2017, CNN reported that 4,444 victims came forward to report sexual abuse by catholic priests in Australia. The Catholic Church has been looking for ways to deflect attention away from the harm that has been caused by their reputation as many are walking away from their Catholic faith. We cannot tolerate our children going to a house of God where men are grooming them for sexual assault.

<u>True and False Prophets</u> ***Matthew 7:15-20*** *Watch out for false prophets. They come to you in sheep's clothing, but inwardly they are ferocious wolves.* **16** *By their fruit you will recognize them. Do people pick grapes from thorn bushes, or figs from thistles?* **17** *Likewise, every good tree bears good fruit, but a bad tree bears bad fruit.* **18** *A good tree cannot bear bad fruit, and a bad tree cannot bear good fruit.* **19** *Every tree that does not bear good fruit is cut down and thrown into the fire.* **20** *Thus, by their fruit you will recognize them.*

<u>The Sixth Trumpet</u> ***Revelation 9:13*** (revised position) *The sixth angel sounded his trumpet, and I heard a voice coming from the four horns of the golden altar that is before God.* **14** *It said to the sixth angel who had the trumpet, "Release the four angels who are bound at the great river Euphrates"* **15** *And the four angels who had been kept ready for this very hour and day and month and year were released to kill a third of mankind.* **16** *The number of the mounted troops was twice ten thousand times ten thousand. I heard their number {200 million, World War I & II}.* **17** *The horses and riders I saw in my vision looked like this: Their breastplates were fiery red, dark blue, and yellow as sulfur {British household Calvary}. The heads of the horses resembled the heads of lions, {helmet with horse hair plume} and out of their mouths came fire, smoke, and sulfur.* **18** *A third of mankind was killed by the three plagues of fire, smoke and sulfur that came out of their mouths {cannon, fuse, and breech load}.* **19** *The power of the horses was in their mouths and in their tails; for their tails were like snakes, having heads with which they inflict injury {modern weapons, missile fire}.* **20** *The rest of mankind who were not killed by these plagues still did not repent of the work of their hands; they did not stop worshiping demons, and idols of gold, silver, bronze, stone and wood—idols that cannot see or hear or walk.* **21** *Nor did they repent of their murders, their magic arts, their sexual immorality, or their thefts.*

The time of war with mounted horses and cannons takes us all the way to the days of Napoleon and British Calvary. Consequently, it had lead us into World War I and II years later. <u>This is another strong clue about the orderliness of the</u>

trumpets and my correct interpretation of results. This would have been the only time in history, we arrived close to these numbers with soldiers. 200 million is a lot of soldiers, we must account for them in this manner. Thus, it is my true blood line of ancient Egypt mixed with Hebrew which has been preserved and flies under the colors of red white and blue. The masons were known to have been wise, yet some went the way of corruption and the black arts. I hope I have done a great justice of the interpretation of John's book of Revelations as Daniel did for King Nebuchadnezzar before his kingdom fell. There was a vast array of nations that defeated evil in World War I and II.

So, where I come from, makes us blood brothers and sisters in Christ, whether we like or not. We fly under one banner, the brotherhood of Moses and Jesus Christ, a common bond.

The time of God's people ascension is very close as we see the destruction of many evil men and powerful kingdoms. The world is becoming ready for the appearance of our Savior and His mighty archangels of Heaven. We, the people, are no longer blind and ignorant to the world's oppression as I see us march the streets peacefully for our causes demanding justice, globally, I know my work will soon be done. We have all become Christ-like, wanting a better place to live for our children and pets. I am proud that we have had come a long way. If you doubt the hand and power of Jesus, please do not. All battles and conquering's of territory are a display of the Lord's earthly power. Heaven stands ready for those who oppose the will of the Lord, now that we have modern day weapons at every corner of the globe. It is not even a contest. I urge a strong alliance to the heavens in the name of Christ to dissipate the wicked and survive all turmoil and turbulences that are approaching. This is the correct placement of the sixth and seventh trumpet.

The Seventh Trumpet *Revelation 11:15-18* (revised position) *The seventh angel sounded his trumpet, and there were loud voices in heaven, which said: "The kingdom of the world has become the kingdom of our Lord and of his Messiah, and he will reign for ever and ever."* **16** *And the twenty-four elders, who were seated on their thrones before God, fell on their faces and worshiped God,* **17** *saying:" We give thanks to you, Lord God Almighty, the One who is and who was, because you have taken your great power and have begun to reign.* **18** *The nations were angry, and your wrath has come. The time has come for judging the dead, and for rewarding your servants the prophets and your people who revere your name, both great and small—and for destroying those who destroy the earth."* **19** *Then*

God's temple in heaven was opened, and within his temple was seen the ark of his covenant. And there came flashes of lightning, rumblings, and peals of thunder, an earthquake, and a severe hailstorm.

The Thousand Years *Revelation 20:1-6 And I saw an angel coming down out of heaven, having the key to the Abyss and holding in his hand a great chain.* **2** *He seized the dragon, that ancient serpent, who is the devil, or Satan, and bound him for a thousand years.* **3** *He threw him into the Abyss, and locked and sealed it over him, to keep him from deceiving the nations anymore until the thousand years were ended. After that, he must be set free for a short time.* **4** *I saw thrones on which were seated those who had been given authority to judge. And I saw the souls of those who had been beheaded because of their testimony about Jesus and because of the word of God. They had not worshiped the beast or its image and had not received its mark on their foreheads or their hands. They came to life and reigned with Christ a thousand years.* **5** *(The rest of the dead did not come to life until the thousand years were ended) This is the first resurrection.* **6** *Blessed and holy are those who share in the first resurrection. The second death has no power over them, but they will be priests of God and of Christ and will reign with him for a thousand years.*

Romans considered beheading a less irritating course of the death penalty. The Roman Empire primarily used beheading for its own people, while they brutally crucified others. Beheading was widely known to be practiced in Europe and Asia until the 20th century. Thus, the biblical end times that everyone talks about starting to take place prior to the twentieth century, when people were being crucified, beheaded by the sword and executed for their testimony of God, defiance of government, religion, and high taxes. It is how we formed the world.

The number or image and the mark of the beast ends prior to the release of Satan which is, but a fleeting time. Therefore, even if we needed or take several countries or organizations, we were bought by grace at the crucifixion of Jesus. Death takes no force for those who have resurrected to become priests in his figure. Even if this number meant modern times, it does not. If it did, none would've had salvation. It is strictly tied to the executions by ancient armies and the four beasts of the earth.

Everyone in this world that has lived in a Christ-like way (docile, wanting peace, etc), already has the seal of God upon their forehead. It is soon time for many peoples' salvation and for some, damnation. This tells you all things have passed except for one event which is still open for a conclusion. You are nowadays in the grace of the Holy Spirit of Christ, who will guide you into tomorrow. United States is my chosen nation of refuge and safety to tell this story. Never has had our president crowned himself in jewels or a golden crown. Why? Because it was the way of our forefathers. We have taken many steps in the right direction and I am extremely proud of this. We have gone a long way from the decadence of the Roman and Egyptian empire; however, it is creeping back into our lives at a rapid pace, making us a modern-day Babylon.

In Revelation, Chapter 20, we have what is called in most bibles: the millennial reign or the thousand years. Scriptures reveals there is a first and second death as told to John the prophet in the Revelations. In Revelation 20:4-6 we see that the first death and resurrection, is for those who were beheaded (killed) due to that they didn't take the name or the mark of the beast up to their execution for their testimony of God. This means the first 1000 years began after the crucifixion of Christ and lasted until Satan was imprisoned in 1000 AD. Those who were unjustly killed were redeemed by the blood of the lamb and reigned for a century with the Holy Spirit. Thus, the thousand-year walk with Christ was <u>spiritual and not physical</u> in this representation. The remnant came to life after the thousand years were over, from 1000 to 2000 AD. This aligns with the complete fall of the Roman and Babylonian Empire and completes the first resurrection. This brings us into modern day America in the year 2000 AD. This is in concurrence with my theory of Satan or the dragon spirit being released in the year 2000 for an abbreviated time to deceive the nations. Remember, he is the god of war and death, and wants our complete inhalation. In the short-run, it shall be, for we, are the glory of His presence, all those in Christ have risen. We can be assured this is the proper timeline, the Holy Spirit has arisen once again. It's a blessing that we have had risen in Christ to see the power of his glory unfold. This was a system set up to witness who the brave and righteous teachers of humankind would be. The devil must be let loose for a brief time to test the brethren of Jesus Christ and Christ is here to give you defense in the judgment.

Here we are in the new millennium and no land has yet to permanently attach a number to a human civilian such as a chip or tattoo for them to buy or sell. This is good news. The danger of any system among humans that is affiliated with being a number or that which revolves around credit, currency, and coin, is economically failing. If a country is conquered or invaded currency can become worthless or lose its value quickly causing famine, homelessness, or even exile. Those who do not take in a system such as this will keep on living as usual off the state while others suffer conditions they're not habituated to. This as well can happen by natural disaster. My greatest warning to humankind is to realize when we populate at epic proportions we give, rise, or need to a greater system to control population, crime, and economies among the masses. Equally so, death tolls become greater with natural disasters because we are more thickly inhabited. It is not the greatest time to bring life into a troubled world. It is like breeding your children into chaos. I say this with love and not out of judgment. We in America, as Christians in an enormous number, can never tolerate humans being marked or chipped like dogs and cattle. I urge you to please take caution in a time of much growing tension in the world. This may be precisely what may take place in other areas of the world. This would be because of famine, refugees of war, natural disaster, lack of birth control, and terrorist acts. As distressing as it is, close to people's sexual need is stronger than the usual sense that their children will starve and be enslaved. Huge populations can be a serious issue and needs to be controlled. Otherwise, we will suffer a shortage of supplies when the demands are high and the same will never meet.

In verses Revelation 20:7-8, the thousand years have gone by and Satan has been released from prison. The deceiver is set loose to lead astray the nations once more. This spirit is now on its way to judgment and final execution by Jesus Christ and his seven angels. Know that nuclear armament is part of this great deception; however, it has a cause. You will never receive knowledge such as this again, of a distant future where every bit is as good and evil. It was very pricy for me to come back to this earth and give you a message. I have suffered mentally and physically much of my life. Know that heavenly beings are here to attend to the physical structure of Christ who was dispatched in the battle of eternal souls. Today, we have time for repose as the Archangel holds the power of the dragon spirit or its great harvest will start. This is the reason for my final message. This is where prophesy also becomes very condensed for the remainder of the book.

In the second death, it has no power over the believer. The resurrection cannot be stopped and demonic powers have little to no influence. This is where scholars must pay close attention to what I'm saying as well as any other person trying to figure out the closure of this book. We are in the time that is called *the new millennium, 2000 AD.* We all have been deceived in some way through time and we have become a system of numbers and economics on the threshold of calamity because of avarice. What is more important, the life of decadence and fame or to return to our position as children of the stars? We all must change to attend a new world.

The Judgment of Satan *Revelation 20:9-10 And they came up on the broad plain of the earth and surrounded the camp of the saints and the beloved city {Israel, Jerusalem}, and fire came down from heaven and devoured them {Israel aircraft}. 10 And the devil who deceived them was thrown into the lake of fire and brimstone, where the beast and the false prophet are also; and they will be tormented day and night forever and ever.*

Judgment at the Throne of God *Revelation 20:11-15 Then I saw a great white throne and Him who sat upon it, from whose presence earth and heaven fled away, and no place was found for them. 12 And I saw the dead, the great and the small, standing before the throne, and books were opened; and another book was opened, which is the book of life; and the dead were judged from the things which were written in the books, according to their deeds. 13 And the sea gave up the dead which were in it, and death and Hades gave up the dead which were in them; and they were judged, every one of them according to their deeds. 14 Then death and Hades {evil, killers and oppressors of men and women} were thrown into the lake of fire. This is the second death, the lake of fire. 15 And if anyone's name was not found written in the book of life, he was thrown into the lake of fire {spiritual prison, time prison, a place of agony}.*

The Six-Day War of 1967, was fought by Israel and its neighboring countries. Known at the time as the United Arab Republic, they launched an assault on Israel and they were defeated by a display of American weapons, aircraft and brilliant strategy by Israeli intelligence. As of recent, Israel rightfully defended itself against in-coming rockets on its innocent citizens and countered a rocket assault against its Palestinian neighbors. Does their biblical must be another confrontation with Israel and its neighbors? Only if you are deceived in whom the Lord Jesus Christ is and the message of peace that I am sending. We see that the devil and the beast are thrown into the fire for deceiving the nations to go against the Israelites. Thus, this is not a closed case yet. A lot depends on the nuclear treaty as well as the behavior of my fellow citizens in the Middle East. If we give power to the beast and the devil, they will reemerge to conquer with hate and greed. That goes for any nation, even America.

When we realize, the angels, better known as the magi had a hand in bringing forth Moses and Jesus for the Holy Spirit to dwell in, things make much more since. It was with great reason they were placed with the Hebrews. I'll provide a more detailed account of this in the chapter *Forerunners of the Messiah*. Jesus nor Moses were the kings of the Jews, they were genetically and spiritually created with one purpose, to deliver the oppressed from this earth. Do you know how easy it was for angels to blend in with the common man? A cosmonaut or traveler could put on the clothes of a Shepard an infiltrate society, with good or evil intentions. Jesus and Moses came into the world in another way, physically and spiritually. The Israelite were sorely oppressed in that day in age, as well through time. I see a great deal of hope with the nuclear treaty that has just been made, although it will have its oppositions.

Dropping nukes on civilians will never be the solution. If this was ever to happen there would be severe consequences from heaven as well as from the earth. We should allow ourselves to move forward as brothers against satanic forces, rather than squander our days on this planet. Since most leaders are arriving to a conclusion, peace is much better solution than a conflicting war. I want to reaffirm, we are in the age where the heavens wish to help us all. If you're suppressing your people, time has a way of making you consume your own medicine. By the force of American knowledge and weapons, Israel made all retreats in the six-day war, a big triumph for Israel! *We do not have to do this*, says the Lord of peace. Plus, on that point is a much safer path. Let us respect borders until the angels arrive.

Now I must spend a moment to try to renew and mend friendships. Are we that different, those who truly want to believe in God and have peace? Many people seek an answer to that in different ways, through many enlightened teachers. This is not my subject. It is the extremist nature of law or thought that yet exists that calls a country evil and seeks to kill their people due to exclusive belief in Christ. Just remember, the Lord and His archangels gave authority, control of power, and knowledge to Satan. Everything has a cause, even if we do not agree with the current events on earth. This is the Lord letting the beast and the dragon have their final run at deception. Those who are unbelievers will doubt me until they see vessels in the sky themselves up close and personal. That would be tragic because by then, it will be too late for many and their actions against the inhabitants of this earth. They do not know the consequences they will bring in the hatred towards the Holy Spirit and its people.

Let's be clear, Satan's powers are regained based on our actions here on Earth. That power is the abuse of power, hate, greed, and lust. We may have a corrupt government in America as many other nations do; however, we are a nation of caring people trying to be stomped out by greed and desire by oppressors of good.

We cannot hold the sins of our forefathers of the past into the future. Today must be a new day. This kingdom was put up with a very specific nature in mind. Even under corruption, the spirit of God still has His hands in all things we do. We cannot say we love God, then threaten to reject, abuse, or exterminate races of innocent women and children. I trust all will express a fresh aspect of the future so that people may feel secure and thrive within their lands. Nuclear power is a huge responsibility to have and it's hopeful that it can be utilized in a peaceful manner and solutions come to us that might alter our paths. To fight a war over words, who's God and prophet is greater, is school yard nonsense! Jesus and Moses were an extension of a very powerful vessel of the heavens. Nothing less, nothing more. That vessel which battles demonic forces and is not human, is the nature of the slaughtered lamb. At the death of Jesus Christ, the incarnated spiritual being seized the hold of spiritual demonic powers. Therefore, many believe that the vessel crucified is God or a portion of God, thus he is our messiah. This is the story of Jesus Christ and I hope that the wisdom it contains will be preserved forever. I take nothing away from those before him or those who will come after and suffer for his kingdom. Glory be to the saints, martyrs, and prophets.

Moses was a very violent man as well as a playboy. He had a high place in the Egyptian kingdom as a prince who held out the crest of the Pharaohs. If this really was the son of God in his infant stages, it would seem he had many examples to learn about many matters and many situations. When Jesus Christ was crucified, he was only truly aware of the Holy Spirit for a very short time before he was killed. In all of history, rarely is it that heaven choose a perfect man to lead. Jesus was a vessel reserved for the glory to come into this world and depart afterwards. For he was spotless in the eyes of God, but not perfect. You cannot lead and be a successful leader in life unless you have walked certain roads. I have walked many roads and traveled an ocean of stars to glorify my risen son. He is the extension of my wisdom, and mighty is the one who will slay the dragon, so says the Holy Spirit of the Father.

The Heavenly Warrior Defeats the Beast *Revelation 20:11*-21 *I saw heaven standing open and there before me was a white horse, whose rider is called Faithful and True. With justice, he judges and wages war.* **12** *His eyes are like blazing fire, and on his head, are many crowns. He has a name written on him that no one knows but he himself.* **13** *He is dressed in a robe dipped in blood, and his name is the Word of God.* **14** *The armies of heaven were following him, riding on white horses and dressed in fine linen, white and clean.* **15** *Coming out of his mouth is a sharp sword with which to strike down the nations {truth} "He will rule them with an iron scepter." He treads the winepress of the fury of the wrath of God Almighty.* **16** *On his robe and on his thigh he has this name written: king of kings and lord of lords.* **17** *And I saw an angel standing in the sun, who cried in a loud voice to all the birds flying in midair, "Come, gather together for the great supper of God,* **18** *so that you may eat the flesh of kings, generals, and the mighty, of horses and their riders, and the flesh of all people, free and slave, great and small."* **19** *Then I saw the beast {reemergence of the beast} and the kings of the earth and their armies gathered together to wage war against the rider on the horse and his army.* **20** *But the beast was captured, and with it the false prophet who had performed the signs on its behalf. The two of them were thrown alive into the fiery lake of burning sulfur.* **21** *The rest were killed with the sword coming out of the mouth of the rider on the horse, and all the birds gorged themselves on their flesh.*

That name, which is written upon the Lord that only He knows is: Death the Destroyer. Though he walks softly and quietly in his claim for peace, his presence alone wakes the dead in a very specific age. I have discovered a bunch of people recently say Mexicans and Muslims should be banned from coming into America and we should not help those in trouble or need. It is an irrational time because of economics and war as I understand that completely and we will soon see life is a conundrum. If either expected or not, events will affect America in the future as we know they will, heaven will treat us as we treated those who are refuges of deplorable economic conditions and oppression. In reality, those who have the most, have much to lose, yet much to gain. If you have not figured it out by now, the whole record of revelation is about the unjust treatment of the Hebrew and Jewish people. The Holy Spirit has written many scripts on the inequitable treatment of humans. Men and women have written such manuscripts all through time and they were usually destroyed.

The spirit of prophecy chose a certain race to be among and certain race to leave this world. That does not imply God does not love all. Heaven has intervened on mankind's behalf, it just so happens the gospels of Jesus Christ have existed longer than any other prophetic manuscript. Why is this an interesting story? The Catholic Church practiced it to spread concern to the citizens of its empire and a means of command. However, the Romans did not know the true meaning of the revelations. It is in modern day, we come to see this revelation with more clarity.

There have been mosques burned down to the ground and little children in school were told to return home to Mexico. How ruthless we have become! This isn't even our land any more than it was for the Indians. If we state the land is under a higher source, then let us apply that analogy. *When I go from this world and the massive city of God lands in America, does that mean, the whole Earth is mine? I have become its general and have the strength to be able to support that statement and impose my will.* <u>In this hypothetical scenario, should I throw everyone out of my lands and keep them from my heavenly city?</u> Or maybe keep the most beautiful and talented for my own joy and sexual desires and kick the rest away? Perhaps it is judicious to act as my king has instructed me to manage. Love all equally and punish those who are just plain wicked. The high or the drug that never leaves is the defense of innocent people and animals from bullies. My reward is when they will practice the same for others, and it unfolds like a disease that can't be wiped out, the magic and power of love. Not a boy meets girl type of lovemaking! The sort of love that stomps out starvation and sexual battery against children and women. The sort of passion that stops wars of greed and builds kingdoms that last forever.

We must take steps to prevent <u>radical Islamic teachings</u> as well any other radical form of religion from spreading in this world. The Muslim civilization is ancient and there is great wisdom in many teachings. The Muslim religion is also very large in population. To combine and set religion aside for the moment in time will make the world a much stronger place. Let's face it, extreme holy terrorist as well as any other terrorist such as the Klu Klux Klan, always have hidden agendas. They would love to find out the world erupt into chaos over religion, organized religion, race, and color. They would take this over sharing technology and getting closer as human beings. They want *the end of time*, so there is reason to spill blood and make money off from the weapons of war. One does not wish the end of times and I can assure of that, one must be heedful of what they bid for.

The spirit of Allah and the prophet Mohammed existed with a purpose. The law was created with an intent in a different time, in the realm of God. The archangel spirit used the Muslim race against the corrupted Roman Empire. This is the empire that killed Jesus and John. Rome's brutality was at a high-level violence. Muslims had an elite line of desert warriors and they achieved many great triumphs in many battles under the jurisprudence of the Koran. The heart of Elijah, is a bond servant to Christ, and the spirit of Elijah, was kindred to Mohammed as well as John the Baptist and Moses. If Jesus studied under the spirit of Elijah and called him teacher or master, we can understand the meaning of this relationship as easily as a bond and friendship that stretches through time. A teacher cannot be a master forever, nor can a student live the law of his master when he finally becomes the master himself. Nevertheless, a pupil must always observe that the many lessons that the masters taught him and studied under; it is the legal philosophy of respect. Therefore, Jesus had a forerunner to teach him all things within the Holy Spirit so he may judge them accordingly. Especially religion, it can be very complicated. Violence will never be the answer in this long equation.

I will say right now, I'm glad for the many nations who knocked the Roman Empire back into their place for crucifying Jesus and killing John. There were such evil men in this dynasty of power. They had bathed house orgies and groomed young men and women in the manner of material body and sexual desires. I tell you my friends, time is a repeating story and will never change. It is no wonder the laws in the Muslim culture existed as the hijab and other Muslim attire. The world has turned into a frenzy of flesh. How can a spiritual teacher not respect this act? That is a very holy gesture to cover the flesh, especially if it is not a forced issue. This was an act not just to restrain women from tempting holy men, as well men from tempting holy women. Muslim women are very beautiful as any woman in the Earth. They were highly desired in ancient days by other kings as strange flesh and exotic. For people to disrespect them and their attire is a very shameful thing. They are guests in our land and we should care for them as such unless proven differently. Nuns and priests carry some of that same value today when covering skin. When going to church, most people cover themselves accordingly as to not to be revealing. The war of God is not against different religions, it is against the deceit of the flesh. Are you deceived or confused about religion? Please don't be. Love is greater than all religions. Jesus directly confronted the churches of Asia in the Revelation of John, as considerably as the Pharisees in Matthew 23. The sprit scrutinizes many religions of their truth and origin and it always should. We are a part of the first resurrection, and many will have the time needed to realize the true statement of Christ. I promise you, time will adjust all things given peace.

There is a lot of testosterone left over from the many ages of war. Nevertheless, to take mass innocent life purposely and aggressively is an unforgivable offense and a misdemeanor of the principles of war and thought in any scene. These are cowardly acts and must be condemned by all countries, including Muslim countries. We must condemn acts of terror on any innocent race of people, even cowboys and Indians. Many must choose in what they must believe, the words of Jesus Christ or the laws of our forefathers. There are many people among us that would sit at a table for dinner with Muslim families and not cast any judgment, including myself. I speak a lot of this hatred because it has existed forever. Many were poor examples of their headmaster and teachers. Let's be clear on that. It is ideologies of men and belief that such monsters have been born. It is monsters among us and those that serve them that keep this world in a poisonous state. I'm not getting to hate or judge anybody over their faith or religious belief as I'm not in that position to do so nor anyone else. I have a family of different culture and faith. The word of God is not a religion, it is a multitude of wisdom which comes from many ancient teachings, the crown of many diadems. <u>Every great kingdom will take from their faults then they may prosper, or go the way of condemnation.</u> Please don't consider the stone statues that people pray before can protect them from what is coming. Everyone is in their right places until we catch the signs of our friends of time and distance. They soon will reveal themselves completely. They wish to repay a debt from long ago when humans were brave enough to care and make a difference in the world. Please give my words a chance and keep peace. If it is victory this world wants for heaven, they must know that the enemy is not of flesh. To have true victory, it is in the spiritual realm of this world.

Many treasures and kingdoms exist in heaven, and we will be brought the rights to such. We do not need to find or discover anything, as it will be a waste of money and time soon in the future. How can we share kingdoms when we act like this? The meek and the oppressed will inherit the land, and to those who have shown mercy to the feeble and persecuted they will go backward into the heavenly kingdoms to prepare them for those who have inherited the world. Serenity will have demons trembling in fright on their way back to hell. This is because they cognize that their time is up and Jesus Christ is here to set everything straight. Their existence (evil) is tied to our <u>unnatural, violent death, pain, and suffering</u>. All these things that we shall conquer as one when we unify and give glory to heaven and the words of the Holy Spirit. We let this evil exist by own actions, it is time to put a finish to it.

My physical father in this life, whom I barely know these days, was working in a defense contract firm. They built components for Tomahawk, cruise missiles, and other very powerful weapons. My father may have worn a top-secret badge; however, I am quite sure nothing is secure in the realm of the holy spirit. I am sure I was not born into a family with a military father, who was an engineer on the designs of <u>electronic missile components</u> just to say it was so. I would imagine this means the holy spirit knows vast info regarding our defense industry. I believe those in heaven have acquired info, <u>spiritually</u>, to disarm military weapons with very high-tech devices. This is great news for those who believe in Christ and will look for his safety and protection! I am super-secret under cover, I'm so deep in this journey, it has taken me many life time's just to figure it out. Remember, I love the USA and its very kind and brave people, **<u>I want us protected at all costs!</u>** I do not love our greedy ways or the poison that flows on our computers and streets. Pornographic candy and the many hard-core poisons which are destroying the minds of American's.

Never do I condone or like war, nor does the Holy Spirit. We, as Americans, and other nations, must protect ourselves from those who would slaughter and imprison us while they rape our women and children. What a fearful manner to subdue a country. As a world, our power should always represent the overcoming of this type of ignorance and hate. We cannot tolerate this kind of hatred to spread like a disease in the celestial sphere or on the dry land. Again, my Muslim brothers are correct, Jesus is not a god. He is the Son of God and is the manifestation of the power of resurrection, who speaks for those who have great spiritual and physical power. However, none will resurrect without the message of Christ in their hearts, that message is of peace and compassion.

As I noted before, the book of Revelations is one of the most complex books written in time. Who would have thought all this has already happened and a finality is about to take place? This can be clarified as we trace the scripture in many places with clear language. *"Seven thousand people were killed in the earthquake, and many were terrified and gave glory to the God of heaven."* Seven thousand is not even a large number today when we look at earthquakes. Per many official estimates, hundreds of thousands of people were killed as well and injured in the Port-au-Prince earthquake in southern Haiti. Not to mention the amount of people that were displaced. The estimated death toll reached just as high in the Tangshan area of China. Now that's damage beyond biblical proportion! It's only going to get worse as the <u>millennial shift</u> approaches. This terminology will be explained in detail as well as the terminology, <u>harvest of souls</u>. This is what the Christ spirit had come to save you from, complete devastation. The spirit comes as your friend, please accept the wisdom. For one day, it will not return as a friend. It will be to completely conquer in the name of heaven and the lord Jesus Christ. We have not been so kind to the earth and its creatures and we've seen it turn against us (earthquakes, hurricanes, etc). The scores of rubbishes in our seas and rivers must conclude because when the spiritual destruction is unleashed, it will be a strong message about change. The Lord will not need military assistance to emphasize this point and bring to your attention.

VII

THE CITY OF GOD

Final season. John's final season of prophecy

A New Heaven and a New Earth *Revelation 21:1-8* <u>*Then I saw "a new heaven*</u> <u>*and a new earth," for the first heaven and the first earth had passed away, and there was no*</u> <u>*longer any sea.*</u> *2 I saw the Holy City, the New Jerusalem {a new place of worship}, coming down out of heaven from God, prepared as a bride beautifully dressed for her husband. 3 And I heard a loud voice from the throne saying, "Look! God's dwelling place is now among the people, and he will dwell with them. They will be his people, and God himself will be with them and be their God. 4 'He will wipe every tear from their eyes. There will be no more death' or mourning or crying or pain, for the old order of things has passed away." 5 He who was seated on the throne said, <u>"I am making everything new!"</u> Then he said, "Write this down, for these words are trustworthy and true." 6 He said to me: <u>"It is done. I am the</u> <u>Alpha and the Omega, the Beginning and the End.</u> To the thirsty I will give water without cost from the spring of the water of life. 7 Those who are victorious will inherit all this, and I will be their God and they will be my children. 8 <u>But the cowardly, the unbelieving, the</u> <u>vile, the murderers, the sexually immoral, those who practice magic arts, the idolaters and</u> <u>all liars—they will be consigned to the fiery lake of burning sulfur. This is the second death."</u>*

Revelation 21:15-17 *The angel who talked with me had a measuring rod of gold to measure the city, its gates and its walls. 16 The city was laid out like a square, as long as it was wide. He measured the city with the rod and found it to be 12,000 stadia in length, and as wide and high as it is long {approx. 1,400 miles}. 17 <u>The angel measured the wall</u> <u>using human measurement</u>, and it was 144 cubits thick {approx. 216 feet}.*

A study of the 79 A.D., Vesuvius eruption of a man named Haroldur Sigurdsson, showed particularly strong blasts during its eruptions. Mt. St. Helens plumed on May 18, 1980 reaching about 101,700 feet, and the highest Pinatubo plume got as far as 147,600 feet per an article from the Oregon State University, *Volcano World.* What would an eruption of the Yellowstone Super volcano look like? *"Science without religion is lame, religion without science is blind"*, stated by Albert

Einstein in 1941. What is impossible for man, is possible for heaven. Per my theory, the city of God occupies in a pressurized structure, self-contained with super thick walls built of a core that looks like quartz or glass. I can guarantee you this material survives and is practiced for something advanced in addition to the urban center of God. That's my little secret for now. The city has an anchoring system that goes deep within the earth, this accounts for the enormous height. At about 1,400 miles high and square footage, it is a super structure that can accommodate a significant number of people. Once anchored, it will be until it chooses not to be and goes elsewhere. This is the kingdom of Christ and his people. It will fare with a very powerful escort.

When we speak of the supremacy of Christ, please know this: I surrendered my kingdom and vessel to the glorification of Christ when I was stricken down from great heights long ago. It was time to pay the piper for the treasures I had obtained illegally and with hard labor of lesser men. This is the battle mentioned at the time of Christ, when the archangel throws the dragon down to earth. As I mentioned, the dragon or serpent are always affiliated to the Egyptian crown that Moses and his Egyptian father figure wore. We understand they had a battle of sorcery in the book of Genesis. The spirit of the Egyptian pharaoh or Father exists within the son, so we may know there are consequences in all things. It also means Moses had achieved a great victory. He lay hold of the serpent or dragon by sacrificing himself in a spiritual battle against the great pharaoh.

The holy spirits exist as easily inside the zone, which is love and forgiveness under such harsh accusation of the foe. Thus, as far as dimensions, they are exactly on the money. Per my hypothesis, the life of Christ is non-human in origin and exists in a father-son manner for perpetual presence on this earth and in heaven. Forever wisdom and power shall rule it. In scriptures, John calls the city of God, New Jerusalem. This city that descends from the sky in John's Revelation is far larger than Israel itself. The entire area of the State of Israel is 8,630 sq. miles. You could fit Israel in the city of God many times over. It is my belief it will be descending upon America, for several reasons. However, the word has been spoken about those who would do Israel harm when unprovoked. The substance that this containment system is made from is indestructible to heat, meteorite debris, nuclear weapons, earthquakes, and volcanoes. In other words, it can withstand almost anything from heaven, or of this earth and endure. With walls 216 ft. thick, one cannot penetrate this fortress with anything. Have you ever seen the movie *The Day the Earth Stood Still?* It's an excellent movie. I suggest we use that as an example of exactly what *not* to do. In the movie, the military tries to penetrate the walls with many different advanced weapons and modern tools. Only to anger those more who had sent. <u>They were hostile to its occupant and tried to press him for secret information.</u> I have nothing left to give, I've have given you all, as a prisoner and humble servant to my Lord and Savior. I have done my time in this hell!

We know these measurements are exact numbers, they are noted in the context of human measurements. That's one huge mother ship, my friends. Because the city is pressurized and has its own atmosphere, it will not need rocket fuel for craft to go up into space. Per my theory, we will also receive a new prototype for space travel that is nonmilitary and strictly for global humanitarian aid. Therefore, the city is built so high with easy access into space. It can also harness energy in several different ways. You will also notice the sheer size of it could block volcanic ash in the mid-eastern United States during a Yellowstone eruption. It will be fixed in a way to compensate and protect as many fresh water sources as possible from contamination.

When the city decides to anchor itself, it will sit raised above the earth and deploy a shield in a very crucial hour. If you were to pull and play with a 1,400-mile squared cube placed on the east coast of America, you would experience a perfect shield and containment structure for most of the United States east of the Yellowstone super volcano. So yes, government facilities will be preserved and highly protected to keep order for a time. This 1400-mile squared city is a piece of technology better than anything we have seen as modern humans. It is approximately 2000 miles from Yellowstone to the White House in Pennsylvania. The world will erupt in different places it is just a matter of time. I will explain this in depth so do not be alarmed. As I mentioned in the beginning of the book, no one must take my word as literal. However, if I have lived many lives and seen many things, then know this book was written out of love. I am attempting to give you the most accurate book possible about history and religion. Those who trust in peace will follow Christ for redemption. Know the glory of Christ is here to lead all people from this suffering for those who believe.

Civilizations since time began have disappeared on mother earth; she is a special creature. Cities were swallowed whole, never to be seen again, buried under volcanic ash and sediment of time. When we Give glory to the Holy Spirit and the heavens, they will save many of us from this fate. People will even doubt and scrutinize the spirit's words, I'm certain. Why? People are stubborn and hard headed. I have deciphered scripture in a very rare manner. This is a great deal of information and history to decipher and write down in a cohesive way. It should give humans a greater understanding of the Holy Bible and why certain things were encoded in the book. It was coded in so we can clearly understand it in modern day and age of Jesus' return. This is a serious business for us as a country and I am here with you. And then feel secure until told otherwise, and then says the Holy Spirit. If God did not love us, we would not be advised to <u>prepare for departure?</u>

<u>Jesus is Coming</u> *Revelation 22:8-11 I, John, am the one who heard and saw these things. And when I had heard and seen them, I fell down to worship at the feet of the angel who had been showing them to me. **9** But he said to me, "Don't do that! I am a fellow servant with you and with your fellow prophets and with all who keep the words of this scroll. Worship God!" **10** Then he told me, <u>"Do not seal up the words of the prophecy of this scroll, because the time is near</u> {open for a conclusion}. **11** Let the one who does wrong continue to do wrong; let the vile person continue to be vile; let the one who does right continue to do right; and let the holy person continue to be holy."*

<u>Epilogue: Invitation and Warning</u> *Revelation 22:12-16 "Look, I am coming soon!* <u>*My reward is with me, and I will give to each person according to what they have done.*</u> *13 I am the Alpha and the Omega, the First and the Last, the Beginning and the End. 14 "Blessed are those who wash their robes, that they may have the right to the tree of life and may go through the gates into the city. 15 Outside are the dogs, those who practice magic arts, the sexually immoral, the murderers, the idolaters and everyone who loves and practices falsehood. {those who cannot enter the heavenly city} 16 "I, Jesus, have sent my* <u>*angel to give you this testimony for the churches. I am the Root and the Offspring of David, and the bright Morning Star."*</u>

When the city of God descends from heaven, we have entered the third and final season. This is the closing of the second season and the time of the second death. This is when death gets its final prize into the kingdoms of hell and destruction for those who denied of the Holy Spirit. This is a representation of fulfillment of all things when Christ finally takes the fallen angels' place as leader of the magi. These foul souls of time cannot be destroyed until the universe completely dies out, and that is a long eternal, prison sentence. It has been a system of punishment here on this earth as some were deserving more than others. I have done my time in this *Time Prison* so that I may save you much pain and suffering. The earth will shed us like an old skin so it may regenerate. How much harm we can make besides pollution and atomic war that will influence many people's fate in this prison I have spoken of? I forewarn you, those who live by greed--and will waste my time and breath--you really do not understand the angel of death as I do. What more can I do to achieve peace in the world before I die? The Holy Spirit has promised you kingdoms made of diamonds, gold, rubies, and sapphires. All heaven asks is stop the sins and return to grace. Let us treat those less fortunate with some respect as they are humans like the rest of us. Treat the lower class with dignity until the angels come, no matter the state of economics. You are not giving free handouts, you are offering an assistance to the infirm and less unfortunate which will be returned to you many times over. When God--the Holy Spirit--is not here on this earth, under cover, He likes to cruise around the universe in His highly over decorated, fortress and city. For those who do not understand, it means he moves around like a king and many will follow.

Men highly underestimated the power of the Lord's word throughout the ages, today is the day the word cannot be ignored. If you want what Jesus has, it was obtained by being a humanitarian, not by spilling blood. He was patient and walked with complete faith in the promises of his Father and the Holy Spirit. I ask you now, as my people, to have the same faith. Look at the ancients, they always had their treasure and tons of gold. The Holy Spirit is as ancient as they come. Our treasures on earth are child's play. It is not how much treasure you have that makes you a king, it's how you use that wealth that determines the prosperity of all kingdoms. All wealth that the Holy Spirit has obtained is stolen treasure from the fallen angels. It all belongs to the slaves of Christ, for by the sweat of their brow these kingdoms were built in space and on earth. <u>Is there anyone who wishes to disagree with the wisdom of this law?</u> The Holy Spirit is now in search for those that will run these kingdoms in a fair and honest way. They will fear the consequences of going back to what is not righteous. This is the nature of all law being established here on earth. The spirit came to give you an example of how we should treat each other. I rejoice in those who have heard my testimony, so says the holy spirit of Christ.

Revelation 21:18-21 *The wall was made of jasper, and the city of pure gold, as pure* *as glass.* <u>**19**</u> *The foundations of the city walls were decorated with every kind of precious stone. The first foundation was jasper, the second sapphire, the third agate, the fourth emerald,* <u>**20**</u> *the fifth onyx, the sixth ruby, the seventh chrysotile, the eighth beryl, the ninth topaz, the tenth turquoise, the eleventh jacinth, and the twelfth amethyst.* <u>**21**</u> *The twelve gates were twelve pearls, each gate made of a single pearl.* <u>*The great street of the city was of gold, as pure as transparent glass*</u> *{gold and diamonds}.*

Now that is a city, my friends. This vessel was built ages ago and I assure you it is not something you want to try to attack. I say that as a teacher and as an ambassador of their good attentions. You should choose God, not them, it is a very simple process. *Outside are the dogs, those who practice magic arts, the sexually immoral, the murderers, the idolaters, and everyone who loves and practices falsehood.* Everything is deteriorating rapidly and this will be the test of great faith. Do we pull together as mankind, or get greedy with everyone for themselves? If you think about it, all great decisions are made with a gamble. Do you want to take the choice of me being highly deceived and a disillusioned man? Or would you like to take a chance on a man who's telling a story of demonic spirits known as the "dead", which are serving out a death sentence by the power of the archangel and his Christ? Me, my bet is for my sanity as being fully intact by the many prophecies that I have already worked with utmost accuracy. Many have yet to be fulfilled. I have enclosed a few sent via emails that were recorded with dates as image files at the end of the book. Could I doctor stuff up or fake it, absolutely. However, I have many witnesses to the level of accuracy I hold. When I get to perform a line of work in the public figure of heaven, know it's going to be exhaustive. The judgment is unescapable and can be very brutal depending on your crimes. My crimes were great, I labored human beings for my own pleasure and gain. I lived to be the top dog and have it all. To live like a king, just to lose it over and over and over, soon becomes insanity. King Solomon mentions it as chasing the wind. Now my treasure is within. By the end of the book you will know exactly who I am and the cost. I have surrendered to the Son of God and yet..

<u>IT COST HIM HIS LIFE.</u>

What is the grandness that is impermanent? This is what many seek, a life with many pleasures with wealth and prosperity. What does that amount to if it's only temporary and then you have to come back into this life again under new conditions? It is because you have not learned a lesson about wealth, greed, and others sufferings. As I have said, "I've done my time in this hell, I'm not coming back!"

The Supremacy of the Son of God *Colossians 1:15-20 The Son is the image of the invisible God, the firstborn over all creation.* **16** *For in him all things were created: things in heaven and on earth, visible and invisible, whether thrones or powers or rulers or authorities; all things have been created through him and for him.* **17** *He is before all things, and in him all things hold together.* **18** *And he is the head of the body, the church; he is the beginning and the firstborn from among the dead {first to overcome death and the grave} so that in everything he might have the supremacy.* **19** *For God (the father) was pleased to have all his fullness dwell in him,* **20** *and through him to reconcile to himself all things, whether things on earth or things in heaven, by making peace through his blood, shed on the cross.*

VIII

THE BOOK OF DANIEL

I will keep this chapter short and move on into greater testimony. In the book of Daniel, the antichrist sets up the fall of many by a false covenant. The scriptures are very vague on who and what the anti-Christ is. I am going to make sure we solve this insight together, so that this subject is clarified. This I can tell you, the main purpose of the anti-Christ is to wipe out those who love Christ and his way of peace and compassion. This is important so that we might know who the last anti-Christ will be to challenge God and the coming of his Messiah.

Per the book of John, the time is quickly approaching as Israel and the Middle East cannot come to a peaceful resolution to their past and terrorism plaques around the globe. We can be sure the anti-Christ will bring suffering to many, before he is stopped. Yes, biblically, he will fail. We will soon see our ancestors arrive in the heavens after a fulfillment of events.

This subject of the anti-Christ begins in the book of Daniel 9:27. John's vision seems to be an add-on to the book of Daniel. I say this because they tie into each other. Per my deciphering of the book, John picks up were Daniel left off. He does this by tying his vision into Daniel's by mentioning the seven heads of the beast with ten horns. However, John's vision is predominantly about the Roman Empire and the siege of Jerusalem by King Herod. Its more aligned to the plight of Israel and its people right before and after the fall of the second temple. Daniel's vision is about the ancient Jews who were taken captive and forced into exile many times. It gives us in depth look at the Babylonians and King Nebuchadnezzar, who eventually destroys the temple in Jerusalem. It also informs regarding the coming of the kings of the Persian Empire who would conquer all of Mesopotamia, Egypt, Israel, and Turkey. It lays the foundation for John's vision and the rise of the Roman Empire.

The events surrounding Jerusalem are also noted in the holy book, 2nd Kings chapter 25, as well as Jeremiah on chapter 52. This is clearly Old Testament information. In Daniel's prophecy, it is noted that Daniel refers to the book of

Jeremiah and the 70- year desolation of Jerusalem. One thing we can be sure of: Jewish prophets were very accurate. Do John and Daniels prophecy correspond or are they entirely separate when we speak of the beasts and the anti-Christ? We must zero in on the facts of John's prophecy and match them with Daniel's. One key fact in prophecy that differentiates Daniel's vision from Johns is the mention of Darius, son of Xerxes, King of Persia 486-465 B.C and King Nebuchadnezzar 635 B.C. Daniel takes us directly to the meaning of the dream by giving us literal names in history to solve the dream of the statue. After the Jews were forced into captivity and exiled to Babylon, we have the rise of Cyrus the Great. Per ancient historians, Cyrus the great releases the Jews from Babylon after having a vision from God. The Jews go back to Jerusalem to build their temple. So, this sets the stage for the building of the second temple which the romans destroy. This is the period we call the abomination of desolation, it changed the way they worshipped. Again, I am not a historian, I am soldier of time. There are so many others who have done so much work in the cypher of history in the biblical verses. I am confirmation of the new and old. The four beasts that are mentioned in the upcoming text, are the beasts mentioned in the first four seals in John's revelation. However, the three beasts are soon devoured by the 4th beast. This gives us clear sign who the two mighty beasts of the earth and sea are in John's revelation. It as well brings the Old Testament into the new.

Daniel's Dream of Four Beasts *Daniel 7:1-28 In the first year of Belshazzar king of Babylon, Daniel had a dream, and visions passed through his mind as he was lying in bed. He wrote down the substance of his dream. 2 Daniel said: "In my vision at night I looked, and there before me were the four winds of heaven churning up the great sea. 3 Four great beasts, each different from the others, came up out of the Mediterranean Sea {Kings of Babylon, Persia, Greece, and Rome}. 4 "The first was like a lion, and it had the wings of an eagle {Babylon}. I watched until its wings were torn off and it was lifted from the ground so that it stood on two feet like a human being, and the mind of a human was given to it. 5 "And there before me was a second beast, which looked like a bear {Asia minor}. It was raised up on one of its sides, and it had three ribs in its mouth between its teeth. It was told, 'Get up and eat your fill of flesh!' 6 "After that, I looked, and there before me was another beast, one that looked like a leopard {Persia}. And on its back, it had four wings like those of a bird. This beast had four heads {Cyrus the Great, Darious I, Xereses, Artaxerxes}}and it was given authority to rule. 7 "After that, in my vision at night I looked, and there before* me was a fourth beast {Roman empire}, terrifying and frightening and very powerful. It had large iron teeth; it crushed and devoured its victims and trampled underfoot whatever was left. It was different from all the former beasts, and it had ten horns {conquered nations of Rome}. **8** "While I was thinking about the horns, there before me was another horn, a little one, which came up among them; and three of the first horns were uprooted before it. This horn had eyes like the eyes of a human being and a mouth that spoke boastfully **9** "As I looked, "thrones were set in place, and the Ancient of Days took his seat. His clothing was as white as snow; the hair of his head was white like wool. His throne was flaming with fire, and its wheels were all ablaze. **10** A river of fire was flowing, coming out from before him. Thousands upon thousands attended him; ten thousand times ten thousand stood before him. The court was seated, and the books were opened {City of God}. **11** "Then I continued to watch because of the boastful words the horn was speaking. I kept looking until the beast was slain and its body destroyed and thrown into the blazing fire. **12** The other beasts had been stripped of their authority, but were allowed to live for a period of time. **13** "In my vision at night I looked, and there before me was one like a son of man, coming with the clouds of heaven. He approached the Ancient of Days and was led into his presence. **14** He was given authority, glory, and sovereign power; all nations and peoples of every language worshiped him. His dominion is an everlasting dominion that will not pass away, and his kingdom is one that will never be destroyed.

The Interpretation of the Dream

15 "I, Daniel, was troubled in spirit, and the visions that passed through my mind disturbed me. **16** I approached one of those standing there and asked him the meaning of all this. "So he told me and gave me the interpretation of these things: **17** 'The four great beasts are four kings that will rise from the earth. **18** But the holy people of the Highest will receive the kingdom and will possess it forever—yes, for ever and ever.' **19** "Then I wanted to know the meaning of the fourth beast, which was different from all the others and most terrifying, with its iron teeth and bronze claws—the beast that crushed and devoured its victims and trampled underfoot whatever was left. **20** I also wanted to know about the ten horns on its head and about the other horn that came up, before which three of them fell—the horn that looked more imposing than the others and that had eyes and a mouth that spoke boastfully. **21** As I watched, this horn was waging war against the holy people and defeating them, **22** until the Ancient of Days came and pronounced judgment in favor of the holy people *of the Most High, and the time came when they possessed the kingdom {military alliances, Germany, France, USA). 23 "He gave me this explanation: "The fourth beast is a fourth kingdom that will appear on earth. It will be different from all the other kingdoms and will devour the whole earth, trampling it down and crushing it {Roman empire}. 24 The ten horns are ten kings who will come from this kingdom. After them another king will arise, different from the earlier ones; he will subdue three kings {King Herod, the three wise men}. 25 He will speak against the Highest and oppress his holy people and try to change the set times and the laws {destroys the temple}. The holy people will be delivered into his hands for a time, times and half a time." 26 'But the court will sit, and his power will be taken away and completely destroyed forever. 27 Then the sovereignty, power and greatness of all the kingdoms under heaven will be handed over to the holy people of the Highest. His kingdom will be an everlasting kingdom, and all rulers will worship and obey him. 28 "This is the end of the matter. I, Daniel, was deeply troubled by my thoughts, and my face turned pale, but I kept the matter to myself."*

The End Times Daniel 12:2-13 *"At that time Michael, the great prince who protects your people, will arise. {Michael casts Satan down, rev 12:1}. There will be a time of distress such as has not happened from the beginning of nations until then. But at that time your people—{Israel} everyone whose name is found written in the book—will be delivered. {first resurrection}. 2 Multitudes who sleep in the dust of the earth will awake: some to everlasting life, others to shame and everlasting contempt {the first and second death, rev 20:14, 21:8}. 3 Those who are wise will shine like the brightness of the heavens, and those who lead many to righteousness, like the stars for ever and ever. 4 But you, Daniel, roll up and seal the words of the scroll until the time of the end. Many will go here and there to increase knowledge." 5 Then I, Daniel, looked, and there before me stood two others, one on this bank of the river and one on the opposite bank {the two witnesses}. 6 One of them said to the man clothed in linen, who was above the waters of the river, "How long will it be before these astonishing things are fulfilled?" 7 The man clothed in linen, who was above the waters of the river, lifted his right hand and his left hand toward heaven, and I heard him swear by him who lives forever, saying, "It will be for a time, times and half a time. When the power of the holy people has been finally broken, all these things will be completed." 8 I heard, but I did not understand. So I asked, "My lord, what will the outcome of all this be?" 9 He replied, "Go your way, Daniel, because the words are rolled up and sealed until the time of the end. 10 Many will be purified, made spotless and refined, but the wicked will continue to be wicked. None of the wicked will understand, but those who are wise will* *understand.* **11** *"From the time that the daily sacrifice is abolished and the abomination that causes desolation is set up, there will be 1,290 days {King Herods siege of Jerusalem, Johns 42 months of Blasphemy}.* **12** *Blessed is the one who waits for and reaches the end of the 1,335 days.* **13** *"As for you, go your way till the end. You will rest, and then at the end of the days you will rise to receive your allotted inheritance."*

In Daniel's vision, he mentioned the beast with seven heads and ten horns. John's prophecy has the same identical description. In John's vision, he describes the anti-Christ or the dragon as the beast with seven heads and ten horns and a man whose number is 666. A more modern beast or anti-Christ, greater and more brutal than all. This was the great mystery Daniel sought after in the dream of King Nebuchadnezzar. This now becomes a little clearer after talking about the beast and his number in the previous chapters. It also becomes clear when we talk about the Romans seizing ten nations under seven kings of ancient Rome. Biblical scholars know them, as the ten nations of the antichrist. This is pretty widely known by those who study the scriptures. These comparison gives a great hope and certainty of the arrival of the City of God by such accurate prophecies of time. There is no debating them, they are highly accurate. The Assyrians exiled the Jews around 700 B.C and then by the Chaldeans very close to 600 B.C., per ancient historians. They were exiled and forced to live in the city of Babylon. So, this certainly gives us a clue to the beast or the anti-Christ in this time and era when we talk of the mass deportation of humans from their homeland. Or when a ruler closes its borders unless you carry or have the mark of the beast. Now isn't that simple folks! It as well should help you understand how Daniel coded his revelation. We must remember the Jews became captives in the lands of the Babylonians, Egyptians, Persians, Romans, and Greeks. They were scattered throughout the lands. These are the clues to a brutal king's arrival in Israel coded by the elements on the statue in the dream of Nebuchadnezzar. Babylon was the head of the original sin or the original offense against God. This would no doubt be the head of gold. Daniel even tells king Nebuchadnezzar that *he* is that head as written in his book.

King Hammurabi was one of the first kings of the Babylonian empire. Under his rule, Babylon flourished and the early Hebrew decimated. We can come to this conclusion by being in the Garden of Eden, which is in biblical history compared to the conquered lands. Therefore, God placed Adam and Eve in the safety of the garden. The sons of God had fallen for the daughters of men and they were claiming territory from the natives of the land. Adam and Eve were the Native Americans of the Middle East and they were decimated. Again, John and Daniel were Hebrew-Jewish prophets, so yes, their prophecy was about the utter struggle for the Hebrew race not to be erased from the earth, <u>much like the Indians</u>. You will notice we imposed the mark of the beast upon the Indian, currency.

If you combine the information I gave you about the first four seals in John's revelation to Daniel's vision, we will know that the dragon and its beast have ruled many nations and conquered many tongues since the beginning of time. Any time we see a figure aligning themselves with Israel, we must be careful of their intentions. Many leaders have brought much pain and sorrow to Israel with false testaments and non-achieved promises. Be careful of the wolf in a sheep's clothes. Will man wage war and trade your spot in the holy kingdom for someone else's black gold? If so, they are more stubborn and blind than my Father would had imagined. God is something more than territory and temples, he is freedom.

<u>War is not what Israel needs!</u>

IX

GOOD AND EVIL

Pharaoh burial mask

Why has life always been so barbaric since time began? Who were these masses that came to this land and began the wars? We know the Egyptians had set up a dynasty that will never be forgotten. They left behind a reminder that all physical kingdoms will one day perish no matter how great it raised when they are not built on righteousness. Their desire to take more territory with men, women, and children to be slaves; it became their downfall. They were self-proclaimed gods. For some of these men, it was too late, their souls became bound to judgment. When a demonic presence fills humans with this much pride and ego, it has done its job. When we do right and righteousness, we become a portion of the Holy Spirit as we transform into a more refined state. With evil, once you drink from the cup of conquest, it is difficult to put that cup back down. Beautiful women, massive treasure, and your image carved in stone, you at once, have become worshipped and adored. Just that small taste, is hard to put the cup back in the cabinet.

These people left behind such glorious architecture and magnificent pieces of art. It would seem if today, the treasures of ancient Egypt, Babylon, and Rome had given historians a great measure of delight. If that's the case, just wait until the days of tomorrow arrives.

According to my hypothesis, it will be no different on other planets than it is today when we progress to jaw-dropping breakthroughs. I will soon tell the story of kingdoms where they paved city roads with gold and diamonds. This was before we fell from grace. These are the realms that were made by my Father, the Lord, and his masses. Today they sit empty like ghost towns after the daylights of the big gold rush. They now belong to Christ and his people, whom are being kept and groomed for His arrival. Even more so than the modern Egyptian pyramid, as these lands were made to support the violent elements of the world. This was managed with a specific cause. Our forefathers did not do things on a small scale. Everything was meant to be a lasting marker of our presence; we were masters of time.

In the second volume of this series, *Masters of Time*, there will be a chapter called the *Stone Wars*. Although it may sound like science fiction, the reality is that it is based on what I believe to be a very true story of a long time ago. When we fought the war of the worlds, higher beings began marking their territory. Stone architecture, idols, and images were left across the world. They stand for <u>different factions</u> that came from the heavens.

When we hear the terminology, God, we picture the Father of Adam. Please allow me to articulate this and then we can clarify terminology: Moses, Jesus, and John, as well as many other figures, are a representation of souls which have been around a long time. They stood for a higher order. I much prefer the terminology *friends from heaven* rather than GOD. The word GOD, has been perverted by humans for countless ages and I would like to be your new friend. Many of those who came from heaven did a great injustice by keeping people blind. I have come to make sure you know the truth of being that new friend.

Let us ask ourselves a few questions: *How did our early ancestors, the ancient Egyptians, know so much about science, human anatomy, and astronomy?* To mummify or embalm a dead person, you must take out all the organs before you begin the process of upholding the human torso. When we speak of the Egyptians, they're very well known for mummifying the dead. This is the very reason a sarcophagus was created, to hold the body of a dead Pharaoh or someone of great royalty. It was not like today when we meet at a cemetery and pray for somebody who had passed away. They did ceremonies in very specific times such as full moons, lunar eclipses, solar eclipses, and very specific star alignments. When the Pharaoh died, people could still call upon his name in the afterlife and worship him as a god. That's why they had many idols. It is so very odd that the only object of desire for these men and women who called themselves Pharaohs, were to build large scale pyramids and burial temples. That's quite a lot of work.

Have you ever questioned why there are nocturnal creatures? It seems so odd for an animal to exist strictly by night. Creatures that are nocturnal have special senses and site that most animals do not. This lets them to prey on other creatures in the dark. Some also have particular skills or abilities that they practice ensnaring their victims such as a spider or an ant lion. If you take time to think about it, we live in a very predatory world. In universal existence, food is one of the major components of life. Most creatures will fight, kill, scavenge, and steal to have a source of ration. Would it not be a wonderful world, or if worlds existed, where nothing is preyed upon? This will be a very important thing to remember as we go through this book.

For the "dead" or that which exists in the afterlife to live, must it have life to be a vessel? This was common knowledge of our ancestors. A host acts as food or energy to sustain these spiritual beings from the afterlife. In these ceremonies, they are calling out for these spiritual principalities of the dead to resurrect into a body that lives with ancient sacred knowledge. Therefore, time and hour was and will always be crucial. The god of war and destruction, is the deity they worshipped by age and time of year. If there were no intelligent life on this planet, these spiritual beings could not exist physically. They would fall into hibernation or a deep sleep in the chambers of the dead, which they created for themselves. How odd is that to think some people might be food or energy that the dead live upon? In this life, virtually every creature has something that feeds off from it in some form or fashion. Do not believe it is any different for us. Whether it is a flea feeding on our blood or a microscopic mite feeding on dead skin cells or spiritual beings harnessing energy while we sleep or in death. This is a cycle that exists. Death cannot exist without life and life cannot exist without destruction. According to my theory, these were the sacred arts of our ancestors who wanted to hold out and rule forever. As you will see, I have not forgotten much through the ages. This may somewhat help prove my many theories as truth.

The symbol of <u>the serpent</u> was a very powerful image for a man and woman to abide by. Equally you can guess, with any ancient art as large as this, there must be consequences when it is used unwisely. This is where violence, death, and mayhem have come to enter our world. Those humans that practiced these arts came from a sacred order who gave themselves over to darkness. They had given themselves over to that which they did not understand. I cannot drop a tear for those who handle the pain and sorrow of man and animal. I cannot tell you how to fix what is broken. The Holy Spirit can fix souls; however, it can't change the way we live unless we believe the words of the spirit. When we speak of free will, it was granted to us many ages ago.

There's no free will today to go wherever we chose in time and space because of our actions in the past. That technology has been stripped from us because of our ancestors. Free will has its consequences in the way we live. For those who cause pain and grief to the habitants of this world, your day will arrive before long. Time teaches many lessons and old souls make good instructors.

In many of the hieroglyphs, we see Egyptians wearing ceremonial masks. When we speak of mummifying the dead, we see the figure Anubis. According to many ancient historians, he represented god of death, the afterlife, and the underworld. I must say that it is interesting as we have someone called the god of death and the afterlife. Would this be the god they say that reins up until the time of Jesus Christ? Could these be the fallen angels the bible speaks of? A god of darkness and deceit, you bet your life on it!

Why did these Egyptians create these large pyramids and burial temples with deep dark chamber's that existed within them? I believe, as many, the pyramids were a multi-purpose facility. As common, ordinary men and women today, we are not giving much thought to these ancient structures that existed, and why should we. All we know as common humans is that it once was a large empire that existed and it was seized before the time of Jesus. I urge mankind to reconsider who these people were that left such a permanent mark here on our planet. I would call for the reader if they have ever heard of, or to research the term *necropolis*. Necropolis is a large city or memorial that exists for the dead. What would you call those who devote a planet to the dead? Possibly, Nerco-Planetary beings (an unfamiliar word I would like to use). The Egyptians were nerco-planetary beings, traveling the universe using man as a shell. Maybe I should not use the terminology Egyptians as a specific. I should say that our early ancestors had become nerco-planetary beings by the deception of alien technology. Why is it currently, our TVs are loaded with shows based on vampires, zombies, magicians, and witches? How is this something that has worked its way into our culture as a permanent fixture? There is a darker set of hands moving in the world in which we live.

Who are the dead and why were they honored with such elaborate stone monuments and called gods? Jesus gives us a very clear sign in scripture on how we should treat the dead. Jesus said to one of his potential followers, *"Follow me, and allow the dead lay to rest their own dead"*. That is a far call from building elaborate dark tunnels and tombs where priests can perform sacred ceremonies. The Egyptian Pharaohs glorified death, for death to them was life. Their people built grandiose temples and stocked them with provisions for the afterlife. It is almost as if the people believed when these mummies awoke from their grave, they would call for amenities in the dark little chambers of the afterlife.

<u>They should have realized they were the provision and amenities.</u>

I believe many are mistaken about why these elaborate social systems were constructed and then sealed. Would what be sealed in the pyramids still be in these dark tunnels and chambers that they created for this god? If it were the god of "death" I highly doubt it. This is the first act of sorcery upon the earth, which is alien in nature. According to my theory, the pyramid itself is a holding place for demonic beings, spiritual in nature, not physical. The defender of the abyss is the all-seeing of the macrocosm, the eye of Horus. The Pharaoh is the beginning of its existence when he is living as well when he is dead, and his flesh completely expired. Then a new vessel is taken by those who take on this dark order with incantations and spells within seasons of time. The pyramids were used more for scientific purposes before the fall and will be discussed in depth when we talk about the forerunners of the Messiah. We are dealing with a conqueror of worlds, everything is efficient with no waste. There is a specific reason this race of humans came and built these structures so that all earth and heaven could see them. They were built to house powerful forces which carry ancient wisdom and knowledge, then they were sealed completely at the Pharaohs' death and the compromise

of his kingdom. Count at the rush of technology from the 1800's to 2000's; cannons and muskets to atomic warheads and jet airplanes. The dead in Christ have risen. If we, as humans, cannot believe these pyramids were made by ancient man to house demonic forces, certainly we must admit they were beings highly different in nature and are known as the "dead". A different breed of human that lived long ago. I asked you earlier, as readers, to think about nocturnal creatures with special powers that we see here on this earth. I asked this question for a very specific reason. I want to point out to you that through time, not all humans were the same in the manner, in which they've lived nor looked. Through time, there were people that enjoyed the bright beautiful sun and then there were those who walked by moonlight and starlight and slept through the days. When I speak of the children of the night, I'm not referring to people who work odd hours or have difficulty in sleeping. When I speak of the children of the night, I am referring to those who practice in the occult. Those who practice things under the shade of night when they call out to the ancient. Although I've never read satanic books or books that were evil in nature, I can tell you some of the contents. The books will recount that you can pull on certain powers to be precisely like the gods with spells and conjurations. It will tell you: *that you do not need the Holy Spirit in your life and just use spells of magic. We are gods and we do not need help in our affairs.* That is foolish and an unwise statement if you ask me. We need all the help we can get in this world. As I first mentioned in the beginning of the book, these powers are highly dangerous. Very few have survived to recount the tale of Abaddon, the king of demonic powers. I have come humbly to tell the story of arrogance and pride that once even flowed through my veins.

The Battle of forever

You are the sun, I am the moon
We take turns rising in this deep ocean blue
You are the son, I am the moon
Wise you've become, I am but the fool
Treasures, pleasures, diamonds, and the jewels
With measure, forever, I stand in solitude
My savior, unchain me, unleash me
Tis my season for some food
Break me, I'll shake thee
The world is in your hands

You hold me, I mold thee
With wings, oh so sad
Forever, your treasure
For timeless is my sands
Hold on, be strong
It's the battle of forever

Many will say, "you don't need Jesus, all power is within you." I will let you be the judge of that by this infinite tale of glory. This is what convinced many of high intelligence a long ago. That achievement did not have to come with arduous work, they could use magic (superior knowledge) and they could cheat the system. They accepted to answer to no one or no one thing because they themselves were self-claimed 'gods'. A form was unleashed upon mankind from a distant space and time. Now we are seeing the results of their actions. Could this mistake have been averted? Why did this *Angel* fell from grace by deception? I would think nothing can happen in this world by chance or accident. Especially something so great in magnitude that it affected all life in this universe. If the god of death holds the keys to time and space up until the time of Jesus Christ, it is then no great wonder to me how the whole planet lived by deception. It could be very well that at first these spiritual powers (miracles), appeared to be miraculous.

A miracle is not actually a miracle, it is a science sometimes beyond our explanation. It is the ability of the serpent or dragon, who has survived and seen many ages. Therefore, a tertiary of the angels believed and observed the *"serpent of the old"*. It is odd that after Jesus was baptized and recognized who Satan was, he performed miracles himself. Before Jesus ever performed miracles, the spirit of Elijah preformed the same and they believed he was the messiah. Prophecy can be summed up as an act or gesture to prove to man that spiritual powers exist; however, they are highly dangerous to the minds of men and women. Some of Jesus' miracles were considered out of context. Surely, I will elaborate on that later in this book. Many of the miracles Jesus performed were scientific as well as spiritual in nature. Because he was much more of an evolved being created by the angels and his people did not understand his wisdom. They certainly knew he was different, but doubted his authority as a man.

I'll go into heavy detail about this demon who fell from heaven, as well Jesus. Who is this evil principality called the serpent, which existed long ago? What is it that mankind has brought himself into? What is it that causes mankind to have crazy terrifying dreams and nightmares? Why is there so much awe and hate in the Earth? Why would there be an evil so great among us that when horrific crimes are committed we wonder how any human can do this? Somewhere in time, humans stopped being humans and became monsters, physically and spiritually. Child rapists, murderers, torturers, drug lords, etc. Thus, when scientists ask the big question: *are we alone in this universe?* You can be certain that we're not. Is it humans themselves that are wicked or is there some something evil in us that grows like a wildfire. No one in this day and age truly knows. And with great certainty, where sorcery and magic were derived. What we know for sure is that magic and sorcery is derived from something very ancient.

According to my theory, sorcery is so ancient that it existed before life and the abyss of space was created. If you'll notice, in our studies of astronomy, there is much emptier in time and space than there is life. The blackness or darkness that exists is vast. The amount of life that exists among the vast darkness is microscopic. According to my theory, long before life came into being as we know it, the guardian of the abyss was released into time. This appears to be the watchdog of time and space with no known master.

A gift left behind from those who had evolved and moved on into the unknown of time doors and space travel. From my many theories and story of time, you will find that space and time was a place for predatory beings who were imprisoned in this great abyss. These guardians carried supreme knowledge and power. Life was meant to be rare and kept in balance by this spiritual authority. Life did not stay in balance because the dark side of life manifested into something that challenged its own creators. Living without law is so much more pleasurable. Many planets with in this universe as well as other universes, were completely obliterated by war. Even in in place in space and time itself, that is now way beyond our reach. The doors of heaven have permanently closed.

Now, by the technology of our ancient ancestors, this universe is flourishing with planets capable of life. This is getting to be the change among more in the new kingdom of Jesus Christ. The universe will be filled with light and the powers of temptation will cease to exist. As I move on to tell my story, you will discover the great tragedy as I talk about certain things. What I also will show you is that with the Holy Spirit, we can be the new kingdom of the ages.

Life cannot exist without death in the present state we live. If we could live forever and you looked at our history closely, you might wish that people could not live forever. There have been blood thirsty rulers since time began. From the time of the pharaoh who launched baby into the depths of the Nile to Adolph Hitler gas chamber exterminations of the Jews. There have been episodes on this earth that have crushed empires in a matter of moments. The Syria earthquake happened on May 20, 1202. Deaths associated to this disaster may have been very close to a million, however, there really is no official number. An earthquake with a violent magnitude, can change the way a city flourishes in a very rapid fashion.

All through history, there is a great tale of suffering and death. What type of eternal life would be of any pleasure when the world you live in is in constant chaos? That would be eternal hell. Is hell really for eternity? <u>Hell is many things, just as heaven is many things</u>. Hell can be a world war with prisoners and death all around us. The pits can be returned to life right after dying. Hell can be physical as well as a spiritual torment. Hell is when the angel of death has free reign on humans to do as he pleases. If ever, the love of God no longer existed on the earth, there would be no hope of surviving the final days. In my heart, I truly hope we will never let ourselves see this day. Change in this world cannot come without great sacrifice. When our world begins its upheaval, what will we do as a race of humans? Our population is enormous and that creates a great problem when the earth becomes volatile. Our ancestors would only go into their ships and move someplace else until the danger was over. Those were the lucky ones. So, let us not fool ourselves about the situation and who our ancestors were. We did not put a space station and satellites up onto space itself by chance. We did not land on the moon just to land on the moon. Everything was made for a reason and what will come for humanity will be greater.

Many allege it is God or Christ, who is omnipotent in knowledge and wisdom. You do not need to see my face or know who I am to understand that this is very true. All things are for His glory I will try to cover everything that I possibly can before my death. It seems so volatile and unpredictable for us tiny little humans to be floating around in the darkest depths of space. Let us remember, love conquers all things, even prophecies of doom that many just don't understand. <u>This is the law we shall abide by!</u>

In the days of the ancient, people that practiced these sacred arts were called seers, oracles, and prophets. The Pharaohs, kings, and their queens held these people in high regard. These '*future tellers*' used them to predict the outcomes of great battles as well as many other things. The accuracy of these people would be phenomenal. Where did these oracles, seers, and prophets come from that man should let them predict wars or political influence upon the earth? Let us say this act of sorcery worked nine out of ten times. At that tenth time that you put your faith into a seer a great sorrow may come upon you and your family and kingdom. You, as a king or a Pharaoh might have achieved a great victory in war and have fistfuls of treasure as predicted. Upon your return home, you find out your wife and son became mysteriously ill while you were away and they perished. An illness has spread in your kingdom and took many lives. Then it all went downhill from there. The spirit will suck you dry until there's nothing left but madness. The realness of this state of affairs is that the psychic may have been correct. She or he did not mention that their vision came with a price as souls and death were exchanged for treasure.

What a dangerous game man has played.

This a predatory practice and I urge caution to many physics of the world. Nothing in this life is for free and you can count on that. <u>The knowledge I give you today comes with a great price</u>, you can be assured. They call it *"dancing with the dead"* and it is highly dangerous. I could not tell you how many times I wanted my life to end. I would try to go to sleep but my mind would not shut off no matter how much I prayed. I finally I had to see a doctor and get on a sleep aid.

Now I'm growing much stronger in the Glory of my creator. You cannot be a master in a world until you overpower the one who has claimed to be superior. The god of death does not only rule upon this earth, this being has ruled in every universe that existed in time and space in which we live, according to my theory of time. This is how I will be able to give you an exact description of the boundaries of time in the chapter *Time*.

This is what makes man special. We are the last soldiers on the battlefield of time in which we now live; therefore, Jesus is labeled the King of the Universe. The power of love has put a leash on a beast that has never lost a war in all its ages. Love conquers all, so it is said. Yes, the end and punishment will come for spiritual entities that are labeled as serpent of the old, devil, and false prophet. These are spiritual entities imprisoned in time and they are demonic creatures used as weapons to engage life and test it to the fullest. They came into fruition by our own grand illusions of greed and power. When they say, the Lord is a conqueror, we get a better sense of majesty.

Let me give you a scenario so that this will make more sense. If you gave just one man, a resurrection and all power and knowledge, like the Pharaoh of Egypt, would he misuse it? If one man is capable of such foolishness, how will all other humans in this world act when they are given that same power and wisdom? This is a complete test of who we are and where we will extend in time and distance. Because this is a very harsh lesson for the angels and humanity to endure, we have been given a mediator. All life in this universe and others are watching the final climax of events. Many creations have endured this challenge and moved on to other places and many have not. It is the mystery of Jesus Christ and the angel of the abyss that tells us this period and the test of life in time and space are coming to an end. All knowledge has been obtained and a master of spiritual law has been chosen. Now that Jesus understands that these beings are spiritual in nature and have the power of resurrection, he has become your sacrifice to understand that which is different than ours. A bargain of mutuality has been made at Christ's victory over the power of death. So that which was "death" has lost its crown, the power of resurrection to Jesus Christ. Only true love could break the chains of death. This is the main focal point of all creation that has ever been, to find something rare. We are the *something rare*, that time has waited for. <u>It is called love and compassion!</u> Everything that was once a part of the fallen father is now starting to exist within the Christ.

When we use the term devil or fallen angel, we are speaking of a man or angel that was overpowered by deception to think that he was a god. This angel was created to punish souls by leading them into deception. And then everything that was once good in this saint has been transformed, like data, over to the body of Christ. In the Biblical scripture, it enjoins us that Jesus is the Father or they are one in the same in creation. That is a very important statement. The father talks of death and Christ is the physical structure of eternal resurrection. Death cannot exist without flesh for that spirit to grow and prosper. It either chooses to grow or it perishes. <u>As I said earlier, nothing in life is for free when we employ these abilities.</u> Hence, here I stood with you one final time to abide in this world. It is simply honest love that will liberate us from the chains of death which held the Father. And it is solely by love that we can keep ourselves from destruction. This is the gamble that was made on our behalf. If we prefer the way of destruction we cannot blame anybody or anything other than ourselves for being a victim to this great deception.

If all the world is filled with volatility, destruction, and death, then we know this was never intended to be our lasting dwelling house. Since our ancestors were brave and have traveled this ocean of stars to come to this earth, we will find grace in the Holy Spirit. What is the Holy Spirit? The Holy Spirit was a created being who was kept in thrall by the power of death. Just as Jesus broke the chains of death upon his Father, it was the Father that broke the chains of death upon that which is the Holy Spirit. This is what is called *the Trinity*. Those of this world can destroy our flesh, but they cannot destroy our souls. I do not expect many people to understand my conception of the Trinity in its entirety. It is in the second volume of the series I will try to give you a more in depth look on how the spirit of Christ came to be. Please know, Jesus is not a son of flesh and blood, he is born of spirit which holds great power. He is the only begotten of the heavens and the bringer of eternal life. From a very powerful angel who once had a long fall from grace, comes the wisdom and grace of Jesus Christ.

What I can differentiate you with certainty is that all the dead have been awakened from the ages and are at once going up around the vessel of Jesus Christ. This is because they were spiritually slaughtered and their people have been saved by the descent of the lamb. And then, I will humbly say this to you, as my people: "It is not that I chose myself to bring out this message. I was chosen to reveal to you the power of Christ and where it came from."

We, as the servants of Christ, are guilty of no crime. We did not trespass on other people's planets or treat them with disrespect. We did not use machines to tear up planets to build kingdoms made of amber, diamonds, and precious stones. We did not create a race of slaves for sexual pleasure or to act as a work force. Yet, we pay for those crimes as if we committed them. We cannot be accused of something that we did not do or we have any repentance for our forefather's mistakes. Therefore, the angel of death holds no power over the body of Christ and his people.

It was a long time ago in the ages of man, I was born of a slave woman. In the story of my soul, I was raised in tribe of lower evolved humans. Those humans which were brought into this world not by choice from a place far way. I do not want to talk too much in respect to this part of the story. I will go in depth on my third book, *The slaves of Christ*. How would you like to wake up one day and know that every beast in the forest wants to consume you or bugs, maggots, or other moving creature all over your skin eating you alive? With that, being alone, frightened, naked, and affrighted. For those souls of long ago, responsible for my family's sufferings and they have not repented of their ways, a special place has been kept for them: Oblivion. It is a home of many lessons; before souls are ruined for eternity. This is something close to a death row sentence. No creature has the right to punish anything forever, nevertheless; it may seem like it. This is the reason that in our society, a life sentence in prison can only last so long, yet they stack up multiple life sentences for multiple murders. If it were up to our judges in modern day times they would punish many forever. The problem with that is, only "death" itself can make a proper judgment on each soul. There are many factors that lead people to committing acts of crime. Some kids are mistreated from the day they get out of the uterus. They learn, from those around them in a vicious world of survival, eventually becoming monsters of society. Only the heavens can hand out the correct measure of justice for everyone. If we did not have Jesus Christ as our defense lawyer, we all would be punished, simply based on our forefathers, who committed unspeakable acts on humans.

Then today, when I use the terminology, God, it receives a different significance than that of long ago. No longer will the spirit come to punish humanity when the final judgment of Jesus Christ has been issued. The judgment will be final as Christ has taken the beating for us all as written in the Old Testament. Grace will live and the rest belongs to the dead. Those that belong to the dead become a source of spiritual food and wisdom of the angel of the abyss. They become a sustainable energy for a being that lives by ages and not by years. A soul hunter, a collector of bounty on rotten dirty souls. <u>Yes, this all according to my theory to keep this book in check</u>. Let's hope I'm wrong and its science fiction.

X

APOLLYON THE DESTROYER

The king of the abyss is somewhat a mystery to the Biblical scripture. Let me introduce you and explain his title. No one will leave space and time or comes into a universe without encountering the angel of the abyss. One can allege it has become the conquering angel of Jesus Christ, guarding his territory with spiritual force until all matters have been carried out. We certainly know from scripture, Jesus could speak to demons and cast them out as well. That is unique talent, my friends. Many great warriors of time that carried out the destruction with armies, were by the power of Apollyon who holds Satan, as a dark prince in a spiritual prison. They are known as the Goddess and lord of death. Who is it that grants them their authority? It would seem to be Apollyon the destroyer king of the bottomless pit. For when he opens the pit the demons come forth to deceive the earth and destroy. What is the bottomless pit? This is a very deep subject for the reader to contemplate and must encounter later chapters to understand or decipher the meaning. It is twofold in nature, as there are many abyss's in the time in space in which we live.

Remember, the devil himself is a prisoner, an instrument of destruction, imprisoned. Is this the same devil or Satan that tested Job? In a roundabout way, yes. We are talking of a Pharaoh who came under demonic possession who tested the loyalty of Job. This really boils down to a mighty angel which is not human, which came into bondage by demonic forces. It is truly not this angel or being that wishes harm to the destitute. It is a demonic principality which infiltrated alien beings long ago to set itself up as a GOD that causes malice. It does this by many forms of deception. Then one day, people wake up to their destruction and realize they have made a terrible mistake. Only when Christ is slaughtered and breaks the seals, would the angel of the abyss gain authority to punish man and falls from heaven like a star. He is the king over demonic forces.

Revelation <u>9:11</u>, *they have as king over them, the angel of the abyss; his name in Hebrew is Abaddon, and in the Greek, he has the name Apollyon.*

These are demons which are set free in certain seasons so that spirit may be essayed in this world as good as others. Demons are manifestations of war, greed, hatred, sexuality, and other sources. This is to gauge what our weaknesses are and unfortunately, there are many. One day, these demons will be destroyed altogether, for they are deceivers with purpose. Even when there is chaos, it is under the direction of Jesus Christ and the angel of the abyss. As in Hindu religion, the destroyer comes to prepare for something fresh. For Christ and his people to build something new, much destruction will take place. If Jesus is love and peace how can he destroy? He does not, he forewarns us that demolition is imminent if we do not take heed.

When speaking of knowledge, I never asked for this knowledge in any way. I never cared about knowledge, science, or space. I loved my dog, hiking, and riding my bike in the hills. I used to walk with my dog for miles and pick fruit off the trees and drink water from streams and be gone the entire day. Then one day, my life changed forever. I trust it was not I, it was friends who once regarded themselves in the personal matters of these ancient people that has cost me this great price. So, the story I tell you is not my own, it is the story of many. I cannot tell the story without that which exists within me and that which resides in me could not tell the story without my spiritual death to this world, transfiguration. Therefore, it is titled the lost books of Jesus and John. This is what occurs when you involve yourself with these types of spiritual rituals and observances of the ancient to ask for something bigger than what you can compensate. It is then it has become a large peril. It should be noted by all mankind.

Again, eternal life is such a powerful thing to talk about. When the Holy Spirit says it will give us eternal life for our service, is it a claim that can be carried out? When we speak of hell and damnation, can the Holy Spirit also make souls suffer this consequence? The spirit of the Lord does not have to see the sorrow and pain of those who do not listen, fortunately. There is already enough pain to last a lifetime. He has no alternative except to let them be punished by that which is very diligent in the punishing of souls. Here I am to embrace, so please hear my words. It is merely because I did not ask for this knowledge to come to me that I am capable to manage the spiritual repercussions. Some would call that a perfect sacrifice, spotless in blame. No such thing as perfect, that's ridiculous! Let me restate that, ridiculousness. There are many men and women that became monks or devout students of religion and had never seen sin. Why were they not chosen to lead man? I will explain to you why. You cannot evaluate the many laws of life unless you have walked the road of agony. I assure you that I have, many times. What a tragedy of endless temptation for our children.

What is the primary purpose of a demonic presence? The main function of a demonic presence is to cause deception, confusion, chaos, fear, and death all around us. This is the way it feeds upon our energy or life force. This is how the demons achieve power in this world. The more pain, suffering, violence, worry, fear, and terror, the more they can cause agony and pain upon this earth. The consume more power that way. We must watch our actions as they are watching us waiting for our next wrong step.

As spiritual darkness keeps getting fed by the horrific actions from the people on this planet, darkness will grow like a cancer. All that it needed was one drink of the poison and it has manifested itself into the spirits of humankind. This was the direction of our forefathers and of the ancient civilizations. Our ancestors broke off more than they could chew when they learned this ancient knowledge of the resurrection. A Great deception swallowed them up. They were full of big aspirations and visions that started well for a long time. One day they woke up and it was time to pay the piper. They were so used to living like gods until their kingdoms came crashing down. It was then a man's journey in the heavens came to a screeching halt. Have you ever heard the expression when they do not want birds to fly *"let us clip their wings"*? When the serpent or the dragon was forced from heaven, he was brought down in a very specific way. He could have easily been destroyed and was not. This was a physical confrontation in the sky that left the dragon no way to go back into the heavens. The dragon or the serpent were not too concerned about being forced into the earth until the day of Jesus Christ, the son of God. The dragon or serpent were not worried because this earth was something that it was very familiar with and he ruled with great power. The reason there would be a concern in the spiritual kingdom is because I've come to give you the truth.

Arming ourselves with the truth, is the greatest weapon that we have. How anyone could be deceived from this day on when I tell you clearly what it is that we are facing. I know nobody truly wants to confront the Lord of death on the Day of Judgment now that I have warned you of who and what this is from the perspective of my eyes. A shark that eats a man or a man that eats a shark is called life, a cycle.

The reality is, our own greed and way of life opened the door to the way we live. As a fisherman fishes with a lure, or a hunter hunts with camouflage, animal calls, or bait trapping, long ago a trap was set for us. Our ancestors have opened the door to be subjected to the realm of "death" and its accusations by the way they lived. This power is called free will. When the dragon and his angels were forced from the sky, they at once, began creating temples under the power and guidance of spiritual forces. Why would God allow it? Michael and the heavens believed they had achieved a great victory, however; the price to the inhabitance of this earth was going to be great. Therefore, Michael the archangel (an incarnation) only achieved a temporary triumph over his opponent, one he did not see. You cannot shoot bullets to win a war against the angel of destruction; it does not act like that. My war with "death" is spiritual, mental, and physical. By his own jurisprudence, in which he passed judgment, he shall be tried. This represents the fallen angel or serpent being held on a spiritual chain by Jesus and the angel of the abyss. Jesus is walking his spiritual creation amongst the inhabitants of this earth demanding glory for those in the heavens and on the earth. It seems this world was built to break you mentally, physically, and financially.

How can we not fear and worry in such volatile times? This is a version of unceasing prayer to Jesus Christ, may you use it often: *"Lord of heaven, I bow to you in spirit and flesh. Let my heart speak the unceasing prayer of your love (repeat) Jesus Christ have mercy on my soul, relieve me from my suffering on this earth as walk through life as a sinner"*. Say this slowly and often to build up a spiritual wall against distraction and destruction. It is like a chant or Mantra, training your mind only to focus on the light of Christ. As you start this prayer, you will often be distracted by other views which will interrupt your plea. They will try to cause you to abandon prayer with many different thoughts. This will occur, especially in times of trouble, grief, or any concerns. This is how you will cognize that there are manifestations around you that hinder your enlightenment and wish you great distress. This will also prove to you that the enemy is very crafty and you will soon expose demons for what they are, "tormenters" of your spirit. With Christ, you will learn to block out these manifestations and feel the light more often and frequently. This is the most condensed form of mediation I can teach to achieve some needed release from the world of chaos. If you are strung out or high and find nowhere to go, I promise you if you're persistent in daily use of this prayer you may not become perfect; however, God will slaughter your sins and make you something new in the short-run. I don't care if your high as a kite or the after fact of a murderer. You rebuke Satan fully and completely as he torments you. Unceasing prayer is a prayer to strengthen your soul and ask for mercy. Rebuking Satan is immediately calling the archangel to your defense to defend you from a life and death situation such as a very immediate suicidal thought. *"Satan, I command you to hell in the name Jesus Christ and his archangel."* Say this over and over! Weather for personal spiritual defense or a friend that's suffering and possibly dying, you then become a dragon slayer. The more this prayer is practiced the more Christ like you will become in spiritual defense. <u>I have taught you what it is that eventually raised my soul into a greater consciousness.</u> You never need to pass a money filled basket to me. I know there are many that have personal issue with money corruption in the church, as well, many egos.

When manifestations interrupt you in your prayer you must give no view or consideration to them, keep praying. When we pass from this world, our mind must be trained not to think about the world and its material values. How did these demons enter this world? That's very simple, our ancestors brought them here. Just as in the yesterday, when beings saw these huge ancient structures, curiosity made them want to explore them. Reminds me of an old saying, "curiosity killed the cat". We have dug up many ancient cities in modern times. Do you think it might've been any different for our ancestors? According to my theory, those who put these ancient structures on other worlds, used them not only to test humankind but many other creations. You just don't go breaking into alien structures and live to tell the story. The pyramid had the all-seeing eye of the cosmos atop of its structure. Everything we do is being watched by the power of the alien mind, and hands.

Can you imagine if you could peel back each layer of time the things that you would see? I'm hoping I can manage that in a certain manner. If ancient life did put it in a hibernation, how would it be awakened? It is never a safe idea to mess around with ancient artifacts or dwellings without proper knowledge of them. Had the tombs seal not been broken, we would not be a cursed race of people. <u>We opened a door, and we have no idea how to close it, nor can it be closed.</u> Any intelligent being that is capable of breaking into a very sophisticated tomb to steal is a perfect candidate to wake the dead. The God of death is not limited to the shell that was taken or borrowed when death occurred. "Death" is a spiritual entity, not of flesh. "Death" is what was sealed in the great pyramid. Flesh is what it needs to survive. Flesh is what it needed to get back into the heavens to rule and conquer. Those that existed on the earth at that time were not capable of traveling into the heavens because of the fall. Death is a patient entity, a machine of destruction set in motion until there's nothing left. Now I have given you some tools to master its presence.

The Pharaoh and his queen were the host for the demonic dead. At their end, they were sealed in. And thusly, it was many that came after their fall and deception coerced them into a delirium of desire. It does not matter where their bodies or mummified corpses ended at, they were the only vessels used in ancient spells and incantations to resurrect these demons back into this world. Once the pyramid was sealed, their work was complete. I will soon speak about the seasons of the dragon who are held on a chain by a mighty angel. A full season in Biblical scripture, from my interpretation, would say cycles of two thousand years. This will lead up to the new millennia or the millennial reign. All of this because we chose to tamper with something that we had no knowledge of. However, great glory will come from acknowledging our mistakes.

Isaiah 47:13-15 <u>All the counsel you have received has only worn you out!</u> *Let your astrologers come forward, those stargazers who make predictions month by month, let them save you from what is coming upon you.* **14** *Surely, they are like stubble; the fire will burn them up. They cannot even save themselves from the power of the flame. These are not coals for warmth; this is not a fire to sit by.* **15** *That is all they are to you—these you have dealt with and labored with since childhood. All of them go on in their error; there is not one that can save you.*

The quantity of time we have as humans are unlimited depending on how we progress and as individuals. When we are in Christ, we become as one. As time becomes limitless, you carry knowledge as I have into your future, which is highly important. We cannot live forever physically until we evolve in the spirit of Christ for many ages. We are not ready for that obligation. We will choose vessels as the universe starts to expand. It will thrive because many are occurring for an exodus as the world goes into upheaval. I would not tell you if it were not so, the father had many mansions. When and where did the great serpent God begin preparation to deliver into the celestial sphere by the power of resurrection? This was mostly before Jesus and in the age prior to Moses. This is when mummification of the dead began and the 1ˢᵗ Pharaohs used the inhabitance of this earth to be the work force. This is when the dragon prepared to battle Michael the Archangel on the battlefields of this earth. The Pharaoh finally realized he had been deceived and had nowhere to go. Whatever gave him source of power would eventually take it away. "Life" did not agree with "death" on the measure of punishment man should receive for releasing demonic powers on an ancient world. I expect everyone to know what it is we fight for, the power of resurrection. To live forever as spiritual vessels. To be allowed the power of resurrection, when we're sworn to a code of universal jurisprudence.

To live forever would need a certain set of standards in both the low and high that dwell among this earth. Many things will have to change and not every human will be cut out for that change unless thoroughly prepared for what is coming.

I've penned this book in advance to tell you many things about our future. One of the greatest bestows a human can have is the power of resurrection. It is a key to finding balance within a world. It is also very dangerous if a world becomes hostile and non-forgiving. Resurrection will not be turned over to us freely by any substance. This is a path for those who have a great love in their heart and are grateful for the sacrifice that the heavens have had given us. All though resurrection or reincarnation is unproven or very hard to prove. I will try to give you some solid proof. First, I will give you the answer to the great mystery of resurrection. The power of resurrection is made up between two spiritual entities. One is "life" and the other is "death". It is something that must survive in equilibrium. Though it once was something used much differently before Jesus Christ, it will become something more beautiful rather than alarming. <u>Knowledge and power become good and evil when we choose how to utilize it.</u> The frightening truth is we can always blame our troubles on something known as the devil and Satan. The monster will say "I live because of your lust, greed, war, and desire to sin". Almost every ounce of suffering that takes place on our earth is man-made. It is entirely figured out by our desires. I consider myself a good teacher of knowledge and truth. They say the gate to hell is wide and the road to heaven is narrow. Again, let us remember resurrection is the most powerful gift that can be granted within space and time. If someone did not love us it would not be so. This endowment was made for our suffering and survival in a wicked kingdom and overcoming it by the bloodline of the lamb. To recite the story of ages is my happiness. I hope many may now know in whom and what we are dealing with on this earth. Yes, Jesus is a man of peace; however, even his patience will wear out if we continue the course that is not pleasing him. What is displeasing to him is displeasing to the heavens.

According to my theory, "death" is alien in nature just like the Holy Spirit. Allow me to explain, "death" in this direction for greater clarity so you may know of the Holy Spirit. The dragon and Satan (the master of death and his Goddess) are creatures which are like hermit crabs who need shells. When they lose their shells, they will find new ones. If life ceases to exist, they carry on when their burial temples of time are discovered, disturbed, and tampered with. They raise to set themselves up as Gods and to punish. This is how magic and sorcery first began and was brought into this world. The force of unlimited knowledge comes from the souls of the vessels they have captured and killed by deceit. This is called claiming and harvesting a soul. They are a far different creation than anything else, they are the cursed dead. They abused laws and powers of the heavens and this was their punishment, the abyss of time. It is the king of the abyss, Apollyon, who watches over them as they have free reign in space and time within seasons. That is until one day someone challenged their ability to liberate us from the grip of death.

We have been lured far away from home into time and place. The consequences of it is our pain and enduring with a reduced life. However, it is longevity to a spiritual race of demons who dwell among us. The sacred art of mummifying and worshipping the dead came down from the heavens with our ancestors from the stars. Thus, our ancestors were caught up in a demonic occult and practiced these sacred ceremonies which came down with them. Just as the Pharaoh and his queen were deceived by these powers, so were alien beings from long ago. Those who were once deceived by this alien race of beings known as the "dead", found a way to imprison these demonic beings by sacrificing two elite figures from their race. Their sacrifice was great and worthy of mention in this story of time. It is likewise a sad story for us. They had no choice but to use us as a means to try to administer the fatal blast to these infernal beings. Long before the pyramids as we know them, the supreme lord and queen of the cosmos lived isolated on a planet alone until death. A male and female of their species paid for their ancestor's mistakes of long ago, exactly as we made out. They are known to me as life and death, the supreme lord and his queen. Know that if Jesus or Moses had a spiritual queen, they would never put her on the front line in the battle of demons. Life is resurrection, it is what brings the king of king's lord of lords into this realm. That is why a forerunner comes and several transfigurations take place between the sons of god. All we see, is a spiritual creation from within the holy spirit of life and death.

They lord and his queen entered a pyramid structure in a far distant place. Who would not be curious of such a magnificent object and what was inside? Like a great big mysterious puzzle, many wondered what is inside, and how to get in. Just sitting there, magnificently, waiting for some to open its contents. If it was sealed or locked, maybe it was with good reason. Demonic powers were soon released and it took them many ages to overcome them. Their sacrifice, came at great cost. They lived alone on a planet imprisoned in time. Their time in prison, was until someone would come that was desirable to wear the seal of their prison. Before they got along the far distant planet to help their condemnation, their kind formed a prison made completely of quartz crystal to obtain energy. Before the lord and his queen went into demise, they mastered all demonic deceptions. They then drank a poison and walked into their *Time Prison* that had been created for them. They suffered tremendously, emotionally, more than physical.

The Holy Spirit has sworn itself and their kind into the service of man for releasing them from slavery. As we may all know, the spirit of Satan and the devil despises mankind. For the lowest being that created on this earth, Adam son of God, rose into a mighty, spiritual creation. He did this so that he might deal the dragon a fatal blow in the name of his father and all who have suffered. It is also to redeem himself and his wife who ate of the forbidden knowledge in the forest. It is the son of God who makes himself worthy to wear out the seals and receive glory and honor from heaven. And because "death" judged man and this world harshly for their mistake, life stripped his office and gave it to someone better who would rule more fairly on man's behalf, and that was Jesus. All judgment of law has been seen through the eyes of the seven sons of God and Jesus Christ. And then there will be nothing left for me to do or tell anybody. I am not in need of a following or a church, I am here to complete what I began long ago. The moment you go into the fight cage with a demonic presence, such as Satan, there is no turning back. And those who have read it or thought it, your damn right, Jesus never tapped.

The alien forces of the abyss have been released; that's why the world is in chaos and death is climaxing. I'll try to die with dignity in this type of world as evil roams among us.

And so "Death's" punishment began for judging the world too harshly and he was forced to walk as a man for many ages before he would surrender his crown to Jesus. This is the harbinger of the Christ, the spirit of Elijah. It is then this being, which now was living in human form, realized it made a huge error in judgment. Jesus accepted the penalty for him setting him loose from his bondage which turned Jesus's life into a nightmare!

Jesus is the only begotten of heaven, a son of the stars, and created from spirit. Protected 24 hours a day, seven days a week from demonic forces seeking out his death for freeing these beings from spiritual bondage. The passion of this child broke the spell of a thousand ages. And so, it was long ago in the days of the Egyptian kingdom, I began two families. One of great stature and the other being broken and ruled over as slaves. My eyes have seen every injustice that has occurred to the inhabitants of this earth. The slaughtered lamb and the souls of time have been awakened. A new kingdom is about to be born. Who would've known?

How can there ever be peace for the dead when we sow the seeds of evil and chaos in the world today? The story never changes, my friends. It replicates itself over and over until time runs down. We either learn how to partake in with these malevolent forces or many will perish forever. There can be no crying in the end, you have been made aware of the great grief we will meet. We must change the way of life of this world as many of us and not just one, are at the edge of turmoil. We are soldiers of Christ, the last defense and hope of all living things in this world as good as others. All of us are soldiers, not just me. I am merely here to be that push to the ending line and tell you we can do this in concert. We can defeat and master this force as a race of humans and be honored by heaven when we live together peacefully.

Many people called themselves gods, lords, or angels in the Old Testament; but, were they? When the pyramids were created, huge and bright, that all those in the heavens could see them, the trap was set in motion for those calling themselves angels and sons of God. We must consider a supreme being or beings, neutral in status in their approach with humans or another being they created. Many sequences of life are played out in order for our supreme creators to gain knowledge about the approach that has been created. When my spiritual father released a demonic being long ago from a spiritual prison by accident, it has taken this long for one human to overcome it and completely understand it.

<u>Forgive me for my slowness, I sincerely apologize!</u> This is why I pay the price; the actions of man were not intentional. It is my price to pay because of a time that has passed. If the creators of humans or at the least the guiding spirit behind them did not create all things, surely it must understand all things in this universe to be our leader. Even if that means sacrificial death. The pyramids of Egypt were a marker of territory to be seen and viewed by the inhabitants of the heavens and the earth. It is essentially saying this is mine, do not come here unless you wish to meet the "dead". The eye of the cosmos was clearly saying, "I was watching you and everything you do". Are people that crazy and so obsessed with gold and artifacts, they would break the seal of an alien tomb? It certainly appears so. Biblical scripture tells us that the judgment was so fierce upon the life that we needed a sacrifice to save us from destruction. As I mentioned earlier, it talks about seasons in Biblical scripture. The season of death will end, and a new season will lead off. "Death" and "Life" must always exist, in perpetual balance. Death does not have to be miserable and painful. Death is a path toward many doors that can lead to light in the afterlife and it can also be the road to damnation and suffering. The Holy Spirit always does, at the end of the time of year, to give humans Spiritual wisdom, which usually is neglected.

XI

MUMMIFIED DEAD-SERPENT

If we remember in Genesis, the serpent is called the craftiest beast of the field. The beast was already here on earth before the creation of Adam and Eve. This is the reason I mentioned different races of humans and stone markers of territory. It is also the reason we can decide whether if Adam and Eve were not the first humans on earth. It is in the day of Jesus Christ that we sincerely get to understand these principalities. This force is unleashed upon his people for their own good. When Jesus is here on this earth, the power of death can be overcome by his teachings. When the Holy Spirit is not on this earth or its presence is not with us, it is open season on mankind. Those who have not built up the Glory of Christ within them before the lapsing of time will know a sadness and sorrow like none have ever seen. We're not in elementary school anymore, this is the big leagues. When the beginning third of the angels fell from the heavens to reign with the fallen angel, the other two thirds came to engage in war against the dragon after they saw they had been led astray; they have never forgotten. They perished in wars, yet their souls exist still upon the ground. This is the war of the worlds, the war of angels, and the sons of God with the innocence of Christ caught in the middle.

We must look with great concern at these ancient orders who took the time to make sure the joints for these Egyptians tombs and sarcophagus would be sealed tight. They were sealed so that not one bead of light would penetrate their breathing position. If you were a nocturnal creature in hibernation, any disturbance to that place of resting such as a light or movement would be enough to wake you. Similar to a spider, which detects movement in its web. This is the way the ancient built their resting positions: to be silence and with darkness permanently sealed inside. Those who robbed the pyramids and temples went to great lengths to break the seals on these structures to get what was inside. <u>Today, we call that a thief or grave robbing, and we are sent to prison for those offenses.</u>

I mentioned in the beginning of the book what is good and what is evil. There are laws in heaven just as there are laws on earth. Who is the enforcer of those laws of what is good and evil? To believe in good and evil we must believe that there's a supreme enforcer among all universes, even if we address it right and wrong instead of good and evil. If it is not one single enforcer then it would be many or more than one. This is very different from the creation and protection of the planets themselves. It is a Force that understands truth to the highest degree. In one way or another we must meet that truth in our journey. That truth is Jesus Christ. God of Adam and the sons of God may have brought forth creation to this planet; however, they are not the protectors or owners of the planet itself. Much of creation did come by the hands of our superior ancestors and this has caused a major confrontation above the skies of the earth. There are many factors at play, playing themselves out right here on earth. We will notice an intelligent human being comes on earth after an extermination, when the ground has taken root. It is minus many prehistoric creatures on the earth. Man arrives with domesticated and undomesticated animals, which started filling the earth. Just like when our ancestors came from far away England, they brought plants, seeds, different animals, and technology. What happened? A question that will take many answers. We must understand that the grace of the Holy Spirit saved us, yet we must also know there are enforcers of law in many forms and fashions. Jesus is the word among a council on ethics within and around him. When the Egyptians arrived in Egypt, they were domesticating horses and using them in battle, to destroy.

So today, when we speak of no mummies inside the pyramids of Giza, at a time they were there. It is then the pyramids were sealed after these sacred ceremonies took place. Unfortunately, many followed in pursuit of the fallen angel for the mystery of iniquity was still at hand (the suffering of man). I assure you it was a big mistake for the pyramids to be disturbed without proper knowledge of them. When a moth or a fly, flies in a web, is it enough to wake a spider?

The title was granted to him the Lord of the flies, Beelzebub. <u>Only a superior man could have gotten into the tombs main chamber to steal the artifacts.</u> According to my theory, this means whatever spiritual beings were sealed in the pyramids, they spiritually sealed all knowledge that existed within time and many universes. They are hunters of intelligent life and souls, which are <u>diverse types of creation.</u> Being predatory in nature, they had walked through time unchallenged. This is the reason there is a king and queens chamber: when they awaken from death, life quickly turns into hell as they reign as gods over who or whatever was stupid enough to break the seal of their tomb. This is known why Apollyon was called the destroyer. Destruction has been freed from its prison. With the freedom of Apollyon, the mighty angel asked, "who is worthy to take the seals from my hand?" When Jesus took the seals from his hand, <u>he was instantly spirited and slaughtered for the salvation of man-kind</u>. The seven spirits of God are then revealed to him.

According to my theory as well as many others, the pyramid is a multi-purposed facility. Beyond what I have mentioned about it being a Territorial marker and a space of spiritual ritual, it is also an indicator of the position from which they arrived. There would be another mark in the Orion's system that fits the proportions used in Giza. This will as well bring us back one step further from where we came from no-ticing the next alignment in the heavens to the pyramid in the Orion constellation. The process of markers continues until you get close to the center of the universe, from which man came abound, according to my past life theory. These marks are constructed of many varied materials, depending on the terrain of the planet. They will always have a mathematical tie to the previous pyramid built. It most definitely is going to be a puzzle for the greatest minds of this earth and in heaven.

The bloodline of humans is as ancient as it comes within itself, as a mathemat-ical equation. We are the mix bloodline of the fallen angel, an angel with ultimate knowledge of this universe as good as many others. His days are coming to end. This will tell us it was engineered by the same Pharaoh, or other being, no matter its age. Remember the Pharaoh is only flesh and skin for something greater to conquer humans spiritually and physically. It's a mathematical an unmistakable marker, showing the Pharaoh's conquest of worlds. Every marker will bear the eye of Horace. There is also another very advanced purpose for building the pyramids. I will speak more about that when we talk about Moses in depth. Scriptures will reveal some information that will give credence to my colleague's theories on the pyramids. It will be then that we have more evidence and a greater understanding of how the author of Genesis knew that 4.5 billion years ago the planet was form-less and empty, long before, we humans, existed. As the mystery of God continues to unfold, I am here with you now to begin the new journey. Death no longer holds my soul by way of the blood of Christ.

Now the earth was formless and empty, darkness was over the surface
of the deep, and the Spirit of God was hovering over the waters.

If you look at a picture of an ancient mummified human, it seems like a body sucked dry of life. It has a similar look to a butterfly or a moth caught in a spider's web. Rather eerie and frightening to me. Just burn me and scatter my bones and ashes to the winds and to the sea. Mummifying the dead was an action passed down by a race of humans, we fully don't understand, we never really give any thought to where mummification originated. The only way evil or punishment can manifest is by our weaknesses and temptation. What better way to set a trap than gold treasures and artifacts. I mentioned earlier about mimicking our ancestors, yet we must understand what we mimic. We could accumulate all the treasure in the world and still never be happy. It is an emptiness of the soul that can never be fulfilled. It is only in serving others, we truly fulfill happiness in spirit. It is a feeling that does not fade when all the money is gone and you're old and gray. We must reach for a higher state of conscious to defend ourselves from the chaos which preys on our souls. When we all become teachers of spiritual defense and kindness, our enemy will lose on this battlefield of time. They have already lost against me in their great deceit, therefore the spiritual hunt for souls is at an apex. War, serial killers, child rapists, and others of the same, these are things of the past that awakening in our future. I am here to teach defense, so that many may be saved. Unfortunately, I know the strength of my enemy and that is a concern to myself as well as heaven. Weakness of soul is the cause of much suffering in many who are not enlightened, both rich and poor. It's hard for heaven to watch those suffer even when stubborn. The worst thing we can do in this world is starting a blood bath and that's when the "dead" or the vultures appear. We will notice on the crest of the Pharaohs a vulture sits beside the cobra. Let us investigate the meaning of the Uraesus, the sovereign crown of the original mighty Pharaohs. A cobra has a vicious poison that kills, (knowledge mixed with greed) the vulture comes when it smells death, so it may feed on rotting carcasses. The king and queen are paired hunters, hunters of souls.

I can beg and I can plead, but many will not hear the words of Christ. When the heavens ask if I give it my all to help the people of earth, I want to give a strong answer. I want to say there was nothing I missed or didn't think of for the glory of your salvation. That is just my job, I am a soldier and teacher of spiritual knowledge and warfare. I would hope someone would do the same for me if I did not understand from where I came from and the absolute foolishness of the world that surrounds me.

I would like to write a little about vanity and beauty. This is one of our enemy's greatest weapons. As we age and our bodies get old, some spiral into depression over fading looks, sagging muscles, and flesh, we could accept all been equally beautiful and equally healthy; however, on earth, we were chosen to walk a different route. We are living a life where we are on our own and choose what to do with that life.

The penalty for the fallen angels is high for their treason. They intermingled and mixed with races not ready to develop fast enough for the standards of companionship. So, they beat them, chained them, and tortured them like animals until they were good servants.

I have no doubt in my mind the roots of my origin. I also have no doubt why God chose me to deliver a message on behalf of man and beast. I once was that naked little boy running free in paradise, till a crafty serpent deceived me, and embarrassed me before my father. Now comes justice.

Beauty is very powerful in both women and men. At that point, is something about a beautiful man or adult females that can cause someone to do nearly anything. Love is good; control and manipulation is not. I possess such a tough time with beauty. I feel nervous and stutter my words when I should be confident and able. If human beings fell from the sky to lay down with their institution, they must have perfected the science to a high point. Women were made beautiful for pleasure and to serve man. We can see with time there was abuse of these beautiful beings.

Things like lust, jealousy, envy, phallus size, good or not good in bed, brought a whole lot of trouble and death to humans. This is the enmity that God speaks of when he chastises the serpent for deceiving Eve. And it is alive and well as we speak today. It's a deep-rooted hatred in which God spoke of. God remarks, his seed, and her source. To me that means his kind and her kind. If the serpent is an Egyptian wearing the crown of the Pharaoh or soldier, this will later explain my version of Cain and Able. Despite being at a tad different from the ancient version, it explains why Caine was not like his brother, Able, whom he slaughtered. *"I will put enmity between thee and the woman, between thy seed and her seed"* It's as clear as day. God is addressing Satan, the serpent or Pharaoh, for subduing a lower race of humans.

In America's past as well as modern day, Caucasian men had a big problem with Caucasian girls being with black men. Black men were killed and tortured for this in many places. This is something that has existed forever, prejudice of mixing races. When I was young, one of my best friend was a huge black guy. I had never thought anything of it. He was a good person and had a very respectable family. Feeling of prejudice in my own soul came later in time when girls came into the picture and my dad got robbed at gunpoint and was almost killed. Why was that? There's a deep-rooted hatred between races that goes back further than the bible. Especially, when we speak of interracial marriages and sex. It is nothing new, it has just resurfaced in many ways through time. Whatever negative feelings I have, they are not of merit and satanic from my perspective, it is tactics of evil within my own being. So being self-recognized of the many ugly feelings we have in this world is very important. I surely did not have hatred towards my friend for being black. If I grew up and was raised by Indians as a white man, I would love the Indians and their causes. That would be the same for my African American brothers. Yet, many would dislike me breeding with their women. It is changing their native bloodline. I think this would be much more about the hatred of my people for taking their land and slavery than it would be about my race and color. To hate somebody simply for the color of skin seems like learned behavior, not something we were conducted with. Do you believe it was the same with Muslim and Hebrews, or Egyptian and Hebrews or any other variation? There are many stupid reasons for hatred and prejudice. This might explain why God became angry in the garden in the Old Testament. Eve became pregnant right after being deceived by the serpent, which is quite an interesting fact when talking about the seed of humans.

These are the things we will have to leave behind someday. Why, may you ask? We are a flawed and imperfect creation by genetics, it is nothing we did on our own. Christ forgives us, as he is merciful and understanding. When we choose to become something new in Christ, we are training ourselves spiritually to take greater vessels. When we prepare to walk into the gates of God's city, many things we will have to leave behind knowing we are only but a shell waiting for a new shell. We will have more equality in the future, being equally beautiful and intelligent. Many will not be able to live such a holy life as this right away. The lord has a plan for all of us. Many changes will take place on this earth. Create no mistake when it is the last call, those left behind will likely to be doomed.

We must remember the sacrifice heaven gave us so that we might not be destroyed. The powers of hell are trying to recreate the same scenario that has always been since the beginning of time. The whole universe is closely linked as we all know, we are not the only beings that exist.

I believe my people to be smarter than our adversary now as time has taught us so many things. We must learn from our enemy so that there are no surprises when the end of times arrives. Me, I'm already dead, what does it matter? I am here to be a strong voice for your salvation and spiritual defense. When a teacher teaches, he hopes his students will listen to his wisdom. Especially, when it comes to something as important as saving souls and protecting ourselves from demonic forces. Remember if it was not for evil there would be no God or Jesus Christ. Just as if there were no crime we wouldn't need police and court systems. Jesus Christ was manufactured out of a need to establish law for human here on this earth.

Dead on Arrival

I was dead on arrival, I say with a smile
Who is in denial, not me the Egyptian Child?
Wings of the Nile grow like the wild
Timeless their grave the sun was the dial
I was dead on arrival, I say with a smile
Who is in denial, not me the Egyptian Child?
I give hail to the son, time's gladiator
I would do it for fun, just for the savior
I'll light up the sky in his theater

I was dead on arrival, I say with a smile
Who is in denial, not me the Egyptian Child?
Caskets have been broken, spells have been spoken
Like oil and dust, with tear drops of rust
How did we fall from the clouds?

Plastic Shell

Why is something beautiful dangerous
It's the falling of God, the falling of men
Why is something so beautiful dangerous
Only time will comprehend
Why is something beautiful dangerous
Ruby Red lips and a crown of gems
Beautiful faces make beautiful races
With ribbon and bows and all the laces
Beautiful races make beautiful faces
Let's kill all the ugly, and leave nothing but traces

Why is something beautiful dangerous
It's the falling of God, the falling of men
Why is something so beautiful dangerous
Ruby red lips and a crown of gems
Beautiful faces make beautiful races
With ribbon and bows and all the laces
Ugly faces, make ugly races
Dirty hair, teeth and skin
Beautiful faces with bright silver braces
Yeah, I got that smile that captures men
Why is something beautiful dangerous
Only time will comprehend

What is life when it's all so fake?
Plastic tits and a plastic face
What is life when it's all so fake?
Plastic trees on a plastic lake
I surrender to the highest realm
Life with a plastic shell!

XII

TIME

Time

Time, is like a river flowing,
Time, I'm always knowing
Time, forever showing
Time, time, time

Time will come, time will go
Time will wash away like snow
Maybe we can learn to fly again
Maybe yes we can

Time, is like a river flowing
Time, the stars are showing
Time, I'm forever knowing
Time, time, time

Time will come, time will go
Time will wash away like snow
Maybe we can touch the stars again
Maybe yes we can
Yes, we can my friends

Genesis 1-2 *In the beginning God created the heavens and the earth. 2 The earth was formless and void, and darkness was over the surface of the deep, and the Spirit of God was hovering over the surface of the waters.*

This whole chapter is based on my theoretical view of the universe. As I mentioned in the beginning of the book, no one has to take my words as fact. This is a very elaborate and complex vision of the universe, and those who hold it. Some may say that it is God who controls all things, not Christ. Again, I don't truly like the terminology 'God'. I would prefer 'friends from heaven'. Yes, all things are under control by your friends in heaven. That is one thing that we can be sure of. If you look at these verses, it will tell you exactly how long man has been coming and going from this earth. As I've told you, when you break certain events down and look at them carefully, things become very clear.

What the author of Genesis, Moses, is describing is the early discovery of the earth long before it came into the orbit of a sun and started giving life. This is an account of what one day we shall find or meet as modern humans when we travel through this universe. The verses speak for themselves. The spirit of God was hovering over the surface of the waters. This is another huge statement telling us about God. In certain bibles, it is translated God moved above the water. Does this translation suggest it could be his spirit only? Hovered would mean an object, not even necessarily moving, but floating above another object. This tells me God is in some form of craft. What makes this strikingly clear that we're dealing with cosmonauts. The author of Genesis was able to draw the solid ground and its state long before modern man had come to see it themselves. *The earth was formless and void, and darkness was over the surface of the deep.* He is giving us a clear example of early astronomy, long before most men knew about it. <u>This also tells us water was here before God came, as we know him scripturally.</u> If God as we know him, father of Adam, didn't put water here and scientists have no clue where it came from, karma may affect those hunting ancient creatures such as whales and shark fins with malice and impunity. We are messing with the wrong race of alien beings' majestic creatures, we understand that.

The author is giving us clues to where he came from in a day when men did not understand. Because the world was dark and crossed with water, the author recognized that in time that this planet would be perfect for supporting life. All it needed was more sun. According to my theory, non-human creatures who arrived on earth before human beings, started the expansive water world. They started bringing amphibious and reptilian creatures to this earth when the light was less significant than what it is today. Working with reptile and amphibious eggs is bare, and they breed rapidly. Juveniles are very durable and thrive in a short amount of time. They put dangerous creatures on this planet to deter humans from mining the planet of gold and diamonds. Her great beauty was set in motion. I'm sure you don't think the creator of men would put such dangerous creatures on the earth as we saw in prehistoric days. For we are the image of the father. If God created, pterodactyls, crocodiles, poisonous snakes, and sharks, I sure would wonder about God and his purpose for humans. The book of Genesis is a very vague description of life, as well as the creation of the heavens earth. When you think about lizards, they have super charged DNA. I saw a lizard leap from my roof to the ground and not even be phased. That is equivalent to me jumping off a high rise, for a proportion of scale. Can you imagine the world full of large reptiles? Men from the heavens who were mining gold had an answer for this dilemma of large reptiles. They caused an extinction of giant reptiles. This began the *Stone Wars* and the *War of the Worlds*, which are two chapters in my next book. It is why you see so many different huge stone markers with weird looking beings across the world. This would be the last time humans would make such an aggressive act towards another race and its creations. Evil fought with great power to keep its kingdoms. The army of the archangel had defeated them.

Man knows the value of the Son of God, the Christ, was the last defense against a force so great it had conquered time itself. This was a war that could not be settled with weapons and guns. Into this world was born the dragon slayer and his chosen servant to master spiritual realms among men. The cost was high for those who loved them. There is not one thing any human can do for the son and his father other than pray for their final victory. This is a personal spiritual battle to gain full authority over the power of resurrection. The greatest thing that can be done for man is to break the bonds of satanic sorcery and let you watch the reward of those who serve the wicked.

According to my theory, time in space is a continuum that never stops and never will. To explain the mystery and the creation of time we must look at it like explaining a recipe. Writing and explaining the recipe is rather simple. To create that recipe and have all the ingredients is truly more difficult. How rare is the perfect term for life, especially when you are far from dwelling in the obscurer regions of space? How rare is an abundant source of pure water? I come to you as a teacher for the sake of generations to come. I must clearly explain what God was, and the consequence of action that brought us Jesus Christ. Remember, if there were no evil, there would be no need for a teacher or protector for the inhabitants of this planet. It is not like this any place else or in any other universe which exists that I know of. Here we are all alone in space. Because I speak of resurrection and past lives I will tell you how this war began, the consequences, as well as the story of hope. I don't believe the author of Genesis was writing theory, the spirit was giving us a vision and using coded verses for us to figure out later in time when we became more scientific. Time as I know it, began at the center of the universe. The center of the universe is the center of planetary life. There was no need for light at the center of the universe, <u>for God was the light.</u> This was caused by an explosion which filled the universe with an abundance of residual light and many came. Exactly as when you leave a light on at night outdoors, many matters will come to investigate. It's no different in this universe or any other. This is my last dance, the dance of death.

In the beginning, the time centurions were awakened and were called to the Mazarine planet. Time centurions are the keepers of time and space. All heavenly bodies' orbits and rotations are mathematically calculated and stored for a very specific purpose, planetary evolution, and protection. All planets that were capable of giving life are highly protected. The Mazarine was what you call the seed of life in this world. The beginning of time in this universe is what is recorded by the Holy Spirit. The Holy Spirit tells me all things are created; we are model within a model within a model. This is so that greater intelligence understands all things about life that can be understood. If you were to ask me how life itself began, that is a question I cannot answer. From nothing, comes something and from something, comes nothing. It is a continuum that goes beyond what the mind can even fathom.

Everything we see looks so large in the vast universe. It is not large as we have become very small. To create the heavens and earth, one must be very large in stature. We will talk much on this subject.

We are humble enough to handle, yet big enough to be a risk to everything living thing on this planet and many others. God has reduced the fallen angels into the vessels of modern human beings. We are ants in the time and space in which we live. It is no great wonder why it takes us so long to get anywhere, that's part of the curse. Alone in time and space with no worlds left to conquer or lands of the earth left undiscovered. The choices soon will become very clear for humans. Are prisons being a vast blackness called the abyss of time and space. Everything we see is a *time prison* created for souls to learn certain lessons about life because of our great failures. Not just humans, everything in the cosmos. We just happen to be the last race to meet what is known as the devil or the serpent. The sworn enemy of the living, and the king of the dead. We are also hard-headed, so it has taken us the longest to evolve spiritually.

Did you ever wonder why dinosaurs were so huge as well as whales and sharks? Some weigh close to two tons. Compared to the average man and woman, that's a significant difference. Size of creation is indicative of the creator and their race. All intelligent life may use other's creations for pleasure and beauty. Beware to those that abuse and misuse other people's creations or their own. Earth has become a place of many lessons. The Mazarine planet was huge, nothing like men have seen now. Because of the size of the planet, most beings lived far distances from each other and never had any type of encounter. They did not intermingle as a society but shared knowledge in certain ways. One way would be crop circles or inscriptions on stone or gold. It was from here that life pushed outward or returned from where it came. The inhabitants became aware that there would be a change in atmosphere.

So, to explain our problem today of freakish weather and massive heat waves, let's us keep an open conversation among the brilliant minds of this earth. Some say the earth has existed 4.5 billion years. If we have destroyed the atmosphere since the industrial revolution in the late 1800s, then you shall know why all of heaven is watching closely at the judgment of Jesus Christ. How many planets might we have done this to in our journeys? If this is the case, we deserve to live in a bubble looking at the hell we created so we may never forget the lesson on the type of energy we use and the products we make. To those responsible, severe consequences must be handed out. This will happen anyway, in some form or fashion. Many have chosen money and greed verses the safety of lives and environment. Could there be other mitigating factors causing these weather patterns, quite possibly so. To understand that we must look at many theories such as pole reversal, solar flares, unstable core, ozone, and the magnetic field. I am not a scientist by trade, I'm a soldier of time. However, I know patterns of disaster are something that we are always trying to solve. I will use my common sense of spirit to prove some cause and effect explanations as we go. You may read them with little regard or you may use them for your benefit.

When you are a created being there are two instincts that seem to be dominant in our genetics. The main one being survival, the secondary procreation. Procreation can be achieved in many ways, including science and asexual beings. This is so a race can flourish and fulfill their desire to make other companions. This is not performed so they can govern over their offspring like Gods, or rule other races. When humans were first born into the universe, there were different beings of the same. Because evil did not exist at that time, there was harmony amongst all. Their world was plentiful and had everything that you could wish to live and learn without cost. There was no intellect to fight or in warfare. As some people would say in this world, *"those were the good old days"*. In time, certain races of man would break up and move out into the Universe because of the impending change in ambience. Specific knowledge was given to them to begin that voyage, the rest was trial and error.

Beings were at the forefront of mining techniques and they insisted to extend the excavation of a planet that was rich in resources, particularly gold. You will read later in the chapter *Gold Rush,* scientists believe most gold is deep within the planet's core. Man took a journey down the road of the unknown. First, they would need to start massive explosions, deep within the planet: therefore, creating massive fractures into the mantle. This was made out with explosives far more potent than nuclear. The explosives were set deep inside the planet's magnetic poles as well as many other strategic positions. They set explosives with timers on the planet and went back through the eye of the vortex from which they came. I will explain parallel and singular vortexes in depth very soon. Success was born, after many ages under the constant gravitational force per unit area and shocks from other heavenly objects. The planet imploded when the mantle fractured into the core. It then exploded, expanding the universe as we know it. However, it is many things that happened that give us this universe not one giant explosion. Let us not think of the universe in this way. This was an attempt make a number of smaller planets that could be harvested for gold, precious metals, and gems, according to my version and theory of time. Mankind in this age of the universe did not need light, God was their light. Humans soon became *Masters of Time* in this universe and started the process of creation. This is the reason that eternal life would be important to those who create. It is a life long journey to be the creator of all things. To enjoy the fruits of labor you must live many lives or in that case, forever. If you do the same thing multiple times over you would have flourishing universes, <u>all that would be required is water</u>. Fresh water is very rare in the universe. Fresh water and salt water did not just appear here by magic, it was a process. The creation of life itself is a process. Some were made dirty and poisonous and they were purified by time.

There are lots of ice in the heavens, but it is not suited for all life until it is made at its purest. The salty water is from different minerals in rock that melts before it becomes frozen and collided with earth. I believe this one of the general theories among many scientists. To clarify or add this theory, those in the heavens changed the trajectory of huge chunks of space ice forcing into our atmosphere, sending it crashing to the ground before life ever existed. This is relatively simple for those in the heavens. It is just as easy as making an asteroid impact the earth and killing reptiles. Many of these theories come from a story in progress called *The Emperors Servants*. This is what the earth does and will continue to do over time: it purifies the water by several different natural processes. It is imperative we try not to poison it any further, it should be for all the universe to enjoy as well as it creatures. We surely cannot drink salt water and as you can see our water sources are drying up quickly at some locations on Earth. It is being used faster than water can hang or be stored and purged. It's no longer pristine in many situations. The waters, eventually, have become wormwood. We, the people, need to wake up and see who our creators and our ancestors were. We are killing a jewel pumping poison into the sky and polluting its waters. Wherever would you find drinkable or fresh lake and ocean water that life can live in within thousands of light years of us? It is so far, that we need advanced technology to get there. This is a game that man will lose in the long-run. It something that makes me very angry. If I am angered you can be assured the spirit of heaven and its people are equally angered. I say that as a witness to the power of the heavens and earth and as a prisoner of time. When you read John's vision about the City of God, it is decorated with gold, diamonds, and walls of precious stone. It once used to be the greatest pirate ship known to heaven and earth until it was lost in war in heaven. So, when I say Jesus holds the world in the palm of his hand, it is best we know that it is true. Pirate ships are fully armed for battle, and this is one big ship with thick impenetrable walls. I only tell you this so that you may know that when they say the Lord is mighty, it is on many levels, and painfully so. When we take something that is not ours to take, the price becomes very heavy. We are not beaten with a stick. We spend more time in this *Time Prison* and our lessons increase. We become increasingly agitated and shaken at our state of affairs. It always painful for the Lord and for us when he chooses to start the clock all over again. You are playing a game in the wrong place by destroying the atmosphere at a rapid pace. <u>You have the earth guarded with high tech surveillance and weapons that enables no one to assist the less fortunate without having altercation.</u>

It is understandable why our prison sentence on earth as well as the spiritual realm is so long and will continue throughout life. Trust me, a thousand years in a 100-year interval seems like infinity. Try a million or until the universe ceases to exist, that's an eternity if we don't acknowledge the consequences of our actions. Our ancestors were messing around with a universal stopping place for many beings in heaven. Not only for water, but for food as well. They do not consume meat, they do not kill or slaughter. This is an issue in heaven and forever will be with non-human origins. Nevertheless, we were made in the image of those who called themselves God and sons of God and they became meat eaters. This was in the day of Noah after the great flood. God of the Old Testament told Noah to build an Ark and preserve certain species for domestication and beauty. When heaven shows us a more serious room than having slaughter houses and butchers, I will be the first to be thankful for a resolution. I consume very little red meat or pork, nearly none. We don't have heart attacks on earth for no reason at all, in that I'm quite certain. We were not meant to be highly stressed with poor diets.

Going along with scientific theory, when a heavenly body gets sucked into a time vortex it will adopt a new track and orbit as it becomes part of new existence. Time is made up of many cosmic vortexes that exist in the darkness of the abyss of space. A time vortex is basically the force behind a universe in early formation. It is what was used to create an artificial expansion in our universe. It is more referred to me as cosmic wind or a space storm. Our universe is constantly moving and picks up debris like a tornado as this is the reason we now see the universe expanding. At the heart of every universe where life starts, there is a time vortex. A vortex allows floating debris a chance to orbit, changing the form of heavenly debris over billions and trillions of years. As a vortex starts to die out, there is much chaos as the universe starts to compact causing massive collisions and explosions.

The basic law about space and time is quite simple. <u>What goes up must come</u>

down or sits in space and spins around and round. If there is no gravity for heavenly objects where do they go? If there is no ground what do they fall to? Space debris floats in space aimlessly with no orbit or purpose. If there is no gravity pushing it upward, it floats away or gets caught in another vortex. It must fall one day. Nothing can stay in orbit or go in the upward direction forever, it must come back down. What does it fall to? Life is recyclable in every way, shape and form, nothing is ever wasted in deep space. That I can assure you.

The dancing of spheres Let us conceive of a planetary life in this way. Does an engineer design a huge urban center without a model or design specs? Let us conceive of the world in this very same room. Normally, an architect will plan a small-scale model first, before they make the actual size model. All things small, that are approved, are then made into a larger scale. Now that wasn't so difficult, was it? According to my theory, we should think of time as a circle within a circle within a circle. Space for us has an end boundary. At one end, is a salty liquid and at the other end, is something we are not meant to see nor we can never reach, except spiritually. Life, being the reason, is the greatest journey of souls and there are many levels. Thus, we are given borders in which we must exist to take that journey as there are a considerable act of substantial estates to reach.

What happens when you put a magnetic core inside a geodetically created sphere? Then you build another sphere around that sphere and afterwards, fill the spheres with one third water and leave two thirds empty void? You would have two spheres with deep dark voids of water. Also, have a sphere within a sphere that could generate hydroelectric current power by spinning around a magnetic core as the sphere itself absorbs light, just as a solar panel does. To do this, you must master polarity within those spheres. We would ask to use something to alter the polarity at each terminal of the spheres so they would act in unison and magnetically. When a magnet repels, or attracts it is due to polarity. Common knowledge and science suggest a magnetized bar has its power concentrated at two ends: its poles. They are known as its *north* and *south* poles. The N end will repel the N end of another magnet, S will repel S, but N and S attract each other. According to most scientists, the region where this is seen, is called the magnetic field. So, this means if I wanted to make a sphere within a sphere hover or suspend itself within another sphere, we would need to change each end to the same polarity. We can manage this with spheres at infinite, given each one is bigger than the other one and holds a greater magnetic pole. Eventually all spheres will work in unison and can float in an orbit just like a planet. By controlling the polarity of the spheres and the rotation of the magnetic core, each pole is repelling itself from the other so that one pole sits perfectly balanced in the other sphere by force of the magnetic field. I call it the *dancing of spheres* for a reason. When you start to spin the spheres at a very high rate then introduce large magnetic stones, at once, the stones get caught in the magnetic field rotation. Large rocks start making smaller rocks which eventually make sand somewhere else. These are the *Sands of Time*. Eventually everything gets caught in artificial orbits within a 3-D magnetic field. The magnetic stones start to get tripped in the magnetic pull as well as the circular updrafts of wind caused by the interior sphere spinning within the exterior sphere. However, the magnetic pull and wind currents would still be relatively the same until you use magnetics to draw the inner sphere upwards or downwards. This is done by adjusting a pole to the north or south, drawing everything by ascending or descending by force of magnetic pull. This is what creates giant space storms or time vortexes. Would a being think everything just magically stays up in the sky forever? That would be hilarious! What goes up must come down or sit in space and spin round and round. As you start to spin the spheres even faster, you are then creating artificial orbits within those orbits, then you add light and temperature. This makes ice in certain regions and gives light and warmth to others, this is achieved multiple ways in this geodetically created sphere of life. This is what holds all the universes within a very specific 3-D circular magnetic field. There are certain areas where gravity is spinning so fast universes must recede. To go any further, they would be destroyed, they would be burned up in the magnetic field. It is then time for our creators to change the polarity on the sphere's southern poles, causing the interior sphere and its contents to recede. This is entirely carried out with dual layered mono magnetic poles that are computer driven and run at specific intervals. This is, thus, that if our creators could not be present or if catastrophe happened, life continues moving, according to my hypothesis. This is the reason our existence in space is constantly running, twisting, and twirling. Because we are whirling at high velocity in a magnetic discipline, the receding and compression of universes happen in a very gradual manner. The spheres never lose a moment and continually turn, but all universes, then are compressed towards the center where they first began, it's a never-ending process. Each model within a model can be mastered by simply changing polarity after each chamber. When it spins at high velocity, quickly everything changes, it becomes a genesis chamber of planetary life. Like the stories of the great Jules Verne, one day, we shall experience many big matters.

Monopoles If you were to look at a sphere created with hexagons, you might realize it can be become something quite miraculous. Each pattern can generate a continuous path of current by linking them all together like a conduit for electricity. In other words, the sphere can contain a charge, under the right conditions. Monopoles, until as recent were a hypothetical elementary particle in particle physics that carry a singular charge or singular pole.

According to the *London Center of Nanotechnology*, these particles are no longer hypothetical. 85 years ago, a theoretical physicist, Paul Dirac, predicted the possibility of monopoles and their existence. At Amherst College Physics, Professor David S. Hall and Aalto University, Mikko Möttönen, have created, identified, and photographed synthetic magnetic monopoles in Hall's laboratory on the Amherst campus according to an article by *Phys.org*. We have broken the ground for the amazing future technology.

As we picture the earth floating around a sun, let us ponder if it would be possible to create a manufactured geodetically sphere made of pentagons and let it float in space with us orbiting our sun. Very much like a large city or a space station, except it is a small scaled replica of something you observed in your journeys in time. It could float around us like a small moon. Could we simulate life on a smaller scale to preserve it during a dangerous time such as war or a dying planet and solar system? What is small scale when I speak of creation? Soon we will find out!

When we speak of moving and lifting Egyptian stone blocks, you can achieve this with mono poles and something I call mono-magnetic quarry plates. With the right combination of charges on the magnetic quarry plates and a vessel with a huge magnetic plate you can achieve levitation: + plus (bottom plates lined in rows), + plus (bottom plate for carved stone, levitation effect), - minus (top plate, attractor for bottom plate, fastened together, block sits in between), + plus (large magnetic plate on vessel, hovers along the path of plates in a line). With several small ships and one large ship, empires were built. Many engineering techniques were used in man's journey through space to build their great empires.

Land of the giants. The Holy Spirit had told me that long ago, life failed on a larger scale and had to be reset with certain protections put in place. We did not go on into the great journey of souls for a cause. Outside the inner sphere in which we live, heaven or utopia, was almost destroyed in the same way the human race was headed by planetary wars.

Time Prison, is the explanation of those failures and what our purposes are as humans. When we fail on a smaller scale, it is a setback for the great *Architects of life*. This is the cause of our fall: we challenged our creators and their laws, and we lost. I am no better than any, I am spiritual prisoner serving out a sentence. I only give you wisdom to save you and set you free by the mercy of the higher being. The only missing piece in this puzzle is where it all comes from. We are in a universe full of secrets. Many universes put together that were built by giant sized beings for a specific purpose. Exactly as our ancient ancestors created life on worlds and had landed for scientific reasons. It is no different as we go up the ladder. Natural planetary evolution in our universe would be very slow, so we created artificial expansion. You will soon see all the things we think of are an extension of our creators who were giants and in time, reduced many of them into new and smaller versions of themselves. Yes, time physically reduced and separated; and multiplied human beings as it shut its heavenly doors to its higher realms.

Intelligent vessels that exist are a manifestation of this knowledge. In the book of Enoch, it mentions that the sons of God or the angels fell for daughters of men who gave birth to giants at about 3000 cubits tall. This is observed as well in the book of Genesis; however, it makes us no clue to where a giant comes from, what a giant is, nor looks like. How could something 3000 cubits tall could be supported to this world? Excuse my forwardness, how does his penis fit into a human female or he be delivered from the womb (unless the angels decreased their size to human level, that's IF they had that power)? It seems something is mistranslated in this book. If we are talking literally 3000 cubits, I believe this refers more to the offspring of the sons of god ascending into the sky. At about 4500 feet, it may refer to the cruising altitude of manmade vessels. We know Enoch and Elijah are associated with a wheel and chariot which ascends and descends from the sky.

One thing we do know for certain, God told Eve her labor pains would be greatly increased in the first book of the bible. Was this because she was very young and not quite a woman yet? Could it be because there would no longer be science or doctor to provide quality care for the young couple expelled from Eden? Or could it be these fallen angels were quite larger than ordinary men and women long ago? Quite possibly it is a compounding of all affairs. Many of the fallen angels were bred and created for warfare, they were legendary among the dwellers. Again, when we talk of giants, I am not sure the translation is quite right. I think it is more affiliated to the wisdom of the progeny of those who came from above the ground. They may have been very tall and muscular compared to a Hebrew man because they were of a greater DNA structure, as their lineage came from above. If you plant a human skeletal well over 9' tall, I would have to use up my theories for lunch. To me, 9' tall is a giant, when I am less than 6 feet.

A story to form a conclusion about giants is the narrative of David and Goliath. If the Israelites killed a giant Palestinian well over 9' tall, they would have mounted him up him like a trophy and carried him around until the end of time. If humans came from the stars in space, dressed in full battle gear, with the serpent or Babylonian crest, they would be larger than life for any unevolved human. These are the men who laid down with women and these violent creations, were born (giants). When you mix wisdom with the unevolved to fast, it suits a serious scenario.

In the Books of Enoch, The Bible of the Watchers, the early verses explain how giants came to be. It talks of these giants which came from the holy men. The giants removed the toil of man until they could no longer keep them. *The Bible of the Watchers, says that these giants sinned against the chicks, reptiles, fish, and they devoured one another's physical body.* These giants drank the blood of their conquest and taught women, daughters of men, magic, and spells of charm. They read them the cutting of roots and tree, and with that, building of homes to pose down with their beautiful conquests. From these accounts of the prophet, we can see that women in the early phases of evolution were wild before becoming beautiful and desirable to the angels. It seems their offspring's sexual appetite and earthly desire for women was more than humans could endure. As they grew in numbers, they devoured territory and every resource in it. The fallen angels and earthly women formed an unholy union. *The record of Enoch said there was a conspiracy and cover up by the saints to hold away their plan effectively.* This means to me, they swore an oath to keep these women and children a secret from the rest of the angels. I'm sure that will make much more sense when the army of Christ approaches. The angels made a private heaven. A space of savage beauty and sexual desire. I do not blame all of them for many reasons. Life is a path, and if a path is not taken, <u>we cannot</u>

understand the consequences. Great mistakes were made in the fall from heaven. Oaths and secrets were shattered for the love of gold and precious gems. Those that brought such men now pay the price for others ignorance and the mistreatment of the inhabitants.

There are various descriptions of giants in the bible, yet we never find any bones from the prehistoric age or any other age that would make us believe they existed physically. Let us not confuse giants that I spoke of in creation, *The architects of life*, with spiritual demons or spiritual giants. These are the expressions of these giant creatures of long ago who became unholy monstrosities. As I mentioned, time had shortened them. Human life has passed through so many stages. Hence, the reason men and women's appetite for sex and violence is so ravenous. We were a creation created with vicious and foul intention as our messiah understands the weakness of our flesh against the foe. They are masters of manipulation and deception against our human body. The more children in the world, the more power they are fed in specific seasons of great turmoil. It is a very elaborate intentional infliction of sorrow and pain upon our souls. Once again, the only need for mass population is to build heavenly and earthly empires which wage war. In the beginning, we were bred as servants and soldiers of war. He is a man, nothing more, nothing less. I emit into your soul, life, and truth, and then you may become a new foundation in the name of the Father and the Holy Spirit. What needs do you have for wars, territory, and billions wasted in finding spirit in the cosmos when heaven promises a vast elaboration of life that have been already made? We must have the passion of control because manipulation, war and violence will be an obstacle to warfare.

Oh yes, those giants love to impregnate women. What women would kill their own flesh and blood, a piece of their body and soul, even if they got to realize they were evil incarnate? They instead worshipped the land they walked on when they decorated them with precious stones and used their overwhelming charm. If they experienced exactly how evil the sons of God had become, they would a have heard God long ago in the days before Enoch and Moses. We now know why our world suffers. In that respect, the evil you see is controlled by giant spiritual beings living their final days and desires through humans. They recognize their time is short as heavenly angels approach.

Do you think when a grown man molests a baby or child, it is instinct? Would they give their whole life out for a life sentence in the penitentiary for one last crazy fetish? A chance to dominate a baby or small child, to exert control, for a moment's pleasure? Not only that, then they snuff the life out of precious little girls and boys to sustain them from finding their predators. This is as unholy as it can be. Yet, it was carried out many times in earth's history, repeatedly in battles in which men conquered territories.

Such weak souls that are so easily influenced by these demons of the past that in my opinion, <u>do not deserve the breath of life</u>. Their time in prison is nothing or will not be enough to prepare them for what is ahead. In prisons on earth, one will receive a shank if granted. Even they cannot abide to be in their comportment. Nothing is unseen or not passed on judicially in this Time Prison. Yes, spiritual giants exist here on earth in this present day, they are recognized as the "cursed dead". Some have taken the way of the righteous and some serve lust, destruction, hatred, and warfare. Recognize this, my dark brethren, you are jailed with no way out and resistance is futile. You can kill my voice a thousand times; however, <u>you are surrounded</u> with more that are like myself. I have sent my chosen ones to testify and see these words. Yes, I have become smaller, yet, I am a giant in wisdom. I am proud of who I am. I have transfigured through time, doors, and windows to be your guide. I have risen from the dead, resurrected for your glory and spiritual defense. We're not going anywhere until we achieve complete victory.

In modern day America, we witness human sex trafficking, adult shops, mass prostitution, and sex machine factories. According to an internet article by *Fusion*, these sex machine factories are building life like humans for our sexual pleasure. We have run the direction of Babylon and far beyond from temptation of Satan. Do you think it was any different long ago in other places in time? Oh, that's right, many of us believe we evolved from monkeys and just appeared randomly. Nothing really matters, they are bound to no law or regulation other than their own laws of money and flesh. Time is such a repeating cycle! We shall come and fall very hard. *In The books Enoch* and *Genesis*, the giants who prey on earthly women are the very reason the Lord taught the Islamic culture to cover their flesh many centuries ago. This was in the beginning when these fallen sons came from the sky. Many of the original Hebrews and Muslims were natives of the land, just like modern day Indians or Africans, before they were conquered, robbed, and raped! Islam has been very devout in this routine for many ages and it is an extremely old culture.

Some might see America as unholy, but <u>not necessarily evil</u>. Many of our laws are loose and revolve around money, not the word of God. Some call that freedom, I call it doom. There are many Christians and others who feel the same, I can assure you. We love our country and the hard-working people as well as the compassionate. We are not perfect by any means. We love righteousness and truth; however, it is a deceptive world. Many today, live a very loose lifestyle much like the Romans who indulged in all pleasures of the human body. As mighty as we are, every great kingdom one day must answer. If I am here today with you as in the past when the spirit-judged Rome, you will know a judgement is approaching, rightfully so. Our leaders have let corruption fill the lands. However, as Americans, we don't kill people arbitrarily on the account we have exposed their corruption. God will judge them so, and with great power. Today, I say to the masses, to defeat evil, we must be one and not divided. Do not have titles, race, and color of our skin divide us and subdue us. <u>Stand as one, as a giant, to be reckoned with.</u>

Biblical scripture suggests that the creation in this universe were by human beings who were far more advanced than we are today. They were known as Gods by the inhabitants of earth. To create the heavens and earth, one would be of much larger stature than modern day common man. If we know God was hovering the earth when it was dark and void, we know that is billions of years ago according to science. If a large dinosaur can devolve into a smaller species that flourishes, so can humans. Especially when cross mixing with different species of female humans. When we are small we take less from planets. Because we breed at epic proportions, this devolution has been a blessing for heaven and great curse for human life.

Now, we can see there are many infinite possibilities that are not explainable to the human mind. Yet, just as life along this earth plays in a loop, and then does all of time and creation. <u>This is to know every possible aspect and outcome of life so that nothing will be missed.</u> This would be the supreme master of time and space who carries out this wisdom. Jesus is basically a young vessel on a journey to a larger claim. Who said that *big things come in small packages*? They were right! To ignore Jesus Christ and his word is like upsetting a race of giants and that wouldn't look good for the earth. Essentially, Jesus was the byproduct of a giant being living in a body in the flesh. I mean, we are talking about <u>the supreme Lord of all universes</u>. From a human mind, all things exist and have come to be. Even the most awkward creations in all universes have come by or were brought about through his hands. What a great challenge and act of bravery it is to throw yourself down into your own system and creation, when creation has become so dangerous it threatens to obliterate itself. Not only were the fallen angels cast down to the earth, the doors of heaven closed upon them and forbidden to return. They were divided, multiplied, and slimmed down until time to put them in their correct place, a remnant slave race of man. Capable of going nowhere fast and bodies that age rapidly, many of these angels will perish before the city of God. We will die with honor as soldiers of time, the elite. Many will simply just burn in the carnage. If we read carefully in the first judgement, the earth started to scorch man as meteorites began to plague the earth.

This means the earth will be brutally hot and plunged into a darkness as the cosmos reigns down its fury.

It was always the Christ that loved the creatures of every kind and spoke in defense of all affairs. Fourth dimension, as well as this universe, sees Him as a wise master of jurisprudence and for that, they have sat him on a stool that cannot be taken away or thrown off. *I am the Alpha and Omega, the beginning, and the end of all things to come. I will love my people like no other when they hear my words! When you hurt, I suffer, it is not a pleasure for me to be here under such circumstances. I will still be in the background, living out my final days. It is much better that way.* They think the angels do not see, they *do* see everything.

XIII

EFFECTS IN TIME

Space storms, hurricanes and tornadoes. If time is gravity in all known universes, we would float for many ages than be compressed into oblivion as gravity dies out. Humans chose a rare parallel time vortex as they wanted to master something of greatness. This can be verified by scripture when it speaks of the heavens rolling up as scroll. This is an event that has happened forever in many universes and is widely known by cosmonauts such as the one who wrote the book of genesis and the prophets. We will always notice in scripture the prophets speak of celestial events, why is that? This is why they were chosen as prophets, their bloodline in the linage of angels.

This vortex I speak of pushes gravity one way, then pulls it back across an imaginary point known as the center of time. When a parallel universe shifts in time, the expanding universe initiates to collapse inwards on itself as it packs together in close to the kernel. Basically, like a tornado that turns into a vortex in the sea of blank. If there is no ground or barrier to hold back these massive storms momentum, it is exactly what this universe will act because of its monumental size.

Isaiah 34:4 Come near, you nations, and listen; pay attention, you peoples! Let the earth hear, and all that is in it, the world, and all that comes out of it! 2 The Lord is angry with all nations; his wrath is on all their armies. He will totally destroy them, he will give them over to slaughter. 3 Their slain will be thrown out, their dead bodies will stink; the mountains will be soaked with their blood. 4 All the stars in the sky will be dissolved and the heavens rolled up like a scroll; all the starry host will fall like withered leaves from the vine, like shriveled figs from the fig tree

Per my theory, this is precisely what happens as the universe ages and sets forth to go away. It and its knowledge are carefully rolled up like a coil to become something new. Everything we see revolves around compression, decompression, and attractors. We will see this on the earth in the form of massive natural disasters. The objects closest to the core of the universe will get drawn in with a rolling twisting motion. Equally, you can guess, this will change and can be VERY destructive.

If the storm did not evolve into another type of space storms, everything would collide and explode and the universe would cease to exist as we know it. It would become part of another universe or fall from the sky. It has always been contained in a powerful 3-D circular magnetic field. Because these events all take place in an abysmal sum of time, this change will also be a beautiful thing and many things can be kept in line by the heavenly beings. This change happens slowly, it is not even measurable to us. All we see is residual light that was, not what is taking place in the straightaway. Just as earth sucks a satellite back into our atmosphere, the universe eventually sucks us back towards the midpoint from which we arrived. The biggest pieces of stone or a planet that did not travel too far in the expanding universe will be influenced the most. This debris will not have travelled very far from the center. As heavenly bodies get caught in gravity when it reverses itself, many of these objects will collide and explode before they pass through the eye of the vortex. It will soon become part of a parallel universe. Whether a planet explodes naturally or there is a forced implosion the results are similar. You can be sure the idea was originated from a natural event and then elaborated upon. Collisions are an occurrence when you have a busy universe, many are little objects instead of the few larger kinds. <u>Expansion of time and time travel always have risk.</u> There is no getting around it.

If we were to think of a vortex as a space hurricane or tornado, we would know this occurs when cold meets warm air in our atmosphere. Therefore, I would call it a vortex, space, wind, or a space storm. It is pretty much the same concept. We recognize that we can fly through the eye of a hurricane if we approach the same in a very specific manner. In time, crossing this imaginary point will be as easy as flying into the eye of a hurricane with the right spacecraft. Because of the quantity of time that this will guide and the many changes the earth and our universe will break through, we must leave this legacy of wisdom and knowledge behind. All knowledge exists for us to move around once again. We, the soldiers of Christ, must first have victory before we take in the distinguished prize. This is then the ugliness on this land will never exist again nor anywhere else.

With this vortex we occupy, it starts to compress and there's no place left to go, we will be completely evolved enough to leave the universe and find another or be taken there. Universes have ages just as many heavenly bodies. They can only last as long as the current conditions will allow. Trial and error, this was a first for humans in mastering such a complex entity as a parallel stream. We have been around since the birth of time. We are some type of ants working away on our colonies?

The important thing is, God has chosen us, humans as His creation and the rest of this knowledge is a bonus. It is not how long it takes to find the road heading home or to journey on into the unknown, reaching our destination is what most counts. The journey of souls was not meant for a slave race or an airstream that was mistreated by others.

All this extra time it takes me to impart information on how things work in the cosmos is <u>my pleasure</u>. When I tell you the tale of time, know that time is long and the road will be bumpy if you cannot hear the words of the spirit. Every toxic spill, every death, every starvation, every rape, every child sold into slavery are recorded with great clarity. So be careful of what company you are surrounded with. The book is not called *Time Prison* for entertainment value. It should scare the hell out of the many evil thugs controlling this world. When the spirit finally gets you alone in death or in life, you're done. The recording will run endlessly with all the results of your actions. Maybe those above you in a corporation, their actions were wrongful and detrimental to earth and its people and you might have turned your head for financial gain. It is a guilty verdict in heaven just as it is on earth. <u>I personally like leakers with such valuable information.</u> Come forth quickly to the proper authorities with your info on crimes against the earth and its creatures. Heaven may spare the leaker from the worst. We tip, for heaven. When man took slaves, he is paying for that consequence, if not, this man will cease at the realms of destruction. Our fathers and their offspring don't get a free pass for killing a state full of natives, we are working to reap that cost one way or some other. Either by becoming human and loving our fellow brother and sister, or we become a nation plagued by violence. We are meant to be an example of Christ today. Most that do not give their life to Christ will never make it on to the next phase unless they carry a will to live stronger than the power of the angel of death. That is a rarity and unheard of, my friends. <u>Trust me, only one man knows</u>. They will be broken by Satan and very powerful demonic forces. Consider yourself warned.

<u>Millennial shifts.</u> Each hurricane or typhoon on this world are unique and never quite the same. It is why they are named and the same is done in heaven. Have us look closely at a tornado and how it behaves when it travels across the globe. When a tornado is at the peak of expansion the top of the tornado, it does something unique. It enlarges and compresses multiple times before the tornado eventually dies away. In other words, the peak of the storm is called <u>fluctuation.</u> To grant recognition to the Mayans, this period is close to ending, then a complete shift will begin to happen. This is where the universe takes a big dip and it will affect the magnetic field dramatically. Think of it in these terms. One movement in time in this fluctuation, would be the equivalent to about 2000 of our earth years passing by. That one movement towards compression or decompression changes the whole scope of our universe. In gradual increments, the universe is drastically manipulated. Life takes its great bounty and death does the same. They join hands in this great dance, even though being complete opposites by natures law!

A universe comes up and decreases based on how much momentum it can hold. If we conceive of our creation in the same manner as a tornado, we then know at the peak of expansion, we will experience various periods of fluctuation before the actual total compression of the universe. This happens about every 2000 years, some shifts being larger than others. Therefore, the saints will come along at exactly almost 2000 years later, with a warning siren. The Father and the Son each have risen. Observation will tell us when this effect is happening. What we will soon see in time, is massive meteor showers and volcanic activities, just as in the days before and after the arrival of Jesus. This is a natural occurrence; yet, it affects planetary life in diverse ways. This causes massive compression in the magnetic field which then causes compression to galaxies and solar systems. Everything in life as we know it, is magnetic and space made of stone. We are entering a new phase, or a new age if you will.

Hence, this is big news, it is not the death of the universe. Jesus is not stomping on the ground and shaking the earth, nor does he hate us. Yet, if we proceed to use fossil fuels and nuclear energy, there's a great chance we can damage this world and make it uninhabitable for our kids and us at a later time when things settled in the wake. This will be because of violent earthquakes and eruptions that will rock the foundations of this world, causing ruptures and leaks similar to the Fukushima reactor in Japan. Harm can be contained to certain countries if we educate ourselves. As well, we are emitting too much poison in the sky, which worsens our current conditions. It is not an appropriate time for a pipeline to be running right down the middle of our country.

Time is a series of births and rebirths. Our ancestors saw signs of the millennial shift coming in this universe. This is when they made their homes in the mountainsides of the world due to objects falling from the sphere. When the masses started to stir, they eventually understood there was nowhere to hide on mother earth. When the earth was in the stage of Pangea and the continents started to shift, this was a sign that millennial shifts had occurred. Some millennial shifts are much greater than others. Nevertheless, we, as humans, do not know at precisely what point in time the land will become plagued by earthquakes and volcanoes blowing up the continents again. We can make an educated guess, but it is best we weren't on the earth at that time. It becomes excruciating hot and a vast number of humans will die that were not saved through Christ. <u>This is noted in biblical scripture in several places and refers to a place called hell</u>. This type of violent stress on the magnetic field as well as the size of the storm (universe) only occurs in the upper regions of our existence and is a <u>big indication of imminent change</u>, per my theories. It matters not, for we are in the hands of the Lord, the master of the universe and everything it. Can you not tell His most holy wisdom?

A millennial shift is almost immeasurable in time because it is based on gravitation and magnetic studies. Our technology has only been developed as of recent because of the fall. These events in scripture in the book of revelations are an unmistakable sign of the millennial shift. This will cause added compression on planets which have tectonic plates. These cosmic events can be explained in relative simple terms. If you take two magnets and hold them in the correct way and roll them around each other they have fluidity. When magnetic objects are spinning in a fluid motion and you start to compress them even the slightest or the magnetic field is compressed, it changes the scope of that magnetic field. It creates a strain on that magnetic field or it releases pressure. So, we are not even talking planetary movement or the movement of the sun, we are talking about the entire field of gravity which surrounds us. Affairs will become much hotter and more intolerable. There is always heavenly body movement and we are just getting intelligent enough to track it. I had read an article from *New scientist* written by Kelly Beatty, *Sky and Telescope.com.*, that said we are removing ourselves from the sun at 15cm per year. Thanks to radar beams pinging off various solar-system bodies and to tracking of interplanetary spacecraft, *they* have pretty accurately measured the sun earth distance by means of the *astronomical unit*. Magnetics is a very peculiar science, you don't need much movement to shift the field of gravitational attraction. Something must compress when things recede and something must expand when it grows, it is the law of physics.

Many planets and heavenly objects are basically like gigantic magnets in the sky, some having unique or different attributes. Reason being, our ancestors were very aware of planetary alignments, knowing it had certain effects on the planet and the cosmos. We are nearly at the peak of expansion, making ready to compress. We will begin to start to experience a millennial shift in the year 2020, signaling a large compression in the universe. <u>This will make natural disasters and weather patterns much more fierce and frequent.</u> If all we see is residual light, there is no way in earths modern times to tell when our universe is compressed until we feel it or see it. This will arrive in the shape of monumental quantities of stars falling from the sky, meteor showers, epic earthquakes, and volcanic eruptions. This measures up with biblical prophecy and goes beyond. This is the intellect that I am here, to complete the meaning of scripture.

Universal shift is such a tiresome process of unfathomable amount of time. Those who love God should have no fear. I would not be here wasting my breath if I did not love you as my people or thought we were not capable of love. Resolutions are being worked out for our survival among the stars. Thus, the Mayans left a universal time clock and we can see it in full. It was given to them spiritually by alien beings just by meeting them. I trust it is exact, not quite as exact as myself. Unfortunately, we have a host of problems to solve before the earth becomes unstable and I'm sure we cannot do it alone. Thusly, the Revelation of Jesus Christ as well as the Mayan calendar and even the predictions of Nostradamus are huge warnings about worldly and cosmic events that took place and will continue to take place as time advances. Many beings are involved in these matters I speak of. There is genuine concern for us even though our ancestors were cast from the heavens in a galactic war. Why should we pay forever for their hatred and mistakes, as there are too many kind people in the world? Believe that you have the word of God and his extension of mercy, the mediator of man.

Again, all we see in the cosmos is what was and not what is in the contiguous. The difference in time and structure, is astronomical at the top of our universe about where we now live. It is spinning way too fast for life that is not the direction a cosmonaut would want to go towards. The Pharaoh, unknowingly, left us a map to get back to what 'once upon a time' was our home.

He never thought in any imaginable way he would lose his throne to the power of the demonic dead and lose the power of resurrection. I cited when we spoke of the exodus earlier that prisoners usually make their room back home and to their people. It is given, by my Lord, that it will be when all things are satisfied, I shall reclaim my ship that dwells in the city of god. This was part of my unconditional surrender, a transfiguration with the Christ child. He now sits on my throne in heaven, I stand here with you in all the glory as his mighty archangel. There is now a bond between that which is human and that which is not, that cannot be stopped. This is what causes transfiguration between the son and the father, they are a simultaneous event.

We must look at Orion's constellation for the answers. There are only two options so it's very simple: the Orion's system was either the last system man was on before earth and/or the Egyptian's Pharaohs wanted to travel there to explore. The pyramid is obviously the clue. The Pharaoh never left the earth, he was defeated in battle and the way of the ancient was lost. Man was traveling away from the center of the universe looking for gold and the existence of life. We must go back in that direction. This is where we would find the clues that we are looking for. Per my theory, a pyramid is just not lined up with anything random, it is an indicator and marker of origin, so ancient people would not get lost among the stars. It is a large mapping system among many other matters. I would say if we ever experienced a space ship to go once again, Orion's constellation would be a desirable space to begin our exploration. Do we have a ship? A star captain or great lord, never puts his vessel or his crew in harm's way, for they are his sole hope of extraction and retrieval in an unknown country? That is the nature of the city of God. I will enter back into by death, but not physically. The Lord has come to help the earth first, then claim his heavenly kingdom built by the master builders of time, the race of the Egyptians and their Pharaoh. The closing day of the serpent god is approaching.

Somebody did us a great service which took many ages. All for what, some gold, territory, and fine looking women? Now they have thrown it all away. They left a map of their legacy and it belongs to my children, the children of Christ. When a lord conquers, he seizes everything. Hence, in perspective, Jesus is a Shepard of the lost, a beacon of hope, and salvation shining in the distance. "I am the arch-angel", a voice saying, "give heed to my admonition for my Lord's army in heaven approaches." Anytime a human begins to think he himself is a god alone, I guar-antee something else will come along and express him how small he is.

Equally, I have averred, I have become very modest, but I am a giant in wis-dom. Know that help is on the way very shortly. Yes, many beings are coming to acknowledge us as great creators in time and space. First, they must let the Son of God and the Holy Spirit have completed their victory over death. You are my people, the hope of all living things here on earth by the power of spirit and knowledge. I am your soldier, the pit bull of heaven. This is because of demonic powers that were imprisoned long ago in this abyss of time. A physical war as well as spiritual warfare has become inevitable due to the fact much innocent life has been infiltrated and got in the admixture. The opponent of them likes his new prison too much. The herald of death will shortly pass. These are real and causes dangerous battles to the mind and souls of humans, which effect spiritual events upon our earth. It is also a very real test of what is greater, love, forgiveness, or domination. Many would give way and many have collapsed under the torment of death. As I have said, I am not a scientist, I am a soldier of time and space. Death for me is imminent. My prize will come in the distant future when I awoke from death and you have heard my message. My eternal spirit with humans is based on success not failure. Oh yes, I have almost passed away many times beginning at an early age. Recognize the cost was high for me and many others.

The narration that I differentiate you is how time began. Whether people believe in my thoughts along these many subjects has no carriage on my determi-nation. For if I am deceived, you will know the depth of evil in this world. This would be the most elaborate hoax ever recorded as you will find out by the end of the book. In college, I studied drafting and civil engineering. I never studied astronomy, science, history, etc. Education and history is very important as you can see. I have many regrets that I did not put as much as I should've in school. If I did not walk the path that I walked, there were many things I would not have learned. Hence, these are someone or something else's thoughts on time and space in the spiritual sense, not mine. Yes, it is almost forceful and hard to put the pen down because it seems the hour is late. I hope one day you will see that.

As you will realize I have cracked down the Revelation of Jesus Christ with great authority and my love, shall always be the same. The single affair that we know for sure by now: a world without change, is a world that will suffer many consequences. The changes in the earth will be dramatic as time passes. The changes will come whether we are still habiting the earth or not.

Revelation 21:1 *"And I saw a new heaven and a new earth: for the first heaven and the first earth were passed away; and there was no longer any sea.*
Revelation 21:23 *"And the city had no need of the sun, neither of the moon, to shine in it: for the glory of God did lighten it, and the Lamb is the light thereof."*
Revelation 22:5 *"And there shall be no night there; and they need no candle, neither light of the sun; for the Lord God gives them light: and they shall reign for ever and ever."*

Blue Moon

Out in the distance, out in the distance
Two suns are rising
Catch the flicker from the candles glow
Twin sons of different mothers
All of heaven awaits their throne

Two moons rising in the house
Son of God speaks the tongue of stars
Two moons rising in the house
Once, in a blue moon, that's for sure
Mercury in retrograde, I'm burning up, I'm burning up
From the ashes, I am reborn

Two moons rising in the house,
Son of God speaks the tongue of stars
Twin sons of different mothers
All of heaven awaits their throne

A gigantic sun. The end verses of revelation are referencing to the city of God, in which, I have had many visions of since my early adult years. It bears a perpetual light and is self-contained. On the day of the great disaster, this will be a crucial element for our people. It is to say, when the bible says no one can redeem you but Jesus Christ, it really is not a moot issue. The Son gave victory to the Father by freeing his soul from bondage. All materials, including this vessel at present belong to the Son of God, who sits by the father figure physically and spiritually.

A rigid set of laws are required to go in this city, then the world and its brutality can never be played again. So that you should know, everything in life is predestined by the messiah and his backers. I will present you a detailed vision for many historic periods to arrive, without any encoding. Now that I am in full force of the heart, I can interpret what was, is, and will be. Recollect, we will not always live on dry land, this is the reason the city of God descends from the sphere. That city will be our part of our new Earth.

New Jerusalem, as delineated by John will descend on America for a period. It is not so much of a matter in preference of location as it is about safety of humankind as well as His chosen. As many ages pass and time goes by on this earth, we will have two moons. This will be a correction to balance out the tension along the earth's magnetic field. This can be performed without adding warmth to the ground. It will add a cool spectrum of brightness to the night and has a magnetic structure that runs in concurrence with our current moon and ground. This bluish colored moon will cast a spectrum that will magnify future bioluminescent animals and flora species. And then, we will nonetheless have a day and night because of earth's rotation, not within the city, for the metropolis is the brightness. Nights will be much different looking with violet, crimson sunsets with the new moon giving off a very magical 3-D surreal effect on the world. According to my vision, in a great distance of time, a light will appear a distance from the ground. Its size will be monumental to our criteria and it will eventually light up the world without all the solar radiation. A manufactured gigantic sun. This will happen as our sun starts to die out and the earth gravitates back towards the center. This will alter what we know as day and night, and we will go in yet another stage. These consequences will be for the glory of Christ and his people when we become his chosen. We, then, will reclaim what is rightfully for the creators. These are the steps the angels of the Lord will demand to set and pull through the world. Simply because you cannot see this sun, does not imply it is not there waiting to draw near. This is what all movement in space and time is creating: energy for a liquid cooled magnetic core that will perch up the world and its cosmos. Strength and duration being controlled by heavenly beings. Whole countries, all tongues, everything in heaven is free of commission when you believe in the public figure of Jesus.

In my vision of the earth, the sea will start to disappear as the universe compresses, causing massive plate shifts. These violent plate shifts will form huge land masses everywhere trapping water in big ponds. The land then will hold much real estate as well as tonic water as time purifies it. This is when a correction will be established to yield stability in our rotation and magnetic study. We will be knocked off the axis several times, repositioning, and changing continents. If you want to know the vision of earth of the Lord Jesus Christ and his creation, please visit on the internet: "The Dazzling World of Christian Riese Lassen". I absolutely love Christian's Lassen's art, he has such a heavenly talent. This means even if the sun dies out or loses its brightness this world would go on living for a long time. God is our light just as it was in the beginning and will be in the end. Nothing is by luck or chance, everything is knowledge and wisdom. Glory be, to those who choose to serve it and woe to those who oppose the will of all creation in this very special kingdom. The Holy Spirit has given and will give the ultimate choice to humans on the day of "new Jerusalem" or the city of God which descends from heaven. When we enter, we can never look back to the way the earth is now. Many will not prepare the journey as they love the way of evil, even when God makes them the ultimate choice in which direction they prefer to be. They would rather reign in hell than serve in heaven, and then it will be. I cannot enter those gates, so my time will be short. I am spirit of many positions and many things, even so, I will constantly dwell in spirit with you. My voice cannot always be with you and therefore, I have made you an intermediary to prepare the means of the masses. I must spiritually leave the earth for very specific reasons.

What is flesh? It is nothing when we leave the body. It is the soul and the wisdom in which we have found in this life that carries on with us into the next journey. No human or being in creation can take that away from us when we belong to Christ.

Effects of time. Let us say you travel from the center of the Universe to a planet such as Earth through the darker regions of time and space. You would not understand completely the aspects of time until you arrived at that journey once again. This way, you can measure the growth and change of specific creatures based on time and distance of travel away from the point of origin. This is the original reason the Annunaki or the Sons of God (angels) brought animals and Cro-Magnon men and women to the earth. As stated earlier, Annunaki were Sumerian gods who many believe came from the sky by their many stone glyphs and statues that they left behind. Many are depicted with wings. The Cro-Magnon man and women in which theses superior humans brought to the earth are the earliest form of human that we know of. According to science and carbon dating, they roamed Europe 35,000 to 40,000 years ago. They were lab rats to test the effects of time. How fast we age depends on the environments where we live in. In the outer parts of this universe time is spinning much faster. The angels did notice a dramatic change once they came back to land. Time had run at a much quicker pace than expected. This would give them the ability to create and return to the earth, to enjoy the fruits of their labor in a rapid manner. This pleasure comes at a price. Humans in the fall, had aged rapidly, which is a curse. This occurred because of a time variable which should have to do with gravity and the centrifugal force. Another element in this equation, is traveling forward and backwards in time. We, as humans, base our measurement of time in hours, minutes, and seconds. We also base it on the amount of time we live and how we take charge of ourselves. This is where time is relevant to the position you stand now into your existence. You would find that humans live much longer or shorter life if we based it on hours, minutes, and seconds in another place in time. Because of the velocity at which we rotate by centrifugal force and the effects of the solar radiation, our physical structures are worn down rather quickly here on land. Human's journey into space brought glorious results; however, <u>the price became higher the further they traveled from home.</u>

    Orbits of universe. Very much like the Ptolemaic systems of astronomy, where time is based on revolution around the sun, the age and the orbit of universes are much the same. All universes rotate around a super magnetic core. When their orbits finally come close enough, it will act as a gigantic sun and give off much life. Again, just because we don't see it, doesn't mean it is not there. Everything is a journey to find out which souls are worthy to move on to the grand prize. And if, what I say makes a lot of sense, it is because I have done this before. It truly is painful to execute it all again because of pride and haughtiness. However, it makes me a great teacher to my chosen son, who I once loved long ago in the garden.

There are many factors to take into consideration being that a universe is multidimensional and constantly moving, turning, expanding, rising, and receding. As you can see, to measure the universe in its entirety in relation to all things, you would have to support many factors. People might say I'm an idiot or crazy and I don't experience what I am speaking about, and it's all right with me. I am not here for a dispute or to be known among my peers for scientific wisdom. You may get hold of it with a grain of salt. I am not a professional with a degree in this field in any way whatsoever. I offer you merely a detailed vision as what I seek is different. All wisdom now exists for those who trust in Christ. I am not here for the concubines of women, crowns of gold, diamonds, fame, or popularity. I have discovered the rewards of those who attend to the textile universe and its ways. When you hurt the animal realm and the precious earth you are hurting me deep down. If you have ever watched the movie "Powder", you might then know how highly disturbing it is to the spirit when it looks the way animals and people are treated here on land. I truly don't wish to be here; however, time has chosen me to carry out an obligation.

Let me give some personal thanks from heaven to those that have found success and have given back to communities and very important organizations who protect animals and children. Many have done this in faith or out of the goodness of their soul, you will not be forgotten. I look through it every day. Athletes, movie stars, musicians, and everyday people who just want to make a difference in our world. We keep doing the honorable deeds today and perhaps, we will be in the pages in the books of history in the future.

Hence, do not think your activities are not noticed nor acknowledged. I am here to see all things that are fruitful to the kingdoms of our Lord. You are ambassadors of Christ's good will when he cannot do it himself for obvious reasons. You will be rewarded in full many times over for your graciousness. Empty the vessel, and he shall fill it exceedingly. One day we will all be Christ-like and have many talents and skills. We must know how to use them effectively. I recognize who I was as a kid and what I have become. I am a spiritual warrior sent to execute a specific task in a specific fashion. I must suffer because of demonic forces I met when I was a Pharaoh of the elite Egyptian order long ago in the days of Moses because the Egyptians worshipped a God of darkness and deceit, murder was done without much thought. Moses killed many men. In Moses, spiritual walk of resurrection and finding peace he is haunted by violent demons of long ago who influence his anger and try to get him to do things he would never think of in this life. Laws are much stronger in these days for these types of crimes. Even if I believe the people are in rejection of the word of God.

For he is my father and I, his son, yet I am the father and he is the son. We have become one in the same. I will grant many scenarios of time and analogies in my series of books. This will be done by the way of the seven spirits of the Lord Jesus Christ so they may be recorded as such. This should occur over the next decade.

Eternal life and eternal youth. In the ancient days, the bible talked about people like Methuselah, who lived what seemed to be a legendary amount of time. Methuselah was a man who lived very long ago. It is reported he lived the longest of men, dying at the age of 969 in the Hebrew Bible. His father was Enoch, one of the great prophets and legends of the earth and the author behind the stories of giants in the *Books of the Watchers*. Cosmonauts, who would travel forward and backward in time, became legends for the inhabitants and were known to them as Gods. Thus, when we apply the word 'time travel', it can stand for several different affairs. Time travel, when man has achieved this when going forward and backward into the universe, which essentially is traveling back to the future, or future to past.

Moved over the skill of time travel it would be comfortable for those that were masters of space and time to create kingdoms and even be able to love themselves by traveling backwards and onward in the plains of time. It is also a way to become a God or a dictator over your creations. Once you travel from point A, center of the universe, to point B, to earth, then return to point A, you have time traveled. To travel these distances I'm speaking of, you would need a vessel that moves itself through space at high velocity to go anyplace in a good measure of time. This process did not occur overnight, it was the aggregation of many lives and many historic periods of human beings that makes us this world.

The one thing that humans seek out today is the one thing they have never mastered and that is youth. Although, man has never overcome this technology; yet, there are others that have in many ways. You must hold the proper shell for eternal youth as the human physical body is delicate. There are dangers in time travel, eternal youth and living forever. You can be certain that every lesson that we go through is so that when humans finally do master these types of technologies, they are not perverted. When we manage to overcome these kinds of skill sets and use them in coincidence with the harmony of creation, then we have become as our creators. We are on our way to that next stage. However, who we truly serve advancements of long ago and left us responsibilities in good faith and with proper teachings. Hence, to create and be scientific is to be as God. To keep what you have created from an opposing force even when it seems all hope is lost, then you are like the spirit of Jesus Christ, a soldier of God. There is a difference in my mind when it comes to these two terms. How neat it is to be a scientist and able to create your own existence. Unfortunately, it was not well protected. I invite everyone to the challenge of preserving mankind and this world as we are the last of our kind.

Yes, there's a possibility we can lose it all, how foolish would we be to be to let this happen at this point in the game. I've devoted many years of my life studying the ground and this Time Prison in which we exist. It seems humans don't care and will demolish everything in the quest for lust of wealth. Or is it possible they do not care of the consequences? Then in truth, they don't realize what the imports for the soul are. If they did, they would be on their knees today asking for forgiveness. Since there is such thing as the eternal soul which can also have its dangers, all gifts must be wielded wisely. When we experience the resurrection power of John and Jesus Christ, we recognize that having an eternal soul had cost them in a heartfelt way. They were killed to silence them from testifying to the words of the Holy Spirit. They were both killed in a very cruel way. I am sincerely sorry for man and women's suffering, for the punishment you have experienced because of my fellow human beings. This is why Jesus and John paid a final debt for mankind. I apologize on behalf of those who came from the sky and did not think about the effects of their activities. I know time can be harsh given the state of affairs we are invested in. I came to pay a price one last time for mankind and I hope I will gain your attention.

When God saw the solid ground and it was still in darkness, it was marked with astronomical charts and calculations so man could return to it afterwards. Thus, we must ask ourselves that is a long time for one man to wait to savor the beauty of the planet, unless there was time travel and power of resurrection.

In **Genesis 1:3**, *God said: "let there be light and there was light and it was good."* As the earth came into the sun's orbit, God of Adam, or the spirit within the father of Adam, saw that the earth was beautiful. He began to bring life and possessions, just as we do today when we move from place to place.

Really, what we have in scripture is the journey of seven angels and their leader. Their souls have been in existence since time began. Thus, we experience what is called the father of lies with a cursed existence and the father of animation with an endless existence. This is also why I can distinguish you the story of the father and the prison that was created for him and his kind. For that serpent of the former, was a deceiver of worlds and many heavenly beings.

When the son of man speaks, know it is with wisdom. We have the living voice of Jesus who spoke to the Father from death. This combination must exist to right what is wrong and that is how Jesus recognized Satan at once at his baptism by John the Baptist. In the end, he had come to sympathize not only why his Father had forsaken him, John the Baptist did the same as well.

Is it right to manufacture a world and use lower life forms to serve you or to be used as guinea pigs? Is it right to let others abuse them after you have the results of a scientific discovery and your work is finished? Could this be considered a violation of universal law?

According to Jesus, it is.

Space: Made of Stone

Jaguars, leopards, panthers, alley cats
I keep up with the night that brought you
Along to this twilight zone
Space made of stone, space made of stone

Atlantis where are you lost lands of long ago
You came on wings of silver, so the story is told
Red winds blowing cold, Red winds blowing cold

Red winds blowing cold, crystal sands beneath my feet
The rising son gave birth to color
I have come within reach

The morning star can be seen

I am but a man with the voice of a lion. We, as servants, soon realize we are only a vessel for a greater cause with each having a skill set. Mine is military, spiritual warfare and deciphering encrypted coded messages. In that respect are very old souls of the earth who left a message in advance from long ago. They were chosen to lead the way for the Christ spirit and his people. So, when we speak of Christ and knowledge, we are actually speaking of Elijah reincarnated into a lower vessel of man as a form of punishment. It is very hard for a great star lord to be abased, and live a lifetime of poverty and physical torture. To live in a body that is not like the gods of Rome and Egypt, that spirit gets a closer observation in why oppression leads to depression and people go crazy. Why poverty makes people criminals and they just want to party and forget the ugliness of the world? As I noted, it is a predatory world and it has become a sad existence for many weaker individuals.

The spirit of Elijah has walked the path of life far more than any other human being. He will deliver the fatal blow to the wicked in this world by a sacrificial destruction. We may not have an idea the authority he has been given, to punish in this world. The one man, whose will alone will be strong enough to conquer death, for by evil deception he became a traitor to own his own flesh and blood and his price was severe. We will talk about this in the chapter *The Prince of Egypt*.

Jesus Testifies about John. ***Mathew 11-15*** *Truly I tell you, among those born of women there has not risen anyone greater than John the Baptist; yet whoever is least in the kingdom of heaven is greater than he.* **12** *From the days of John the Baptist until now, the kingdom of heaven has been subjected to violence and violent people have been raiding it.* **13** *For all the Prophets and the Law prophesied until John.* **14** *And if you are willing to accept it, he is Elijah who was to come.* **15** *Whoever has ears, let them hear.*

When you play god with lower forms of man, one day somebody greater will come and show you exactly what a god is. This is the case of Elijah; to walk the earth over and over until he finds the Messiah, the "chosen one" of the Holy Spirit. The Holy Spirit is alien in nature and there is no better teacher, which has been for countless ages.

The ring of fire is by far one of the most destructive natural features this earth has ever had. When it starts its eruptions, and gets rocking, the earth will be knocked back into the dark ages.

For those souls still living here, their final days on earth and judgement has begun. They will have to live the way like the Cro-Magnon men and then they will know the law of karma. All the rotten souls of time will fill vessels that still exist on the earth in a moment's notice. They will know their fate and the reason for the same. They will recognize their wrongdoing and they will grind and gnash their teeth at the judgement of our Lord. These souls are those responsible for the greatest crimes of the earth, one being <u>trafficking humans.</u> Let every man see the law as it is in heaven and how it is served on behalf of the innocent.

So, let us remember the first thing that will occur to let us know our earth is changing into something new, is air temperature. If the change in air temperature is followed by eruptions and more frequent earthquakes, this will be a good indication that the ring of fire is becoming active. This will mean it's not just carbon emissions and pollution that is causing climate change; however, it is being made more extreme by carbon emissions and poisons being pumped into the sky. We are creating our own hell by polluting the sky, accelerating the conditions for money and profit.

As the judicial system of this earth has judged me in this life, so you too shall be judged on the corruption of the laws on this earth. California will be the crucial key that scientists will have to keep their eyes on. Its fault lines run along the whole western United States and Mexico. This is a key fault line when looking at the ring of fire. Wyoming houses the world's biggest volcano in Yosemite.

Before there is ever a massive Yellowstone eruption, a warning eruption will spew massive ash first. On that point is some scientific evidence proving this from an earlier outbreak. When we house our kingdoms with foolishness, I pray for those when that time comes. Who in their right mind, builds civilization around a volcanic ring of fire? Just like a fogger set in motion, a volcanic eruption causes shortness of breath and soon death by inhalation or annihilation. The sun will darken and chaos will erupt for those who are still living or not protected by Christ and the angels of heaven. This is the judgment God has saved for the wicked, as it was in the past. It is no different.

Those in Christ, their souls and flesh will have already been delivered from the earth. If humans were to know that the whole western coast could be covered in dark ash at any day, panic would erupt. I will fix a humble address to our acquaintances and <u>good neighbors in Canada</u> before we end this book. I am here in plenty of time to forewarn you as my friends and people, give glory to your Lord who will show great mercy in the *Day of Judgment.*

Every great kingdom in time has literally failed from greed and corruption within. It is time to change as a society or we will be left behind. Only one kingdom will survive: the kingdom of Jesus Christ.

<u>A new law goes into effect.</u> In the days to come, we must vary to ever introduce the urban center of God. They don't have liquor stores and crack, brothels, or porn. They don't have cigs, gaming consoles, nor television with cable. It is not a place of fashion, sexual activity, jealousy, and neither greed. It is not a place you can hunt or eat meat. These are why laws were passed long ago in paradise, nevertheless, things rapidly went out of hand and the earth was deluged. They were trained, unevolved men and women to one day leave the earth.

Time is a field of stars burning in the blackness of the night. I often wonder what it would look like when someone finally turns on the lights. <u>We are a long way from home; we have ventured as far as any race of human has ever achieved in this realm of time. What a magnificent accomplishment for us as a race.</u> Who wants to keep this journey alive? I am here to help. Imagine you're self-shrouded in the many colors of the universe. The sky is forever changing and never a dull moment when you awake. Beautiful crystal pools of water, animals, and plants that would blow your mind. This is what God wants us to have. However, we cannot be given such treasure and treat it as we have treated this earth. It is a crime worthy of far worse than the punishment of death, maybe a thousand deaths.

Fields of The Sky

The fields in the sky are always turning
Inside my heart is burning
<u>*My son of time he has been crying*</u>
<u>*Inside my heart is dying!*</u>

I'm walking through windows
I'm climbing through doors

I come from high places they say is yours
I'm dancing with shadows
I'm playing this game
You be the master and I'll be your slave

The fields in the sky are always burning
Inside my heart is turning
I still feel the son, he is shining
It lets me know, he's not dying
Shame on you who crucified him
<u>*I hold the chains that surely bind them*</u>

The fields in the sky are always turning
Inside my heart is burning
The moon maiden, she plays me forgotten songs
The loved we shared was never wrong!
I'm walking through windows
I'm climbing through doors
<u>*I come from high places they say is yours*</u>

The fields in the sky are always turning
Inside my heart is burning
<u>*My son of time he has been crying*</u>
<u>*Inside my heart is dying!*</u>

When I spoke of Enoch and the titans, men drinking the blood of others and having a voracious appetite for flesh, many matters will soon make sense. We have come a long way in the evolution of God, from our earlier state. This is after being wiped out many times here on earth, as our flesh is not perfect. However, many lessons will be learned. I will send you many teachers to prepare you to enter this mighty kingdom. They will pray continuously to redeem all heaven and earth. That may not be the life for everyone that doesn't mean I or God will not love you. Your life and death will be left full of suffering if left behind on earth, even if you believe in Christ.

There will be remarkable stories to tell among its people. It is simply a place of refuge in a time of great tragedy. Many will make the pilgrimage to his holy temple, the city of God, from every place on earth. They will have readied themselves to enter the gates. Many will have to make this choice.

One day the inevitable will happen, and there will be plenty of warnings. There will be a massive quake in California like anyone has never seen. This will be the first evolution of this planet. Notice the huge mountain ranges in the state of California. This did not happen by a one little 6.9 or 8.0 earthquake. This started to happen when the universe was experiencing strong millennial shifts and there were multiples, with duration and over extended periods of time. Every island and every mountain were moved from its place. Why would God put us in a volatile world? He didn't, his own people took this world by force and challenged His law so they could harvest gold and laid with women and have children. At present, we bear those results. I know everyone thinks not in my time, it will never happen in my time. <u>Yes, it will and can</u>. I'm here to tell you if we don't change our fate while we are stuck in this *Time Prison*, humans will suffer and wish for death but death will not come.

There are very few choices we have, as people on earth, unless we are part of the political power that is feeding this system in which we exist. The people that are in control of this world are aware of many things that I'm talking about. They will never reveal what they are hiding from humanity. To be honest, that is why a great deal of people does not believe in God or Jesus Christ. They know with the current technology that we own; many things can be explained by scientific discipline. Who ever said Jesus was not a man of science? Especially nowadays, that we can create men and women in a test pipe or by applying in vitro fertilization. It alters the narrative of how we feel biblically about miracles and creation. The universe would be foolish to believe that the citizenry that are running this nation and others evolved from apes without any intervention and have become what they are today. Let's ignore the lies and get down to business. If people believe that bull, I may as well give up now.

As I mentioned, bloodlines are very old in human beings, they just have been mixed down instead of upwards. We all have become more equal with time. The hatred of skin color and the abuse of mankind by their word level is being annulled by the passion of Christ. We now regard ourselves as one race: humanity.

We all must love, according to John 4:20. Do not be deluded by lies and manipulation. It would be better for death takes you then to raise your hand against
your brother for religion or race. The fierceness of the Old Testament had reason
and is very difficult for many to forget, but behold, it is a now a new day.

Some genetic bloodlines are more advanced than others and many secrets
have been preserved. Mankind was made beautiful in the creation by God. Thus,
much of that, mankind was filled with pride, arrogance, and thought himself
greater than any institution. Such was the pride of Lucifer, one of God's most
beautiful angels in the celestial sphere. When we see a mirror, it is a tribute to the
vanity we have created. God did not create vanity, humans did. Did you think any
creation other than ourselves in the universe sits in front of the mirror and puts
on makeup and brushes their hair many hours in the day? Mirrors were made for
women and men to experience their own beauty, not to be self-absorbed. I think
it makes grooming less complex, indeed a miracle in that since. Especially for one
who spends much time alone. If we all looked the same, there is no need for beauty.
However, if there is beauty, it is only in the eyes of the beholder when no mirror
is reflecting their faces. More of a reason many ancient laws existed. Those with
good looks and strong bloodlines live with great favor.

We live in a modern day political science, based realm. To have an empire
and be masters of space and time, many workers must exist in addition to a ton of
resources. Think about that statement. Once again, the only reason to have huge
populations is to build an empire or to go to war. If you've lost your fleets in a
warfare that survived in the heavens long ago, you must reconstruct. <u>Would you
be ready to oppose a war against an army that already defeated you and knocked
you back into the dark ages?</u> How long would all that take? Would you have enough
time to rebuild before the next extinction without aid from those in the heavens?
I think not, to all these interrogations, says the Holy Spirit.

By the conclusion of this book most of the world will feel the same about those
who will dispute the law of heaven and Jesus Christ. They will think many to be
quite foolish after the events I have described. I like it this way, for you will need
me and my people just as much as we need you. Your drive will not carry you far
enough and mine will. We are in this together, all of us. Whether you're the bloodline of the angels or common man, we all bleed the same. Our footsteps are very
predictable. It likewise produces no sense for an uprising among our people here in

America. Whatever our corrupt government sees as fair we must accept that, in an economic sense. I know many are on the brink of total starvation and loss of health care. The people of Christ are in no situation to subvert a regime which retains a real specific intent at this instant in time. Peace and love will always be the result.

<u>We must protest unfair social status and inhumane treatment and always stand as one.</u> I will offer a solution to man, which is the word of Jesus Christ and his compassion for the earth. This will be the true test of faith for those who believe in my words. For if I am a crazy man, and you listen to my voice, and give what you can to the poor and needy, what did you actually lost? Some health care, dental work, and a little compassion for those who struggle in life. If I am the voice of a king who sits on thrones, of many worlds, and you ignore that voice, <u>you have lost everything!</u> You would be treated by that king equal to that which you have cared for his people. <u>You can count on that for certain!</u> Jesus was a refugee of war and hatred. He was turned down by his own citizenry as well as the Roman Empire. Just remember, the rejection when we go closing our conquered borders or exiling people back to a hellhole. If we are the chosen, let's act accordingly.

The city of God has a medical facility that we cannot even fathom. This is what makes life fair and just, the laws of Jesus Christ. My people will not help those who do not love their brother and sisters and show no mercy and compassion. You will be refused from going in its gates. They will laugh at your paper money, silver, and gold and ask you if you think that will save you in hell. This world has a lot of thinking to do, let's hope for the best.

We must break the cycles of oppression. All the information is here for you to decide just who might be the author of this text as well as biblical text. I am just the vessel of a voice which can impose its will upon every soul in time in space. This is called by me, *the walk of time*. Just so it is clear, my soul once lived among a family of great wealth in the Egyptian dynasty among the great Pharaohs. I was a great prince who had everything I wanted. Now I must suffer for having all those things I had. For heaven to take its anger out on me and punish my soul is proper. I am willing to die and pay the price for past crimes and what I believe. That's why I am here. To torture a man like they did Jesus for revealing truth to humanity sends chills up and down my body. Heaven cannot and will not forgive such brutality. My life has already been a living hell, please know that. I have given you everything I know through the voice of my chosen son.

XIV

THE SECOND COMING

Crop circles are a captivating case for me. On August 15, 2002, in Sparsholt, Hampshire, England, a crop circle was found. According to Michael Barber's internet article *Alien face crop circle: a second look*, this crop circle was conceived to be deciphered. It was later found that the "record" furthered the bitmapped design by hiding a binary form within the circular tracks much like a thick disc. The message was later decoded by an IT programmer named Paul Vigay, by translating the patterns as an 8-bit ASCII text encoded cipher. I found this read-out to be a highly interesting article. Please notice that I am not a mathematician, this message is out of my league as far as deciphering codes. However, the man who decided this was on the right track, I am quite sure.

Michael Barber's internet article presents some interesting reflections about the message as well as some possible hidden coded dates. A lot like a biblical revelation, this message was encoded to show advanced intelligence. For those who like puzzles, have a look at Michael's detailed article online, *'Alien face crop circle a second look'*.

The message is thought to read as follows:
- Beware the bearers of FALSE gifts & their BROKEN PROMISES.
- Much PAIN, but still time.
- BELIEVE.
- There is GOOD out there.
- We oppose DECEPTION.
- Conduit CLOSING (time door or window closing?)

Is there a significant reason this was executed in the UK? Will this arise out of conflict with Muslims in that region or by large natural catastrophe? Maybe both. What is it concerning? It is in a crop that is very important to all mankind, corn, that should be are first seen. Does it have to do with BREXIT? Could it have

something to do with the super volcano that is 390 miles outside of London underneath Lake Laacher? According to an article by Ted Thornhill entitled: '*Sign of
the times*', written on January 2012. This volcano has been due to erupt at any time.
Unless it should do with what was written by Brian Clark Howard, December 2016
in *National Geographic's* where he tells us Italy's Campi Flegrei may be awakening
from a long slumber, scientists warn.

The message must have some type of great significance. It says much pain, but
there still is time! This is about the safety of many as well as the earth. Please do
not take these messages lightly. If those having money and power think they can
keep it forever, I assure you, it will not be so.

According to myself and theory, many crop drawings cannot be duplicated by
human beings during this time nor anything close to it, especially in one night. It
is a computer generated from a device which then relays it to small craft. We are
on the edge of this technology, but not close enough. The image is captured on
a device which is about the size of a smart phone with a camera. This technology
goes much like a printer. The small ships act as printer heads at super high speeds
that never goes down. Yes, they are like us in many ways, but a good deal more
progressed in engineering science. Humans had to do almost a complete start over
in technology. That *really sucks*, as our younger generation would say. If you look
at the image online in the article previously mentioned by Michel Barber, you'll
notice three distinct blips in the background. It is much more noticeable with high
resolution shot. This stranger is standing on our earth's surface transmitting data
to the ships which then they apply their technology to trace out the shapes. The
stranger is taking an image of himself and sending it to us as a raceway. A *selfie*
right before selfies even existed. Amazing, right? This would be drawn out with
a compression device which bends the corn stalks without breaking them. This
technology is associated as well with the use of mono magnetic poles and magnetic
waves. According to my theory this is where all science is headed and it will alter
the destiny of humanity. I would be in utter amazement if human can replicate
this crop circle with any closeness right now. The complexity of the foreigner from
an aerial view is marvelous. This would be a great technology to create if you
wanted to have an active conversation with an alien life. So, this is my message to
the skeptics: create a message overnight equal to that which was sent. That way
we will know it's a fraud.

These organisms will not break up their location by transmitting signals to this land. That would be the equivalent to breaking military secret locations by our government today. According to my theory, these animals are equivalent to a cosmic military and their arrival should not be chosen lightly. This gives us very graphic detail of what this race of aliens looks like. These are allies of the incarnated Holy Spirit.

In the second coming there will be <u>arrivals in intervals</u>. According to my vision, the first mass appearance will be when a volcano erupts near the California/Mexico boundary line. This will be a mixture of intelligent life forms gathering data on volcanic activity around the mob of fire, as well as there were many races of humans once upon a time, there are many races in the heavens. As I mentioned, humans have had some issues through the ages, they did not play so nice with others. Yes, we all can confirm this behavior of our antecedents. Not only mankind was their racism, they imagined to themselves greater than every race of being in paradise.

In war, it was so for many historical periods. That is until greater beings came into this realm of time to defend. A great and far different weapon was used on us called "time". Shortly, we will move around once again. This universe is being given to humans because we were the original creators of its existence.

Most beings in the heavens are nocturnal and thrive in low light conditions. Notice the size of the eyes in almost every description given by people who have had visions and drew them out or claimed to have seen an E.T. As well, we see that in crop circles. It is a sign that they live in the darker regions of the universe. Just like some creatures dwelling at the bottom of the ocean in its dark depths, so it is equal in space.

Our status as humans, need an exceptional home with proper lighting. One day, this world will flourish with many different races of humans and all others are welcome to see. We will create exceptional homes for them to gather and reconcile their needs. Subsequently all, they are becoming ready to be the blessing that we have long been waiting for. This is the big reason behind the judicial decision of the all-seeing eye of the world, as well as universal creation itself. We cannot continue as a race if we continue to bring suffering to creation, our own, and others. We need to learn how to respect all life forms and planetary creation before we move on. We must acknowledge our status as fallen prisoners of time. We must also be concerned about our desires to use knowledge correctly and suspend advancement of weapons that are used for war. A war of necessity will be fought to free the weak, thus, this is a message for the future when we finally have the desire to be at peace with freedom for all.

Suns evolve, planets evolve, and universes evolve, this is nothing new as it has been the same since the beginning of time. My return suggests that the many changes needed are soon coming for humanity. Something has stepped forth into my being to explain our existence and the fate of the same. I hope humanity will respect the time that was given as well as the mercy of those that live in the sky.

We have spoken many times of Satan or the devil as the feeling of deceit behind a system of suffering and grief. I know America will soon see something clearly at last. All kingdoms that were large will be collapsed by greed, power, and racial discrimination. How much more proof will man need that these beings exist, as well as our long-lost ancestors who inhabit the city of God? We are working towards wonderful things in medicine and scientific discipline. One day it must be free of charge. If heaven is to give glory to physicians on health, they must love serving humanity and the animal kingdom for that reason alone. It cannot be about prestige and money. There are no physicians of that nature anywhere but here on earth. Your pay is eternal life in the many mansions of heaven. I ask you, is that not enough? <u>All souls are here with great intent.</u> The medical, dental, and mental care system in our state is a prank. I walked through every organization there is in some shape or manner. I have picked up the waste and corruption first hand, long before today. When the spirit of heaven judges this world, it must know all things about the way we live. To figure out how we live, the Holy Spirit must walk the globe many times in many different vessels.

We must acknowledge the many who have taught and suffered under this world and its conditions to show law and fairness here on this earth. It is no longer a one man show as Christ is within many. I worked many years as an assistant manager for a pet shop in California. You don't want to be hunting my exotic creatures and driving them into extinction. The owner of the pet shop is not nearly as friendly as I, <u>that I can assure you.</u>

Allow us to make certain we know one thing for sure as being in humanity. There's a lot of real estate in the heavens and you're going to have to go through the law of Jesus to obtain it. It is only by eternal life we will even see this real estate.

We're not light years away from other planets that support life, in whatever form by accident. We are prisoners, make no error.

Everywhere you look, around us, are our dead planets. Even if we, as modern humans, completely killed ourselves off as a race, we cannot escape the lessons of time. Intelligent life has already taken that into consideration. It would be a complete start over for humans and that would not be beneficial! We are being taught spiritual lessons within a season of time. All souls are bound to this earth until it is finished. Even if we had the technology to leave earth, we would run into resistance before we ever came across a habitable planet. This already took place long ago. Our technology was crushed and we had to start over. It has taken us thousands of years to get to where we are now, most of it in the last 100 years. That's quite odd. This is because we are ready to hear the message of Christ and we will comply or deny, it really does not matter to me. We can save ourselves so much suffering by at once following Christ. We are not going anywhere far anytime soon in space travel, on our own accord.

We are here to find out how to treat a planet and the creation that is upon it. We are hither to learn not to breed like animals until our population is so great we run out of resources. We are here to find out how not to kill each over wealth and dominion. Many do not have it in them to take the lessons that I am speaking of which poses a quandary. Therefore, our ancestors were forced down from the heavens in biblical history to face penalty for their offenses. Although, at that point, is much innocent life mixed up with this mass, we sustain the capability as humans to make things correct and change the way we're leading.

We have some of the most brilliant minds that we can imagine right here among us from every race and country in this world. It cannot be about money, fame, and notoriety. This world should be about the advancement of mankind. We don't need a spaceship to save ourselves from this fate. We don't need to reach the stars. The stars will come to us with authority of Jesus Christ when the time is right. Remember, the father had many mansions, if it were not so I would not tell you.

All my theories, all these visions will soon make sense when we see the E.T and UFOs in the horizon of the sky. It's not if, it's when. I will die once again in this world, so please keep faith in my words. I cannot be of service in a fantastic way until my vessel expires. We can struggle and defeat each other off as the earth gets volatile or we can help each other until we consider the signs of those in the firmament. This is the army of Jesus Christ and the arrival is coming soon, we can bet our lives on it. When my friends arrive, and reveal themselves, any aggressive act interfering with humanitarian aid will bring detrimental results to the state which shows aggression. I say this not out of arrogance, but for the safety of nations. Some countries' technology may be spared for them on the day of the Lord's arrival. Much of that will depend on each country. We do not choose who they help, that is something they will have already chosen based on various genes, according to my theory of time.

Humans and races of humans often disappeared from the earth in volatile times until we became more advanced and place satellites in space. This had scared many away from our planet. These vessels are servants to the higher being. Let me say this again, the vessels that are coming into our orbit are <u>friendly in origin</u>. Do not bring consequences against your people by aggressive behavior, please do not. When they reveal their existence and they see no aggression, they will return. <u>They will arrive in a very specific way according to my words. This will be to prove I have risen back to the throne in the city of God.</u>

As I said earlier, the first major appearance will be associated to a volcano that will become extremely dynamic. It is no secret the spirit is here enlightening all mankind. The next appearance would be to show us a display of advanced technology. They will organize a lap in the volcanic steam and harness the thermal energy. They too can harness energy from lightning bolts within volcanic discharge or lightning storms. They will give us a spectacular light show before they leave. This would be a show of friendship and an acknowledgment of our destiny. Once more, this issue looks to be connected to a volcanic eruption somewhere close to the California/ Mexico boundary line. After trust is fully proven, they will announce themselves in an emergency as we do with multiple colored flashing lights and loud warning sirens that will be heard across the earth. Much like rescue vehicles we see along the road, we should stay out of their path. This will be the final signs of massive imminent volcanic eruptions here on solid ground that will affect most life. This will be in conjunction with the city of God descending on the area that I have appointed in America. This is when a wondrous time of preparation must occur. I will draw greater attention again to the fact the city is depending on freshwater resources; let's try to keep it that way. When everybody does their part, we will thrive.

Eden Restored *Revelation 22:1-5 Then the angel showed me the river of the water of life, as clear as crystal, flowing from the throne of God and of the Lamb **2** down the middle of the great street of the city. On each side of the river stood the tree of life, bearing twelve crops of fruit, yielding its fruit every month. And the leaves of the tree are for the healing of the nations. **3** <u>No longer will there be any curse. The throne of God and of the Lamb will be in the city, and his servants will serve him.</u> **4** They will see his face, and his name will be on their foreheads. **5** There will be no more night. They will not need the light of a lamp or the light of the sun, for the Lord God will give them light. <u>And they will reign for ever and ever.</u>*

John and the Angel *Revelation 22:6-7 The angel said to me, <u>"These words are trustworthy and true.</u> The Lord, the God who inspires the prophets, sent his angel to show his servants the things that must soon take place." **7** "Look, I am coming soon! Blessed is the one who keeps the words of the prophecy written in this scroll."*

The Lord has come to save his people from this destiny. Then now you know how much the spirit loves us by imparting this message in advance. It is not a time to fear, it is time to gather and celebrate the coming and show to heaven that we are the race capable of dealing against demonic powers as their final blow. When we deliver the final blow, all of heaven will gather to show us glory. We shall not be deceived any longer, not on my watch. Please acknowledge my wisdom and move ahead as if our life and world depends on it.

Everything I do is based on signs of the earth as well as my interpretation of scripture, history, and my knowledge of time itself from my many walks in life. That doesn't make me greater person, it makes me foolish and hard-headed. Considering I was so high in stature that I would not give in to the wisdom of my son of lower intelligence. Now he gets the last laugh! *The Son is the image of the invisible God, the firstborn over all creation.*

You will know soon my accuracy is far greater than any human that has walked this earth. This is something the Holy Spirit has seen many times since the terrestrial evolution.

Hopefully, there would be no need to silence my voice or track me down for further information. This is my soul being crushed by the son of God under interrogation, you can be certain I have spilled my guts.

<u>I recognize the capability of my government and others.</u> I have no favoritism of anybody, as I'm just a story teller. When you found me, you would suppose it was altogether a misunderstanding or a bad prank. One thing is for sure, it is not any kind of joke and my suffering in this kingdom is surely not a laughing matter. I am a doctor of souls and a warrior. My path is separate from those who lead this country. There's a lot of pain of addiction and spiritual illness, so this is very much connected to my destiny. I am here, I am there, and I am everywhere. You would just notice someone who once was a great ally to many who had suffered, someone who is a common man with common problems. Yet, he would be brave enough and willing to help someone that was in great distress. Once more, this is what time has waited for since its existence. It has waited for love, compassion, and tears for others' sorrows and pains. <u>This is what leads to great kingdoms.</u> This is everything I know that will lead us to prosperity, it is in your hands now.

For the astronomer conducting a radio telescope at Arecibo, Puerto Rico, and if you choose to do so, you can send a message on my behalf. Aim it in the direction of the Orion constellation (beings in heaven are masters of camouflage, living in the sub terrain of planets as well as in the oceans). You don't have to wait thirty years for an answer they will know you sent it as soon as it happens now that I am with you. They have been here for a long time watching us. They are everywhere, so please, hear my message. Could deception run this deep? I highly doubt it.

<u>Message:</u>
Glory of heaven and the victory. We seek your aid. Millennial shift begins in 2020. We await your arrival and further instruction. 1400 cubed squared. Welcome home.

I will silence my voice in the affairs of the earth. Thus, they selected a common man to save the message. Of course, a scientist would or should have explained all these results to you. Even so, that would have made even more skepticism. What this tells us is that spiritual beings can make who they choose to be great, it is not really anything we do independently. I am speaking for someone who appears to have a science background and has seen many places. I can oppose off the desires of the grand deception. Distance and time mean nothing to me. I recognize it's there and I know its contents, and I am in no haste to get my award. There is no need for a following or gathering; all truth has been exposed. I want mankind to succeed, my future is your future. I trust that one day, people will say that I was a great teacher with forbearance.

It has been twenty years of thoughts condensed into something man can sympathize a little more distinct than the Holy Bible. I have interpreted it for you, into the common tongue. I have not converted or altered any prophecy, I only have given them depth. I am not a miracle worker, I am advanced beyond my long time in thought and interpretation of the Holy Spirit. Spiritual knowledge and power is something that cannot be sustained forever. It is a means to an end and a fresh beginning. It is something like an atomic bomb for souls. It is practiced merely in the most desperate places in life. That great power is death, Apollyon the destroyer, and the monsters of the abysm. This was heaven's choice rather than our utter destruction. To touch or hold the power of death is cruel. It is mentally and physically draining on the soul. It is a constant accusation and correction along with multiple teachings of life. It is not for every race in heaven, that's for certain. We are tough because we come from a lineage of bondage. With that said, I have set up and recorded many great laws concerning good and evil.

God bless to each, and every nation who hears my words.

XV

SEASON OF DEATH-THE BODY FARM

Ten years after-Karma of my Lord

There are winners and losers, truth in time
10 years later, larger than life
Walls of white where is the door?
Hell is burning fire in the core
I'm the genius in the silence
I'm the genius of love and violence
In the silence I waited for his call
Listen to my wake so you don't feel the fall

Stop, Stop the killing
I am alive, I am awake
This dream is no different than the next
Ignorance is death!
You fear what you do not know,
I wanted to know
I tasted the nectar at the well of your hearts
And the blood of a 1000 Years

When Jesus appeared on earth, this was known as an incarnation. It is a final incarnation of the Lord as a new age ushers in. This is very similar in Hinduism and Buddhism with their deities. In Buddhism, it is called "becoming again." With any religion, we never get the full meaning unless the master is present to explain it himself. We can label things good and evil and right and wrong. But who are we to label? A perpetual balance must exist.

The image of the serpent on a Pharaoh's crown is posed beside a white vulture in many cases. They formed this image when upper and lower Egypt united. Have us take note that the snake and the vulture appear together on many of the male and female Pharaoh's crowns. We, as well can take note of the extravagant use of gold by the Egyptian Pharaohs to create their burial masks.

It is a high tribute to vanity and ego. Permit me also remind the reader, a snake enjoys dark chambers and tunnels. The female (queen) goes deep inside these chambers after a time of nourishment to bare offspring. These chambers were intended to protect the expired remains of the Pharaohs until the seals were gone, which awakened the dead. It is the equivalent to waking a vampire from a deep sleep or should I say many.

Such an odd creature to choose when wearing a crown of gold upon a human head. Or were they not human? Certainly, I would guess it could imply they were highly dangerous. What is my proof or citation of information? A long, long, walk in life for making similar mistakes in some shape or manner.

All the events I spoke in the chapter *Time*, are being put down on paper for the second book *'Masters of Time'*. Floating universes, inside-out worlds, dancing spheres, giants, and time doors, what a story it's going to be. I hope somebody sees the vision of a starving artist who wants to make a difference in this world. I would like to take my story to another level.

The Uraeus is a symbol for the Goddess <u>Wadjet</u>. This would contradict Eve as being the first woman upon the land. This would suggest that man worshiped the Goddess in the early times of the Egyptian and Sumerian dynasties. We also can come to this conclusion about women, by early stone carvings. They portray the female Goddess predating Adam and Eve's encounter with the snake. So, women as well have been around a very long time. Nothing is new, it has only been changed.

Now that we know that the Egyptian Pharaohs and their queens wore a crown to symbolize their authority as rulers here on earth, let's ask the reason of this. *Why they chose the <u>serpent and the vulture</u> as entities to be forged in gold on their crowns?*

Let us look at what each animal stands for. The cobra, a vicious serpent with a poison that kills and a vulture represents "death", a scavenger who feeds on dead carcasses. So now mummifying and burying the dead might make sense! The serpent lays a trap with deception and poison (wisdom mixed with greed), the vultures come when they smell death in the air (the end of a season, war, and death). It would seem the king and queen of the Uraeus are paired hunters with supernatural powers beyond many. They signify spiritual creatures who feed off human oppression and death. Even a dead man or woman can emit energy from their flesh in the long-run.

Welcome to the body farm, where nothing goes to waste. I know, it's scary stuff; be glad you have Jesus at your defense. This would not be so bad if it wasn't based on the deceiving, torturing, and killing of souls to harvest that energy. This is a form of evil or a form of punishment that exists. This has nothing to do with Jesus Christ or his Father, it stems from free will. Ultimately, demonic presences want the world to be in fear, chaos, deception, and greed. This is so it may cause many casualties in the final season. That is the best time to harvest souls. So, I have come to forewarn you of their trap and deceit upon your flesh. Please be aware of that.

The Egyptians lived in great deception until the days of Moses. They thought they were Gods over men. What was behind their great power? Were they some type of cosmic vampires in space and time, with power of resurrection and eternal life? This will explain the many altars set up across the world throughout time, with cosmic alignments. This too will go to explain sorcery and miracles. Moses was high-ranking magi who lived the life of a prince and a pauper. He did not recognize who he was until the day he challenged the Pharaoh. This was so he can see the suffering of the people. Moses had two types of people that loved him. The pitiful, they loved him because he was honest and treated the masses with respect. There were the Egyptians, who loved him as well since they believed he was the messiah, the chosen magi of the ages. He was ultimately betrayed just as Jesus was. Moses was their messiah; however, the curse of death does not break easily. Many did not wish the Hebrews to be civilized, they understood them as animals who bred at epic proportion. Thus, they were treated less than human. This was until the daylight of a new order of magi, a secret society which tried to overthrow the chains of darkness.

Although many things cannot be proven by me physically, I will ask the great questions once again. Why make out we have stone temples and altars all over the universe with cosmic alignments? Who are the mummified dead? Let us remember, hunters hunt within a season. As it is in on the earth, so it is in the heavens. This is the perpetual balance I speak about.

As we learn spiritual lessons, they will not be forgotten as we travel along with the Christ. The Egyptian, Pharaoh, who fell from heaven is a manifestation of a demonic presence. This was a great star lord who fell by his own avarice and desire when given ultimate knowledge and ability. He and his queen were cursed above all creatures and have become the "dead". This is not anything new, however, it is a replay of events that had occurred over and over. This dark black art is built on deception to trap intelligent life that becomes enamored by their own material ways. Our own desire has brought this judgement. As we had read, Moses confronted the Pharaoh, it is in redemption for the deception of Adam. This time the spiritual father allowed his son to handle his business with the crafty serpent, a father figure to Moses in the Egyptian empire. It would be the same in the day of Jesus, just in a unique way.

One of my favorite host on ancient aliens once said, "We live in infinite time and space with infinite possibilities". How true and correct you are, my friend. Many responses will come presently, that is my promise to the multitude. If anything, we all deserve answers in this life.

No matter what your thoughts and views are upon my manuscript, I am pleased to tell my tale. I will break down a season upon this earth to show you, to the best of my ability, of how it works as far as perpetual balance within this cosmos. That way, you have a good estimation of when the destruction will be released in full capacity. No, it is not the end of the earth, but a change for us, as humans. Let us not think that the Mayan calendar was off, it's right on time in my perspective. It is correct within a period of about seven years, by my calculation. This was the end of their calendar because life in this cosmos is about to change drastically. It would appear the Mayans were tracking the <u>millennial shift,</u> just as Jesus and John. I believe natural disasters will start to grow and produce more violent as the year 2020 approaches. They will continue to worsen, unfortunately. We are in the period called <u>fluctuation.</u> Hence, the Mayan calendar is exact in respect to this issue, it has already taken off and we will not consider the full effect for many years. The universe has been taking dips and rising back into position for many ages. When it finally stops fluctuating, the universe will start to lose momentum and power as it must recede or perish. When we recede the magnetic effect on earth is at highest peak. We then experience compression along with the dropping effect in the universe (space storm) instead of the rising expanding effect, or fluctuation.

These events are controlled in heaven by mono magnetic poles which I explained in an earlier chapter. In a sense, everything or in roundabout way, heaven controls with great purpose. Somewhat like a computer driven algorithm that constantly plays itself out. We once were very large in creation when God hovered above the earth when it was dark and void billions of years ago. In his image we are created but as smaller versions. After years of war, planetary death and lack of territory, a smaller version of humans survived the great quest, they were known as angels and fallen angels.

On the account, my editor believed the full contents of my story would be served best at later date in another book, I have condensed my tale of time. It is obviously a great task to prove the many things I say. A prophet of spirit may never be able to do so. I believe I will present a strong case of evidence men came from the sky.

According to my theory and timeline, the Annunaki (the original Sons of God) were creators in the firmament and creators of life on earth, *Masters of Time*. They became divided and known as children of the night and children of the light. They ruled this universe since time began. The children of the night became the Egyptian race ruled by the great Pharaohs under deception. These are basic timelines that match closely to modern historians. They are not intended to be exact dates; they are meant to show activities in a 2000-year season in the countries that makes up biblical history. Modern dates are based on my encounters with individuals such as John and Daniel.

Stone glyph of Annunaki

Sumerians. There is some proof, per ancient historians, that there were settlements of civilization which existed in ancient Mesopotamia somewhere around 6000 BC. These were the aborigines from the land whose daughters became beautiful. According to my theory, they were the creation of the Annunaki, in which they fell for the daughters of men. The bloodline of God's chosen ones comes from the middle east because a great injustice was done to early Muslims and Hebrews when the Sons of God fell. For they were weak and illiterate, God made them strong and witnesses of his word. This is when man began to pollute their bloodline from the stars. They basically were having sex with beasts, young men, and women that were developing. It is more like rape and seduction than sex, equally they were easy prey. In some instances, it was the equivalent to Einstein having sex with a modern-day native of Africa or a native of the rain forest. A Scientist having sex with their lower creations. This is the huge mistake that I have spoken of: the pollution of the bloodlines.

Many were not ready to become advanced that quickly. According to my hypothesis, the Babylonians conquered Adam's native territory and ruled like kings. A very similar story exists here in America when speaking of the Indians. Time is repeating itself. Will we ever learn? Yes, I understand we fled persecution and high taxes, many did so to persecute others. The Babylonians drew first blood with God by defying his orders to allow these innocent creatures alone, when they were driven to the borders of the ocean. <u>For that they were later decimated.</u> Many men who came from heaven, eventually chose women and children instead of science and space travel. Therefore, we live somewhat a cursed existence. Our ancestors gave up longevity to experience companionship and children here on earth. Spirit is full of many roads and paths, free will has its results. Children are not meant to be born in outer space that I can assure you. The world is an exceptional home for all life when having offspring.

Pharaohs of Egypt. Some were around 4000 BC the serpent king and his Goddess emerge upon the earth waging war. Pyramids were under construction, yet, we really have no exact date of their construction. There is no telling how long the Egyptians walked the ground before building the pyramids. 10,000 BC seems to be the magic moment of change upon the earth. I should believe this is when the Sons of God started to lay down with the daughters of men, which is mentioned by Enoch and in the book of Genesis. Per my theory, the fallen angels were conquering man and women since their existence began on earth. Prehistoric Humans were meant to be servants and trained for mining and war as they evolved. However, man had different plans once they saw how beautiful women had become in creation. They gave up their place in heaven to live on earth. The angel's spells of magic and seduction that they taught women, had men dropping from heaven like flies. It seems the magic spells mentioned in the book of Enoch were very powerful. This is how the angels were cast downwards, by the force of their own magic and beauty.

The 2000-year Season expires

Shiva- The Trinity of Hinduism

The Statue of Shiva

Lord Krishna. Somewhere around 3000BC, the Shiva incarnation appears, which holds death, the destroyer. A cosmic being which holds the balance of peace and devastation of the serpent king and his mummified dead. An archangel of heaven. A duality.

Lord Vishnu. Shiva incarnation, approximately or is to be. associated with the time period of 1958-2000 BC, according to my timeline and theory. The incarnation, which holds death, the destroyer. War is waged in heaven. The *Bhagavad Gita* speaks of an ancient war in heaven and it reads in the following way: "*There is a war that opens the doors of Heaven. Glad are the heroes whose fate are to fight such a war.*" This war is now upon the earth. From 2000 BC to AD, the first season has passed in the judgement. This aligns with the seven prophets of God coming forth to the earth. These are the seven angels or spirits who stand behind Jesus Christ in the book of Apocalypse. This is the first part of Revelation. This opens the door for the second book of Revelation, the second death and second season.

Revelation 1:20 *As for the mystery of the seven stars which you saw in my right hand,*

and the seven golden lampstands: the seven stars are the angels of the seven churches, and the seven lampstands are the seven churches.

> Joseph-prophet 1
> Moses- Son Of God- the incarnation
> Elijah-prophet 2
> Isaiah –prophet 3
> Daniel –prophet 4
> Ezekiel -prophet 5
> Jerimiah -prophet 6
> Zachariah -prophet 7

John the Baptist, AD the beginning of the year of our Lord, the incarnation and forerunner. Balance takes place with birth and crucifixion of the messiah, Jesus, Son of God. Power shifts to the son of man at the awakening of the Holy Spirit, the baptism. Semi-victory over death as rebirth begins. A new age is given to mankind by the blood of the Lamb.

Revelation 20:4-5 *I saw thrones on which were seated those who had been given authority to judge. And I saw the souls of those who had been beheaded because of their testimony about Jesus and because of the word of God. They had not worshiped the beast or its image and had not received its mark on their foreheads or their hands. They came to life and reigned with Christ a thousand years.* **5** *The rest of the dead did not come to life until the thousand years were ended.*

Those who were beheaded or killed because of their testimony of God or did not worship the image or take the mark of the beast, came to life, and reigned with the Holy Spirit for a thousand years. This period covers from Jesus' death to 1000 AD. The rest of the dead did not come to life until the thousand years were completed (1000 AD to 2000 AD). The dragon, that serpent of the old, is let loose.

These are physical dates of my colleague's births in modern day America, they have since passed on. I do not wish to reveal their full names for privacy reasons as I will not reveal mine. I am a ghost in a ghost writer's tale.

AD 1928 (exact date unknown), Daniel the prophet comes forth. Physical death occurs. Dr. Daniel was born in the region in Pasadena California. He specialized in holistic healing and medicine. He was close to 70 years old when I met him.

AD 1958 May 16th (10 years, 6 months apart), John the forerunner of the Christ appears. <u>Physical death has occurred.</u> Once again, this is the incarnation who holds the destroyer. "*A mighty angel came forth with a chain in his hand and seized the dragon.*"

AD 1968 (10 years, 6 months apart), Prophesy soon will be fulfilled. The appearance of the army of Christ will soon appear in the heavens. Son of God appears, <u>spiritual death</u> has occurred, his spirit now sits on a heavenly throne with the two witnesses. This also is a balance in the zodiac: Scorpio and Taurus. Summer solstice and the winter solstice. A balancing of scales or spiritual power

The year 2020 will be a very significant date in this age, maybe as well as for myself. Not the end of time, but a time of drastic modification. This is the age when "death" has no power over the chosen. The believer cannot be bound to the earth under punishing demonic forces on the day of judgment. At one time, a spiritual seal has set in place, the saint of death has no power to sustain you in the spiritual land of darkness. The power of resurrection has been achieved by the believer in Christ. Demonic forces lose their power over the believer. This is the conclusion of the second season, second incarnation or the second coming of the Christ life. It is also very near to the closing of John's Revelation.

<u>**The Final Season.**</u> Paradise Theatre was the tenth album by the rock band *Styx*. It was released and used as a metaphor for the changing times in America. This was confirmed by an interview from Dennis DeYoung's in the *In the Studio with Redbeard*. According to mythology Styx was the Goddess of the underworld, the River Styx. In mythology, Zeus rewarded her by making her stream's the agent of the binding oath of the immortals. The River Styx was also a river or stream, which came forth from the depths of the underworld. <u>This made the waters became wormwood, more specifically, the rivers of hell.</u>

Let us speak of coincidence or some hidden meanings in music. In Dennis

DeYoung's _Paradise Theatre,_ he wrote two tracks called AD 1928 and AD 1958. They became short tracks that segued into other songs one being _The Best of Times_. So, they were very short written musical pieces which needed a place on the album. You'll notice, whether by coincidence or spiritually, 1958 and 1928 is linked closely to the Shiva incarnation as well as the modern-day incarnation of the forerunners in 1958 AD and 1928 AD which I mentioned. In both seasons, BC/AD, 1928 as well 1958 are very climactic points of change. A time of change, 1928 AD is the year before we abandoned the Julian calendar and started using 1929 (MCMXXIX), a common year starting on Tuesday of the Gregorian calendar.

Roughly in the age of 1928-1958 BC, a universal war in heaven begins and arrives to end at the dying of Christ. This can be supported by the Bhagavad Gita as well as Michael, the archangel, biblically throwing Satan from heaven. The fallen angels were completely cast down to earth after the crucifixion of Jesus Christ. By 1928-1958 AD we have had several major wars leading up to World War II, which is one of the most historic wars in time and history. Just so that is clear, in the years we formed the atomic bomb and began experimenting with nuclear warheads, our final temptation has begun. We can be sure the powers of Satan are slowly being set loose for the last and final season to lead astray the nations. Darker powers are looking to cause a blood bath and carnage so that death and his queen can cause their last feast on souls. For those who are wicked and greedy, your time on their hands will seem like forever. Evil knows when it gets into its final destruction, there's no stopping it. Demonic forces will drag as many souls down to the pits of hell as they can to share in their suffering. Misery loves company. So yes, we are in time of change. What excellent composition of songs by the legendary Dennis DeYoung and the band Styx. It was I like to call mind candy, a force to make you look deeper in thought!

It tells us in scripture Satan's time is short. If you pick up my message, we do not hold to ease an Armageddon. Let us call it: a day done in prophecy and start on the new heaven and earth. That is very well within our rights and aligns with scripture. Everybody can say that they have had a victory with GOD. Sure, there are bullies to be dealt with, but let us deal with them as soldiers of Christ and quickly. Their continued arrogant hostility towards innocent nations and people is going to come to end one way or another.

United we stand, divided we fall, join the winning team. Peace or epic war will be achieved by the time of my death. An upheaval approaches in the east as well as the desert sands if peace is not reached.

Revelation 20:7 says this is the beginning and end of the final season of the king of the abyss. Jesus and his people hold out the crest of victory and become worthy to be in the new heaven and earth.

A lot of our future now is dependent on intelligent decisions, such as peace over war and knowledge over wealth. We are all becoming scientifically aware, time is equaling out knowledge among mankind. It is extremely important what we practice with knowledge from this day forth. What makes knowledge good and evil should be clear to us by now as humans. Just as when you have a child, you can teach it love, forgiveness or hate and malice. The sources of tomorrow are planted today. There is no question in my head, we are headed more toward a result than a doomsday scenario. We do not need the end of times in the way other countries have experienced them. When an evil so great is born, men burned alive in their cages and their throats severely cut. It gets time to lay aside differences in faith and purge the heavy darkness. Finally, when we unite as the righteous, nothing can hold back the power of our Lord.

As you go through this book there will be soft evidence and hard evidence, all evidence is there. I will not mind being ridiculed for such deep thought and vision; it has happened to many times. The sad part is when many events start to take place, just as long ago, they will regret their rejection of the word of God. Right after they crucified Christ, the Roman Empire started to suffer greatly until its complete demise. Babylon was laid to waste, at his word.

XVI

THE GOLD RUSH

Sirens

Here I am like a siren, in the days of gold, bronze and iron
If you look at me I defied them, and I ask that you deny them
Statues growing tall beneath the harvest trees
The air is full of jet fuel, I call it cancer in the breeze
Rockets and shuttles going off, so count the sonic booms
The holes are raining thunder in your high altitudes

Here I am like a siren in the days of gold and diamonds
If you look at me I will defy them, I ask that you deny them
Slaves of the pyramids in a time you never knew
A myriad of Angels, shall rise from <u>YOUR</u> blue
Buildings growing small beneath my golden wings
Christ has come to love you, while the earth starts to scream
<u>*Here I am like a siren*</u>
The Prince of Egypt, Son of the Pharaoh

According to my theory of time, as well as many others, Long-ago there was a gold rush just like there is on this planet today. Gold was in high demand by explorers of space. Gold was the key mineral element used for many things. Gold is the most valuable substance a cosmonaut can have because it lasts forever and does not corrode. Many crafts in the heavens are built with an infusion of gold and other constituents. This gives them longevity with lightness and speed. The gods of space used vast amounts of gold to build empires. The sum of gold that man had been is unfathomable to our imagination today.

The course, in which they chose to find this gold and other precious stones, and stones was in dispute by those who had come before us. There were great battles in the heavens for planetary ownership because of a legacy of dying planets left behind by man. Their methods became extreme and they did not carefully consider the fact that they might have to live on a planet that they were mining. Or they might possess to live where they preserved most of their workers and slaves. The earth was loaded with gold and they were finding it everywhere with the help of a great man known by the name of Eli. Eli was the master of genetics, master of geology, and lord of space travel. How could one man achieve all this in one life? He did not. Because humans had a hand in the creation of the universe, they felt they had rights to all planets and they did something rather foolish. They caused an extinction to many amphibious and reptile species. They managed this by forcing asteroids and meteorites to affect the world. They did this for two reasons: to kill off the larger reptiles and it also gave them the opportunity to mine the impacted areas for gold later in time. This was another approach to mining gold; even so, it had been used exclusively on dead planets. This, as well, would be thought a universal violation of legal philosophy. Remember, this is all trial and error by the wisdom of their forefathers. Man's specialty was mining planets and space travel.

I would suppose this was all theory, nevertheless, it is clear what we are good at and where we are heading towards. We cared less about beauty and only the treasure until we came to earth. It was a great paradise of beauty and it gave man a new quest in the heavens. This is where the account of love begins in humans. This is also where I recount the sad chronicle of those who study and take until nothing is passed on. But as there is a gold rush, there is also black gold, which is something that causes equal destruction to the mines. Thus, spiritual powers chose a human to bear for the voice of many. We are a race capable of great greed, violence, torture, and the list goes on and on. I am not here to preach or tell any adult male or women what to answer or what to believe. I have come to give you wisdom.

Most scientists today think that gold came to dry land from outer space in large meteorites that have come across the planet over billions of years ago. In fact, according to science, most gold on Earth is at its center, where its heavy properties caused it to drop over time. The gold that is set up near the surface comes from relatively recent strikes of meteors that had a considerable quantity of gold.

Nowadays, fracturing the mantle of a planet to implode the core makes sense if you're mining for gold. You can take a huge planet and reduce it down to smaller planets to mine very effectively. Yes, that is a theory, a theory which was proven to be correct many ages ago and it's another reason the Son of God and the Holy Spirit hold me in this prison. It also shows me another reason; we were banned from heaven due to our careless behavior.

We destroyed other beings' homes intentionally and non-intentionally as we raced through the heavens with the slaves of time searching for gold. As I mentioned, some alien creatures live in the sub terrain of planets when they become very hot or are not very hospitable on the surface. We cannot use heavy explosives on planets without investigating if there are life forms that had been or previously lived on that planet. The best way to do this is always leave some type of message far in advance and see if you get one in return. As I mentioned this will make much more since when we become masters of time once again, <u>giants in creation</u>. Some of those returned messages were completely ignored. Just as we ignore crop circles today and call them a hoax. We cannot always assume a planet is empty or deserted, or unowned. Would you believe there are worlds built from the inside in the same way I mentioned the cosmos? The scale of the planet is just a camouflage for great cities beneath the surface of the planet. <u>Who and what are they hiding from?</u>

The further man traveled into space to find gold, the further distant planets became that were habitable. There is only so much available gold on a planet and such is the need to mine many. And then, in that respect, mining and geology techniques did not come from evolving apes and evolution, it came from superior man of long ago. Today we call them the Annunaki and the Alantians. The Bible calls them gods, lords, and angels. Much evidence points us in that direction verses men and women coming strictly from natural evolution. Because gold cannot be made in a lab, the way that many gemstones can be, scientists consider that gold mining in outer space may be the next important matter in the future.

The next set of verses are by a man named King Solomon. If the bible says King Solomon, a man of great wisdom wrote these things, I very much believe them to be true. The universe is a revolving wheel. No thought or idea in this world is unique. So those who think they are blessed above others by God, they are mistaken. They are older souls that have come back into the world, much like myself. Many of them are entering into the world as we speak. We will see more child prodigies than ever before. How they use that wisdom is what makes them good and evil.

Ecclesiastes 1:9-18 _What has been will be again, what has been done will be done again; there is nothing new under the sun._ **10** _Is there anything of which one can say, "Look! This is something new"? It was here already, long ago; it was here before our time._ **11** _No one remembers the former generations, and even those yet to come will not be remembered by those who follow them._ **12** _I, the Teacher, was king over Israel in Jerusalem._ **13** _I applied my mind to study and to explore by wisdom all that is done under the heavens. What a heavy burden God has laid on mankind!_ **14** _I have seen all the things that are done under the sun; all of them are meaningless, a chasing after the wind._ **15** _What is crooked cannot be straightened; what is lacking cannot be counted._ **16** _I said to myself, "Look, I have increased in wisdom more than anyone who has ruled over Jerusalem before me; I have experienced much of wisdom and knowledge."_ **17** _Then I applied myself to the understanding of wisdom, and also of madness and folly, but I learned that this, too, is a chasing after the wind._ **18** _For with much wisdom comes much sorrow; the more knowledge, the more grief._

Referable to the fact man's journey into space took them into the obscurer parts of the world, we demanded to detect planets with orbiting suns to colonize. These are the planets with undeveloped real-estate and where our first human ancestors' journey ended, long before the time of the pyramids. According to my past life theory, it was the spirit of Elijah's encounter with supernatural beings that created the Egyptian serpent race by supernatural power. And he went forth, to conquer man. The deception was arrogance, pride, gold, and beauty. Every man from heaven came to sip from her cup. It was a high-end poison. A third of them fell to worship the dragon, known as Satan, destroyer of worlds.

Man's journey into space was a remarkable success and they had found many planets that could prolong life artificially or naturally. They lost concern for the environmental factors and were leaving behind a raft in the pursuit for gold. They had a mad dream to live like gods and enjoy their kingdoms and gold forever. No one imagined they would ever play out of the territory or planets, so far, they bore to increase technology each time to go further into the cosmos. This is the peril of wisdom, when are we happy or content with what we have? At what point, it is our desire so dangerous to our being? You see it every day: nuclear energy, mining, fracking, drilling for oil, it all takes its toll.

Something or someone gave our ancestors exactly what they were looking for, with consequences. Not only did they lose concern for environmental factors, they did not alert people of the discovery of premature aging. The further they traveled into the universe, the more quickly they would age. They would forget the mining operations with guards, managers, and slaves who all suffered horrible conditions. These people who mined planets with lower figures of mankind are known by me to be the overlords who became fallen angels. The slaves that were genetically and biologically engineered are the slaves of Christ, whom Moses came to set free. At one time, men had no conscience in how they treated these men and women slaves until the day of the Holy Spirit and the word of God. These men started to have a conscience because of a series of freak accidents and illnesses that followed them wherever they went. The facts have become clear as day to me. It is such a repetitive story.

I've arrived to explain these events to you so we may change the fate of humankind in the times to come. This is where I disagree with King Solomon, one of the Bible's most famous names. The crooked can become straight with wisdom and knowledge as they are powerful tools when applied in the right setting and the right time. Otherwise, God would not sustain a city that descends from heaven and we would have still been a race of unevolved beings with very slight knowledge. It is a very complex conundrum life, and its evolution. We either prosper in wisdom or we blow the world into oblivion and suffer every bit of the way. It has happened already in many other places in time. This is the whole reason behind the pyramids and the Holy Ghost. A set of spiritual lessons to be a guiding force for humans, they are known as the "dead".

Yes, humans were masters on the forefront of mining technology and space travel, but a problem existed. The amount of treasure that they wanted could not be obtained with the work force that existed so far from home. The Sons of God developed a way to expand that workforce rapidly, which was very clever. They used the lowest form of man they could find, left behind from the research days of the Annunaki, and crossed their DNA with their own. This theory is highly talked about among ancient astronaut theorists and historians. I know this is very much, the main focal point of my voice. I assure you, I can only confirm many theories. The Sons of God mated with different lower forms of women. I believe I am the byproduct of one the earliest races mixed with the blood of the angels.

This is what the angels carried out in the birth of Christ and Moses, an uplift in the Hebrew genetics.

As we see many stories not published in the bible coming forth, it will not be hard to understand how the bloodline of Christ migrated to America. It is tough to deny many records left in the Sumerian clay tablets as well as all-across the earth of humans who came from the sky. Even the Bible grants us this sign in several different records which I have translated for you. The age of Giza is highly in doubt by modern day scientists. In the book *The Orion Mystery*, Robert Bauval demonstrates that the best fit for the Giza Pyramids is around 10,500 BC. I cannot confirm this theory with science; however, I believe the pyramids to be very old, much older than first, though, and I will soon explain why. I always try to back something scientific with Holy Scripture so we may set up truth by accuracy of the prophets. *The Orion Mystery* is another great read for those who are searching for the truth about our ancient ancestors. I do believe we have proven the Sons of God or angel's appearance in this world when it was still black and void in the Book of Genesis. This is strikingly similar to the story of Enoch, except we do not have giants that are 3,000 cubits tall.

Again, I believe this is a translation error. They were giants and removed man's toil because they were the blood of the angels and very talented in math. They could build larger things with stonemason skills and engineering.

These unfortunate lesser men and woman that got caught in the mix of this mess that originally came from a planet far away, according to my past life theory. The surface was almost completely mountain and stone and they were cave dwellers. They were selected because they lacked intellect and could be well manipulated. I differentiate you these stories because I am proud of the father who became a master of space. Until now, my soul is disturbed by the legacy because he and his people have forgotten me. I am in awe of the great minds that do exist on this earth and have much respect for them, let that be known. You are the hope and fate of those in the existing universe. May you respect me for the knowledge of my fallen father? That's all I will ever ask of you.

My father was a genius (Elijah), he was a traveler of time and space and was highly esteemed by his multitude. His days of traveling ended abruptly when my mother gave birth to me in the early days of the Egyptian empire. My mother was a slave woman who was very beautiful and the Lords of Heaven wished her. My father's work took him many places so I knew briefly about him. The one thing I did know, as much as my mother may have found love in him, she also hated him because he left her with their children. He only came home when he wanted to lay down with her. My father was a master stone mason and a constructor. He had many lovers across the areas of the world. He sowed his seed everywhere he travelled. I talk with a hatred, yet I, as a human being straining to invest myself in the place of a great star traveler and Lord. I ask myself, could I make the same misunderstanding, given I had the same knowledge that he possessed? The response to that query is clearly yes. Thank God for predecessors. This is what time has been all about, lessons and corrections of something very distressing to the architects of life. It is highly wrong to use your intelligence level to have others serve you as a god. It is one thing to make a mistake and try to correct it and another when you don't care at all. This is what brought my father crashing down from the heavens, to lose his throne among the stars. Time would repeat itself many times before his son would become worthy to hold the dragon spirit becoming the <u>archangel of the Christ.</u>

When we are reborn into the world after many generations, we lose all instinct of past life. To be able to remember all these things, it would be a total recall of events in your past life. The knowledge of our past and where we came from would be lost unless something preserved the message, rather than on paper. After all, man has burned or destroyed many books to hide knowledge from the past. The Holy Spirit is the keeper of all facts and all wisdom. It has knowledge in all things. A library of unending knowledge. So much knowledge, it cannot be contained in one man and must exist in many vessels. These vessels arrive at the age of Christ, who will then, have what pertains to his mission.

The story of America and Christopher Columbus was sweet and joyous until humanity came in numbers to find gold. That is when abuse was at its prime among the aborigines. Nobody was going to get in the way of their gold. It is a crime when you discover something that is beautiful and sacred, then bring others who care nothing about it. It is then, you become bound into the law of the universe. This is the reason Christ forewarns you of the results. The consequences are high at the rejection of the word. Because of my father, I paid for his sins and have walked the world many times. It is only in the mercy of the Christ spirit that I am relieved of this duty and the spirit that was in Jesus assumed the punishment.

Therefore, the spirit of the father is in the son and was also in John the Baptist, the spirit of Elijah.

This can be tied to the story of Moses and his best friend, who was the Pharaoh's son. Although by deception, the father lived, and there can be no excuse for such arrogance. It is through his sons and the order of magi that his punishment takes place. It would be what was inside the Ark of the Covenant, which was taken by Moses that would change the Pharaoh's son's fate. Thus, he chased Moses through the desert. The Ark of the Covenant and its contents was his legacy to the stars. The Pharaoh and his son were punished, spiritually by Moses when he broke the spell of darkness that existed within the cities of the dead. They were cursed above all men. Jesus or the spirit of Moses, liberates his friend of this bondage and curse in the age of the Roman Empire. For Jesus acknowledges the greatness of the prince, his mighty archangel, by his knowledge of his fallen father. He also begins to understand the spirit which holds him, John the Baptist, or the prince of Egypt. He becomes a servant of the Son of God when he frees him of spiritual death. This is a bond that cannot be shaken.

Never will we be deceived by race, color, nor intelligence. We see this being fulfilled in the New Testament. The only begotten born of spirit, so that he might fulfill all things. The glory belongs to Jesus Christ, the word of God. For He is the incarnate vessel of all of creation, more than a prophet, and more than an angel. He is flesh in the world, born of spirit from the heavens.

As I have mentioned, it is no time for the world to argue over titles and greatness of titles. We are talking about the safety of all human and unhuman life forms on the planet. How can anyone ignore such wisdom that comes from so high? I can only shed tears at the consequences, some will have to pay. I can tell you all about consequences as I have had many lifetimes of the same to understand them. It is a sad day when we destroy the planet that we live in and turn it into a money machine. Fenced, portioned off, and sold to those who have the most resources. We do not own anything on this planet, it's all just borrowed. I believe most of this book is about a universal force that has arrived and is ready to challenge us on our own as well as our behavior on this planet and many others. If only you knew the price I have paid, then I would gain your attention. If you only knew.

XVII

Moses and the Pharaoh's Daughter

Much of this volume of my book, <u>is my interpretation of scripture and time.</u> My second volume is involved with semi-factual stories of my life before this earth by the recollection of memory and spirit. How can we be sure my accounts that I tell you were founded on any form of truth? I did not just grow up one day and say, "I'm going to tell the world about God and the angels of heaven."

At age 22, after having my son in 1990, my journey began forcefully when I met a very powerful demonic force. I stood before a man named John, who wore a skull ring on one hand and a <u>female alien ring on his marriage finger.</u> I found that rather odd after being raised as catholic and receiving confirmation when I was young. This was way before the time skulls became popular. Nowadays, everybody wares skull rings and t-shirts with various skulls. As well, you see it artistically everywhere. Acclaimed high-end fashion designer Alexander McQueen, known for his rebellious style and unconventional fashion shows, helped popularize the skull in haute couture in the <u>2000's</u> according to an online article about fashion trend by Hillary White. It seems John was a jump ahead on the latest trends and fads. He was very much fascinated by the skull and eastern religion. His explanation for that was that for some people death is life. Now think about that answer, it took me years to contemplate it. Let us remember that the year <u>2000</u> was a very significant date in my interpretation, it is the year I believe, scripturally, Satan is fully set loose for a short season. In Hindu, it is the last dance of the *Nataraja* or the cosmic dancer, the incarnation of *Shiva*. The all-consuming fire of creation and rebirth, a duality. Much like the artwork art depicting the archangel Michael and the Hindu Shiva, the powerful being has it foot upon a demon. This is depicted in many Hindu and Christian art pieces and is representative of the crushing of ignorance and evil.

I tell you of these events with the utmost passion for earth and its people. You don't want to be caught not loving your fellow brother and sister. You do not want to be a foul or greedy soul caught in this judgment of humans. No other creation in life is subjected to our current conditions and circumstances. Many may have grown use to death and destruction, as well, the caging of animals and humans. Never will I get used to it. It kills me inside to watch others hurt or suffer. When you treat something foul, even it's just food or a temporary prisoner, there is much karma involved. If you should kill to survive, it should be as clean as possible and livestock treated with some dignity. If our souls were energy or food to sustain alien life, would you not expect the same? Never underestimate what is at the top of the food chain. If you do, you have ignored the greatest wisdom Christ can teach. Law was perfectly set up long before humans ever existed.

When I first met John, I was his pupil learning what I did not know. We started to discuss biblical knowledge and the subject of Atlantis and Lemuria came up. He asked me if I knew the difference between good and evil, I just looked at him funny. He said, "give me your hand for a minute, trust me, it's all about recognizing energy or spirit." When I took his right hand, he started talking. His presence was so peaceful and calm, relaxing. He then took me by his left hand and started talking, it sent a burning feeling up my arm and he smiled with a wicked grin like that of a devil. I recoiled away instantly. His eyes became glazed over like fire. I became aware of a very powerful spiritual presence in the room. I became lightheaded and very weak, I was overwhelmed and fell to the ground. When I got to my senses, I quickly became aware of Satan as a somewhat of a visual ethereal being, a shadow moving around the room. It was only because I was in the presence of the Holy Spirit I had a good visual and protection from my adversary. I had become aware of the Holy Spirit in the same room and I ran out of the doorway.

When I awakened from being on the floor, I felt strange and uncomfortable, that's why I raced out the doorway. I went home and started reading the bible. I was reading the Bible after this strange encounter and I happened to open to a page referring to <u>Star Wormwood</u> in St. John, the prophet's vision. This was the name of the musical theatrical John was performing in California before I met him. I looked up the meaning of wormwood and it happens to be something you can use medicinally or it can be a bitter poison. Maybe in this theatrical there was a great significance or a hidden meaning to my spiritual experience. There was! I solved many of the writings meanings just about *10 years after*, in the year 2000. I as well began decoding certain biblical books when young in life. This spiritual encounter soon became much more mental than physical, this spiritual being was closing in on my soul and mass confusion started to take place. It felt like my head was in a vice, constant pressure always trying to break me. In a very unorthodox way I became very aware of demons and their hosts. That which plagued John since he was child born with an umbilical cord wrapped around his neck. That which wished I never came into his life to redeem him from such a battle or him to enlighten my soul.

The reason I know for a fact this was demonic attack is the aftermath of thought. Although I was not a lady's man, I surely loved the ladies. When I had this spiritual encounter, I began having very uncomfortable feelings of sexuality, female in nature, if you catch my drift. It was the kind of stuff that would never go through my head, it was very powerful! This was when deception was at its highest point. I had gone away from the situation to places of isolation to battle it out with such a demonic power. I wrestled every day with a host of thought. It soon started going in for the kill, usually attacks on my heart or floods of anxiety over past sin. It really has never stopped, it's always a constant assault. I have grown much in the arts of the magi.

I speak of these spiritual lessons honestly and open. One of the greatest generals of all times portrayed in Oliver's stones *Alexander the great*, was portrayed to have a gay lover. In the fields of war, when conquering vast territories, home sexuality did not exist for military genius's in battle. It gets awful lonely in the isolated battlefields of the earth. That was a time long ago were it was widely accepted in Egypt, Greece, and Rome. Moses, a mighty general in war himself, was very close to the prince of Egypt and the pharaohs daughter. I would have to say He may have learned some pretty nasty habits in the Egyptian dynasty. When I am attacked spiritually, it seems to stem from these sins of long ago. I have put myself through many periods of celibacy, never married. I am very much what you call the hermit.

Today, sexuality has turned into something a little different than in the past. It seems to have much more lethal consequence's spiritually speaking. I understand today that is somewhat of a demonic attack on men and women seeking a much holier path than long ago. We have major gender identity issues crippling America. For those who suffer gender identity issues and unusual sexual desires and thoughts, they are and can be very real. The first thing I recommend is for America is banning free porn from the internet so some child like mine own doesn't type in a word he hears at school and gets a free perv show at an early age.

You see how easy it is to make an unblemished child sin? There are those to be held accountable. The content a child can view without a credit card is quite absurd and a dangerous poison for our youth. Much of this content is abusive, distorted, and quite disgusting. Yes, you think I didn't. I am here to see all sin for what it is. A child can log in to a host of fetishes with nothing more than saying they are 18 years of age, that's absurd. I take this so very personal! This is mind-changing and brutal poison for any being, so says the holy spirit.

I studied with an older man and his wife who were Jehovah witness for many years, he never really gave me the full chance to teach them. He was too caught up in his *perfect religion* of no birthdays, not serving in the military and/or no blood transfusions to save your life. How is it that his religion was greater than all and Jehovah witnesses would be chosen? That's a contradiction to what the first and second resurrection teaches. Those who were killed by the beast and did not take his name or number had everlasting life. The majority of these were Muslims and Jews who executed by the roman empire. The 144,000 who are seated at the throne are of the tribes of Israel from the day of tribulation, the first and second temple, and really have nothing to do with Jehovah witness. He did not want to hear that. He ended up losing his wife after the first 30 days of having internet. She caught him looking at pornography of a younger aged women close to their daughter's age. He never knocked on my door again to finish our teachings, <u>although I wish he had.</u>

One of our dearly beloved pastor in Orlando lost his son when he confessed to having extra martial affairs. I sat in this church many, many times. Wow, what a preacher he is. His music ministry is like a live concert event. I am very sorry his son felt that much guilt in his action. In church, we strive so hard to be perfect like it tells us Like Jesus was. <u>Unfortunately, that is major cause to guilt and suicide these days.</u>

No man on earth was perfect or will ever become perfect in thought, speech, or action, <u>it is a fallacy.</u> We are a flawed creation built for sexual activity and pro-creation, per the devious plot of fallen angels. We were used as sexual servants, war machines, and taught many foul things. Spiritual life was given to us through God of Adam so we could gradually transform into more holy beings.

That is why the angels brought Jesus into the world as an infant to be <u>spiritually slain</u>. It was several transfigurations between John and Jesus that gives us glory, neither perfect, yet they were willing to die so that the spirit could ascend back to the throne to be spiritual aid for the archangels of heaven. Do not ever let lack of perfection be a means of suicidal thought. I know each one of the pastor's people in the church would have forgiven his son for such an error. Jesus as well, at the drop of single prayer. He was forgiven by the blood of Christ when he confessed as a child. It is a very heavy burden for a soul to leave earth in this manner.

Satan caused this Christian son to have an enormous amount of guilt at his sin being he was a legendary pastor's son. *What will the world think, what will the congregation say, my family, and friends? Will they not respect me anymore?* All for a brief period of lust and satisfaction that was bred into us since the beginning of time? It was too much to take in the thought process. After all, we are only human and our minds will break easy if we are not armed appropriately. You never know when the enemy is coming, just like Jesus when he arrives like a thief in the night.

The devil is a master at his game, no matter how much we love Christ. He is an accuser of our flesh! He maybe the danger of his attacks against our flawed flesh, just know that it's not worth committing suicide. It is a very tactful trick by the enemy and our own deciphering of words in scripture. I can assure the pastor's son's soul looks down in great admiration of his father. A very wise father and teacher of many souls. The holy spirit tells me he was a good son, <u>I am so sorry for the loss and his temptation.</u> We must be thankful if we will learn something from my teachings about suicidal thoughts and striving to become perfect in Christ. We fall so many times, and it is best just to get back up and try harder in our path. Continually harness are these paths, each path being a different road leading to the same place, with many variations.

Nobody is exempt from the attacks of Satan, no matter how much we love God. Money, power, popularity, and prestige change the way we think and we sometimes make ourselves bigger than we are in Gods kingdom. We are one step away from being shamed and humbled. Weather we are straight, gay, an adulterer, somewhere in between, or far beyond, these attacks are meant to break you down because you feel different or have major feelings of guilt.

Many people have crazy sexual desires, some much stronger than others. Never does anyone have the right to bash or kill someone who suffers from this unknown spiritual phenomenon that effects many men and women. Sometimes the ones who yell the loudest and commits horrible crimes against this community are guilty themselves. They try to justify their hate and atrocities that they commit as an act of God for their shame. The God I understand does not work that way. We are turned over to darker forces when we lack his protection. That plays out in many forms!

The suicide rate is very high for the transgender and gay communities. I am a Man of wisdom, not a hater. Through Christ I have suffered through time to know all things about that which causes suicides in men and women. The spiritual world is very powerful in the mind. It is because demons are at an apex, each one trying to grab a shell to snuff life and cause affliction and live out unearthly desires. When a man has strong desires, and goes from being a man to a woman that acts like a whore, dressing seductive and seducing men, you have been turned out by Satan. I do not say that to be foul or mean. When politicians and doctors allow transgender gender operations to occur with an almost 50% suicide rate, you my friends, <u>have a put gun in your hand according the laws of Jesus Christ</u>. That is not going to change, no matter how much you perfect such an operation. That is almost a 50% ratio that causes homicide by unnatural cause. And you think God did not send his best? Law and punishment are established differently in heaven than on earth and they are always watching!

If you suffer in this way, my fellow brother and sisters, and wish to change, remember unceasing prayer of Christ. Don't ever let it take you to the roads of suicide. It is better to ask for mercy and redemption if you feel troubled rather than take your life. <u>He will answer if you keep praying, trust me!</u> When He answers, you will then know that He will always there no matter if you're wrong or have confused feelings.

Remember, I have walked all roads for your sins with the most holy Christ spirit at my side. Many times, something tried to convince me that my sin was so bad that a flood of anxiety literally swallowed me whole and started to push me towards suicidal thoughts. It was so very hard to escape and we should never let our mind get that far with guilt, that's craziness. <u>Let me tell you it is never quite that bad.</u> It is 90% mental attack by darker forces. The other 10% may be an acknowledgment by the holy spirit we need to change our destructive behavior. Remember unceasing prayer of Christ and you will rise and strength no matter your wrongdoings. To reject Jesus completely will be your last mistake.

Alien demonic beings affect everyone in this life. It is a simple exercise of giving us free will and let us be tempted by the powers of death. The pain from these suffering and deceptions we create becomes harvestable energy, food for demonic beings. Those who like to cause fear, pain, and suffering are many times unknown disciples of Satan. Power and worship of their brutality feeds the power of the demon masses.

This spiritual event that happened between John and I was very much like the first baptism of Jesus, when shortly after Jesus was baptized he acknowledged the Holy Spirit. When Jesus was tempted by Satan, Jesus fled to the wilderness when nothing went his way. John was revealing something to Jesus which is not human in origin, the spirit of death. He was revealing a marriage; many would not wish to reveal. A marriage that was built on sorcery and witchcraft. This marriage stems from his Egyptian mother and father, not his own. A marriage that descended from the fiery stars of the abyss and was so alien in nature that it puts a chill up and down my spine. However, we must become aware of darker powers and sorcery in this world. It comes from the order of the magi when Moses was the Egyptian princes brother. Now these powers are banned from the angels by consequence of their actions.

Let us remember when Moses said, "he was our lord and God", he had killed a man. This tells us two things: the spirit was forgiving to Moses even though he murdered and ordered murders, there was a heavy price to pay. When we see Jesus declare himself son of God, we really have no idea what his life was like other than after the baptism of John. The recent release of the *lost gospel* states Jesus was married and had children. Whether true or false, it appears maybe Jesus and Moses were very much like many men today except they were caught up in a very ancient order called the magi. To doubt this would be very foolish after I explained how Jesus raises Lazarus from the dead. Miracles are often misunderstood or mistranslated by over ambitious interpreters of scripture.

As time passed after the above first mentioned spiritual realization, I had gone back to question John on many things. I kept feeling very strange. When things got from bad to worse in my younger years of this spiritual encounter, I ended up living in the hills for a time. I became very desperate and did things I was not proud of in that time of my life (one situation where I ended up stealing food and items for my survival). It was soon after I realized I was gaining knowledge as well as skills close to that of John's. I became someone new over a span of three years, becoming a poet and a musician. I began to experience a spiritual heaviness upon me as the years gone by. Massive anxiety, loss of sleep, and uncontrollable thoughts. My teeth were grinded down from constant anxiety. It was soon after in 1993, I met Dr. Daniel, a holistic healer, with whom John was a patient. I had many questions about my spiritual encounter for him as well. He said to me "my son, have you read Psalms 91?" This is one of the more recognized psalms in the bible. It is about protection.

My last conversations with John were very interrogative verses a conversation of friendship. When I inquired him about his beliefs in biblical scripture, he would always say "the Christ spirit is within me". He always would play me the most elegant version of *the Police* "wrapped around your finger". There are many lyrics in *Sting's* music that soon stuck out to me as time passed. When I read this lyric closely, it seems to be talking about a master student relationship. I'm sure to the artist Sting it has its own very distinct meaning.

In my interpretation of this lyric, the narrator is mesmerized by the ring on the finger of the one who considers him only to be a young apprentice or pupil of his excellence. It is only when the narrator departs and vanishes from sight that the subject of the lyric understands exactly who he was. It seemed to be speaking about a choice of two evils or two different drastic choices. The narrator and subject of the lyric become an object of a very important choice and lesson. The newly crowned master is always wrapped around the subject's finger by knowledge and wisdom. The subject of the lyric is always wrapped around the finger of his master, as well a disciple of knowledge or time spent in their many shared teachings. It is a marriage that cannot be broken. I believe maybe that is why Gordon refers to it as a shining band of gold that comes to fruition. He learned his craft from the band *Police* and took it to another level in his solo career. The song speaks of lessons the narrator had come to learn that he did not learn in college. This very much means the author came seeking wisdom more so than anything.

Now that I look back, it should of have been me playing the song to John, not the other way around. I did not know how to play it. I was truly mesmerized by his talent and skill. I was in awe of the ring around his finger. I carried his guitar for him and set him up for shows as I was an apprentice. I may have not surpassed him in music; nonetheless, many of his skills have become mine and they were coming into fruition, a shining band of gold. To think one would then write songs in my presence that I understood the meaning better than he, soon would be the smoking gun of reality. The spirit within him belonged to me. The world is not big enough for two spiritual masters.

Mephistopheles is mentioned in a very odd way in the song *wrapped around your finger*. In folklore writings, *Mephistopheles* is a powerful demon of damnation, a collector of foul souls. We soon might realize this song may not be about the marriage of a man and women, it is a song very much with an open interpretation.

Many people were following John and his music now. He did a variety of acoustic covers from *Bob Dylan and Neil Young* as well as some phenomenal originals. When he did his solos with the harmonica and guitar at the same time it was very powerful. One night, before leaving for Florida, he was performing in a concert. A spider dropped down from the top of the stage rafters and started dancing above his head in sequence to the music. Everybody started laughing hysterically. It was very much not a laughing matter to me, though. It became alarming. It looked like a big black widow, that which devours her mate after having her offspring. I soon would start to realize the nature and importance of meeting this individual. As well I would soon learn of the very heavy spiritual aspect of my encounter. Never will it be a pleasant day in my life that is for sure.

It was just being before I left California in modern day times, John, myself, and my son of three years of age spent some time together. It was then that my young innocent son's spirit was attacked and spiritually slaughtered by the force of Satan. Since he was a threat by nature of his bloodline, Satan quickly went after my son's soul. His spirit was at once seized by a mighty angel up to the throne of God as a perfect sacrifice. Then the archangel descended with all his glory. This is how the Holy Spirit entered the world to come to my aid, a pure vessel of a child. Ultimately, he would save my life by transition of the spirit.

A great spiritual battle quickly took place when my son came forth into the picture. I was close to death many times and in many ways. My spirit, then became the new guardian of the Christ spirit. It was too big of a fight for an immature child and not his battle to fight with. I remember John asking me if I loved my son and I broke down crying because of all the pandemonium that ensued later in his nativity. I do love my son and the son of the Holy Spirit. I finally started to realize what this all meant in more modern terms. It is the final fall of the great Egyptian Pharaoh who was the father and leader of the order of the magi. A new father and son have been chosen in time. It is more about the pharaoh and his prince of long ago than it is about me and my son in present day. The lowest has become highest and the highest become the lowest.

If that is what I was chosen to be in the Holy Spirit, a guardian, so then it must be. Thus, something that happened long ago is playing out around me and through me. I am paying a spiritual price for something that happened long ago when men belonged to the order of magi. This is when Moses and Aaron walked the earth with the lord of Mt. Sinai.

You can punish me for my sins of time. Satan. How dare you attack an innocent child with no sin in his life? My son used to tell me when he was about 11, he had seen dead people. I cried many tears for I could not help him at that time as his life has been full of trauma. My son has not had much realization or memory of this encounter with John, he was so young. I do not believe he understands it today either, he knows I have changed. Because he is not in spirit as he was when a child, it is like a faded memory that he barley recalls.

I remember when he was just a little guy, I seen his body jumping around, as if having an epilepsy, while he was sleeping. It was like something was attacking him when he was visiting with me. I cradled him tight and sheltered him from the storm. I experienced this myself long ago, when I first met John. This is when he taught me the unceasing prayer of Christ. Have this be noted, we are the "dead" and have no memory, for the "dead" prey on your soul constantly. I have developed through prayer and meditation. This offers me a glimpse into the past and future as well as a spirited defense.

I love my son. He was a wonderful, little, innocent bundle of joy. He was snatched from me at such an early age. It very much seems evil was not going to let me embrace this child. I was a sick man with some heavy issues plaguing me; therefore, it was no place for a child to be with me remember when my son was about three or four I had a visitation and I took him to get baptized. The preacher refused to baptize him because of his age. He said he was too young to know Jesus. He wanted me and my son to be a more permanent fixture in the church before he baptized my child. My son took a holy bible out of the pew and said, "Daddy, Jesus is the word!" The preacher's jaw dropped. I chastised the preacher in front of his congregation so that they would know what kind of preacher is among them.

This all, of course, stands for the mass murder of innocence as it was back in the day of the Pharaohs. Spiritual powers trying to snuff out God's beloved child. And for that, the spirits and powers behind this dark sorcery are going to pay dearly. Nobody messes with my son, my friends, and family and lives to do it over again. The day will soon be done for the dark Lord of the night, he has met his match. The pharaoh, with his dark demons of deception will not be throwing any babies in the river anymore, and fear my Lord those who do. The spirit of the fallen father is my greatest treasure of wisdom which is irreplaceable. The spirit of my son has been always remembered of innocence and purity, truly what I came to fight for. Today, it will be defended forever. This world has a new father and time will bring wonderful things. The father known as "death", can never live in the flesh ever again for this great deception. That serpent of the old, a liar, and deceiver by evil forces.

Before I had left John in California, he was starting to be stripped of all talent as he wore a jean jacket where he plastered the words the fool and jester upon it. This took the place of his nice black leather jacket that had a dragon on the back, the object of my intense investigation. I mean, the guy literally started losing his mind and acted in an odd manner, so I knew it was time to leave. He soon would die a horrible death and along the way forget many of the things that even happened in our encounter. This means, he really was only a very temporary vessel for me and my son. When John lost his spiritual talents and I gained mine, whatever was left of him or in him was not human and peace of dung. John gave up his soul in the battle of forever as servant and slave to Christ, an archangel of heaven.

John wrote many masterful original songs that were theatrical in nature before I left. One of my favorites was *The Emperor's servants*. This was done on a 12-string guitar; it was so ridiculously beautiful. Given the nature of this relationship, it can never be forgotten. I believe he is now very much a part of me spiritually. A unique marriage, designed from spirituality. His loss in battle to demonic beings is only a new begging for someone else. Never is the journey over, for now he lives within.

Nobody stays the greatest at something forever. That is the beauty in sharing talent. To watch something or someone shine even above your highest expectations. When money and popularity is involved, it becomes a downfall afterwards. It takes away from a master student relationship or even becoming equals.

Hence, it was prophesied that one would come to show his power and strength over death. Some may be very disappointed as I tell my tale, others will rejoice in hope of the resurrection and eternal life. The one thing I can say for sure, this is entirely bigger than one man who declares the Holy Spirit and fights against demonic principalities. It is now about those who teach mankind on how to defend themselves from the arrows of satanic sorcery.

John the prophet, Jesus, and John the Baptist were an unbreakable trio who held the powers of the Holy Spirit. Without either one of them, the victory of the Holy Spirit would not have been possible. Look through time and see the vessels God chose, none has been ever perfect. Jesus was the perfect sacrifice, for he came as an ordinary child stripped of spiritual authority. He came from the order of the magi; however, he chose to be born in a very low position to show humbleness. This is what the angels decided would be best. Nevertheless, his genetics were very particular, they were not of the common adult male. Untainted by astrology and mysticism, he was an ordinary man until he met John the Prophet and John the Baptist.

This is also true with Moses. He was very normal up until he was instructed by the Pharaoh and his children and the Lord of Mt. Sinai. He became the first earthly son born of the "dead". They taught him the ancient arts of the magi. He was trained in the dark arts as well as self-defense to overthrow the Pharaoh. The Pharaoh cursed Moses for eternity with great darkness. The only problem was it flew right back in his face as heaven's chosen vessel aged in spirit.

All this wisdom I speak of began to play out in the book of Exodus when Moses had a male parent and brother not of the same origin. His father was the Egyptian Pharaoh and his brother and sister were of royal Egyptian blood. Moses was thought to be born from a Hebrew slave woman and man, however that is not entirely true. He was a plant by an elite Egyptian and the Pharaoh's daughter. It was the "spirit of the archangel" which infiltrated the Egyptian kingdom. In the same matter, he infiltrated the Roman Empire with the birth of Jesus. In the days of Moses, the Pharaoh's daughter had a vision of the Lord and was told she would have a son who would rule the earth and heaven in the ages to come. The Pharaoh's daughter was very young; however, she was a powerful magus in the Egyptian dynasty and had the bloodline of the great Egyptian royalty. The genetic replica of her mother, who was silenced for her thoughts on how a kingdom should be governed. Her mother a very powerful seer and oracle of the divine, her love eventually one day strayed from the mighty Pharaoh. The Pharaoh's daughter was sexually abused like many young women and she was kept as some freak prophetess for the Egyptian Pharaoh.

A Pharaoh, many times would put brother and sister together to preserve the royal lineage of those who came from the stars. The daughter of the Pharaoh was not causing it, she failed her father with the aid of the Lord of Mt. Sinai who once greatly loved her mother. She was the sole one who did not fear the Pharaoh's spiritual power and hence, she would teach her spiritual son, Moses, to be a true king. Moses was a kind man to the slaves and the slaves thought Moses to be reasonable. Moses was born from a Hebrew woman, but had advanced DNA. The woman became pregnant without the need of a man in my version of time. This story is close to Jesus's and John's story. Even so, this would be difficult to express in the time of the Old Testament and anyone to understand it. It is also a little perplexing at the time of Jesus until we understand the angels were men of science.

Moses's Hebrew sister put Moses in a basket and sent him down the river when they were murdering infants to stop the coming of a messiah. It was no accident the Pharaoh's daughter and maidens were down by the river; she was there for baby Moses. This was when compassion and love really started coming into the world. People could not resist seeing others be treated like beasts, especially infants. They were willing to die for what they believed.

The Pharaoh ordered all firstborns to be killed when he was made aware of the deception of the magi. The subject of the Pharaoh and his assassination attempt was able slip into the royal Egyptian dynasty as a baby and was raised on his own. When you talk about assassins, the archangel is the top heel. He lived right around the Pharaoh and infiltrated his kingdom as a small infant child. The Pharaoh killed many children so that he can cut an advanced bloodline being introduced to the Hebrews. He wanted to keep them unintelligent, so he could govern as their god.

The people were believers in the power of Pharaoh's daughter, she enjoined them not to abide by the edicts of the Pharaoh and kill their children. Many babies were killed trying to stop the coming of the Messiah. For that, his punishment must be greater than all punishments given. This would be very similar and played out again in the days of King Herod. This is really what we call *a demonic spirit using men to enforce its dark black magic*. What an evil bit of dung this man was to have killed children and did so to preserve an oppressive empire.

In the story of Moses, we now might see why the Lord of Mt. Sinai knows who Moses was and why he went looking for him when he was exiled to the desert. The Lord of Mt. Sinai warned the Pharaoh he was in the wrong for treating these people in a cruel matter, like God in the days of Adam. The Pharaoh refused to turn over property belonging to the angels. If he was banned from heaven, so was everyone else. Pride, hatred, and jealousy, the poison started sinking deep within his skin. There was a very specific reason for the Lord of Mt. Sinai to be chosen by the spirit.

This is when the Lord of Mt. Sinai threw down his crown of gold and betrayed the Pharaoh. He had to send Moses back for two reasons, a final confrontation and to retrieve a "particle enhancer". The device was part of an accelerator that worked in conjunction with a nuclear reactor. I will try to prove to you with certain scripture, they had nuclear energy back in these days. Moses and his people took the part for the accelerator from the Pharaoh guards with force before they left the Pharaohs kingdom. The prince of Egypt, thought to be in modern day by historian's to be Rameses II, was Moses best friend. Ramses, his older brother chased Moses into the desert. He believed Moses stole his father and the Egyptian people's legacy to the stars. Moses escaped that tragedy by the power of the lord of Mt. Sinai. The sea rose and entrapped the Egyptian army, leaving Moses and the Israelites to flee to safety at the base of Mt. Sinai. This was not a miracle, heaven had intervened to give safety and protection for the extraction and retrieval of this very important piece of technology. Therefore, in the bible it talks about bread falling from heaven in the verses of Exodus 16:1-34, manna and quail. Today, we have no idea the act of endurance it took for Moses to lead his people to safety and betray the pharaoh.

The Ark of the Covenant *"They shall make an ark of acacia wood. Two cubits and a half shall be its length, a cubit and a half its breadth, and a cubit and a half its height. You shall overlay it with pure gold, inside and outside shall you overlay it, and you shall make on it a molding of gold around it. You shall cast four rings of gold for it and put them on its four feet, two rings on the one side of it, and two rings on the other side of it. You shall make poles of acacia wood and overlay them with gold. And you shall put the poles into the rings on the sides of the ark to carry the ark by them. The poles shall remain in the rings of the ark; they shall not be taken from it. And you shall put into the ark the testimony that I shall give you."* **Exodus 25:10-22**

Moses gave the device he retrieved to the Lord of Mt. Sinai and its rightful owners. The dimensions of the Ark of the Covenant are somewhere around 36-40 inches cubed. We might clearly see that the instructions God gave Moses are clearly meant for him to build something that houses a radioactive material. For one, the way it was built and the rings which were attached for carrying ease. This was to avoid as much direct contact as possible with the item in the Ark of the Covenant. How something could be so great and packed into such a small package change the destiny of God's children?

If lead was not available and gold was in abundance that is what they would use. We know Moses did not leave the Egyptian dynasty empty handed. This is a big reason knowledge and freedom was kept for the angels and a great friendship was born between those in the sky and the Son of God. There is yet more to prove my nuclear theory as we go along.

Astronomy and space travel were taboo and not to be spoken of. It was the forbidden fruit of the common man. Therefore, God warned Adam and Eve of the Pharaoh and the forbidden knowledge during the garden. The serpent being craftier than most men and women subdued God's spiritual son and his lineage into bondage and labor. Everything you see today is based on wars that God fought to free his son and his people from evil empires. It is Jesus Christ's presence alone that keeps the powers of heaven from coming down into this world to end addictions in human's presence. We will notice when the world had become sexually immoral in the book of Genesis there was a massive cleansing. This means population and humanity had gone out of control. It is only because Jesus Christ sacrificed himself to be our teacher that we even live and breathe. As humans, we could vanish in an instant.

It states in scripture, when Jesus made himself worthy to open the seals that he took the keys of death from Hades. Apollyon the king of the bottomless, a spiritual prison, holds the keys in which no man can fathom. The abyss is a black emptiness that stretches forever. The abyss of the earth is more related to temporal prisons in the lake of fire. Volcanoes that lead into the depths of a spiritual hell were exceedingly hot temperatures that would make souls moan and wail with great agony without the presence of a savior. The keeper of demonic beings thrives in very hot places. This changes all things from the Old Testament into a New Testament. This changes the balance of all things in this universe. With

Jesus Christ seizing the keys to Death and Hades, this establishes new law. The destroyer must now go on into destruction, which was its sole purpose in creation. The laws and punishment of temptation will soon be abolished.

Revelation 1:17-19 *When I saw Him, I fell at His feet like a dead man. And He placed His right hand on me, saying, "Do not be afraid; I am the first and the last,* **18** *and the living One; and I was dead, and behold, I am alive forevermore, and I have the keys of death and of Hades.* **19** *"Therefore write the things which you have seen, and the things which are, and the things which will take place after these things."*

Death is the only thing certain we know in this life, a beginning, and an end. For some, life is a journey of joy, love, pain, and sorrow. It seems to others in this life that they are here to serve darker intentions. They are the controllers of thoughts and nations and say they are of God, yet know nothing of his will or glory. If it were not so, I would not have had lived to tell this story. To say one is Lord or God, we really must understand that phrase and meaning as well.

In **Exodus 20:2-3** Moses said; *"I am the Lord, your God which have brought you out of the land of Egypt, out of the house of bondage, you shall have no other Gods before me."* When he uses this phrase is he speaking of all things about life in this universe or is he simply stating he is the Lord God over the slaves of the Egyptians whom he set free? What was the spirit behind these works and by whom was Moses given authority?

As I have explained many of these verses to you, the truth should be clearer. The problem is that scientists, government, and religious facilities will argue my interpretations. That is because men who sit in high places make their living by exaggerating the truth or hiding sacred documents or veracities. You can be reassured that this has gone on almost since the origin of mankind. Through securing, holding, and manipulating knowledge, enlightened man found humans could easily be mastered by leaders and false religious beliefs.

By Scripture and science, I will write down that these humans who called themselves angels, Lords and Gods were mere travelers of the sky. The Ten Commandments from God were based on the thought and laws of superior men, travelers of time. Lesser Hebrew men and adult female were being overshadowed on this earth under the dominion of the Egyptian Pharaoh. It was at that time, the Hebrew people cried out to a God for mercy under their dictatorial. Many others as well called out for mercy from the tyrants of the earth.

Heaven chose Moses to deliver the slaves from the Pharaoh and his wicked and sinful kingdom. So, it was here, the spirit heard the call of the weak in this great injustice. To set us free from this bondage that we were living in, the price was high for the heavenly spirit. Without the sacrifice of men in the biblical scripture, this world would already be in chains of darkness.

Because we receive eternal life given in Christ, there will be plenty of time to pay off our debts when victory has been carried out. For worthy are those that are selected to receive this natural endowment and may they never abuse it. They say in heaven if you want to build a kingdom, build it on principles of fairness and righteousness. If we cannot do that, our kingdoms will never last. There's nothing that can stop what has been put in motion by the heavens. They have chosen their leader and they are gathering to serve.

It is on this day that I understand why I must suffer as my people had. A leader or warrior of spiritual principles and law can never judge law within a kingdom unless he has walked the road of many. I do understand our weaknesses and our strengths, most of all, the desire to live in peace and free of oppressions.

To understand the relationship between John the Baptist and Jesus Christ and how their lives tie into Moses and the Lord of Mt. Sinai, we must ask ourselves a few questions. We know that Elijah went into the heavens without seeing death in some type of flaming chariot. It would be odd for Jesus to tell his disciples this was Elijah who was to come when speaking of John, the Baptist. And because these were planted children by the angels, what was the spirit of Elijah doing in the same time as baby Jesus? Why was he paired to grow up with Jesus as the fore-runner? The spirit of Elijah inhabits the body of the forerunner, John the Baptist, six months before Jesus's birth and shortly after the Angels came to visit Zacharias as told in Luke 1:11-57.

There is much mystery surrounding Christ's birth from a Virgin. How was Mary able to miraculously have a child of greatness without sleeping with a man? I like to forever keep the righteousness of Jesus's mother, for she is a very godly woman. As a scholar and teacher of Scripture, I will tell you the four brothers of Jesus are never accounted for in this story as being born. There are only two logical questions for this scenario: was he the oldest or was he the youngest? Also, were they full or half-brothers?

Because Scripture does not give us those answers, we must question why these births are completely left out in early or later chapters of the Holy Bible. Or is it possible they were destroyed or completely removed from the Holy Scriptures, as many other manuscripts, to prop up the power of the Church and mother Mary by declaring her an untouched virgin of God? Rarely were women virgins back in those days unless they were young of age.

We are now finding lost manuscripts from different apostles that give a sign that Jesus was married and there was unrest between disciples. I would say if the bloodline of Christ ended up in America, then surely, we can confirm many stories of about Christ having a bloodline just as Moses. What we must accept is Mary had Jesus without having intercourse with a man. Jesus was to be a chosen vessel of God, which is very clear.

Who was this angel that placed Mary to sleep just as it is mentioned when God did the same to Adam when he created Eve in Genesis 2:21? This would make the Angel's visit more miraculous in a time where we say there was not much science. Also, if you look at all the verses I have revealed in previous chapters, you will find that the Morning Star, which the wise men followed, was much more than just a star.

Please know this, this was a very blatant attempt to increase knowledge to the bloodline of Jewish people who were being dominated. Once again, many were being ruled over by the Romans, just as they were under the rule of the Egyptian and Babylonian empires. Jesus Christ comes forth instead of a man called Moses.

In the beginning of this book, I mentioned Ecclesiastes 1:9, which says there is nothing new under the sun, it has always been. We are today, once again, becoming masters of DNA, in vitro fertilization, cloning techniques, and several other skills. We are dabbling with time travel, worm holes, dark matter, particle accelerators, and a host of other things the common man has no idea that we are working on. We are starting to store seeds from many various places in a place called the Svalbard Global Seed Vault in Norway. You can learn about this vault and the many men who are behind creating it and pull your own notions as to what it might be, or might become.

Once again, this is nothing new to man, it is but another journey in time for those having great wisdom. Let us ask the question; How could mother Mary, who did not lay down with a physical man come to have a child who one day would be ruthlessly hunted and killed by men in the physical realm as well as demons in the spiritual realm? Mary bore a son who would be as of today the most powerful and influential figure that the earth has ever seen.

When John the Baptist was beheaded in Mark 16:14-29, this is when Jesus starts his rise to power in the ministry of God. This is when he also chooses apostles. This is when he also begins direct conversations with the Holy Spirit as well as Satan or the serpent. This is confirmed in Matthew 4:1-11 in the last temptation of Christ.

The next fact, I will give you in explaining this relationship between father and son is when Jesus goes to the cross. In Matthew 27:45-47. On the cross, he cries, "Eli, Eli, lama sabachthani," this can be translated to "my father or my God, why hast Thou forsaken me?"

The Death of Jesus *Now from the sixth hour darkness fell upon all the land until the ninth hour.* **46** *About the ninth hour Jesus cried out with a loud voice, saying, "ELI, ELI, LAMA SABACHTHANI?" that is, "MY GOD, MY GOD, WHY HAVE YOU FORSAKEN ME?"* **47** *And some of those who were standing there, when they heard it, began saying, "This man is calling for Elijah."* **48** *Immediately one of them ran, and taking a sponge, he filled it with sour wine and put it on a reed, and gave Him a drink.* **49** *But the rest of them said, "Let us see whether Elijah will come to save Him.*

As the author of this book, I cannot help but to be so sad that something like this had to happen for us to receive His glory. Notice the context in the verse on the last paragraph. Some of them that stood have heard what Jesus had spoken about. They said, "This man calls for Elijah". It tells me that Jesus got more than he bargained for in the baptism of John.

This gives further weight that John the Baptist was a vessel for the resurrected spirit of Elijah as well as the archangel, the Lord of Mt. Sinai. Now we can explain God even further as we speak of Elijah and chariots of fire going into the heavens, and look back at Moses and the burning bush.

If we read these verses in Exodus 3:2-3 closely, we can conclude that God is in some form of craft or vessel putting out bright light yet it is not catching anything on fire. We knew back in those days there was no electricity and something like this would really catch your attention. The light was bright enough to catch Moses's attention and draw him away from his flock to investigate what was happening on the mountain. In Exodus 3:3 Moses said, *"I will now turn aside and see this great sight, why the bush is not burnt."*

In the rhyme that follows, God sees that Moses has come up to investigate and calls out to him. A spiritual being would not demand to see Moses to call out to him or grab his attention. Moses was afraid to look at God for he was in fear. We must discuss this verse in depth to understand it. God mentions this more than once, *"man shall not look at my face"*. This is a very peculiar request by the Lord on Mount Sinai. Adam and Noah as well as many other figures of the bible, used to have conversations with the Lord and he never mentioned for them not to see his face. As Moses draws closer, God instructs him to take off his shoes because he was about to enter holy ground.

In trying to introduce himself to Moses, He gives himself a title, God the Father, the God of Abraham of Isaac and of Jacob. Thus now, we must look at this carefully and conclude the same based on this specific statement of God who leads Moses and his people out of the captivity of the Egyptians. To do so, we must look at the God of Abraham and at what time did he walk upon the earth prior to Moses. When we speak of the God of Abraham, we are speaking of the lineage of Adam which is almost 625 years prior to the encounter between God and Moses.

We can also see from the text in these chapters that God already knows who Moses is. In Exodus 4:10-14, the Lord becomes angry with Moses because Moses believes he is not eloquent enough to speak for God. God instructs him to use his Brother Aaron as a mouthpiece for what Moses was to learn from the Lord. So not only does God know Moses name, he knows his brother's name as well?

I will ask the reader to use their common sense. Was God among the Egyptians when the Pharaoh exiled Moses? This is where we, as human beings, must use intelligence in studying Scripture as well as science. How could a man or being that was 625 years old still be talking to Moses on the mountain and giving instructions on how to deal with his people and the Pharaoh of Egypt? As I mentioned earlier, we can be 100% sure this was a physical being because he gives Moses physical items such as the Ten Commandments. This also would show very clearly that the Lord of Mount Sinai had stone mason's skills equal or greater to that of the Egyptians. He was a Mason of the highest order.

We start to notice in biblical history, the many times that people encountered with angels, it is on a mountain. Elijah ascends into the heavens on something that can only be described as a chariot of fire or flames of fire similar to how Moses met the descending God of Abraham in the burning bush.

In the New Testament and the Old Testament there are events that are not easily understood by the human mind, especially as it relates to the spiritual realm and the Holy Spirit of God. I can only, as a man, attest and witness to the story that sits inside my heart and soul to give you a greater understanding of the Holy Spirit of God that I have encountered and come to understand.

In **Exodus 19:9**, God tells Moses: *"I will come unto you in a thick cloud that the people may hear when I speak with you, and believe you forever."* So now we have fire and flames and thick smoke at the arrival of the God of Abraham.

Exodus 19:11-13 *And let them be ready for the third day, for on the third day the LORD will come down on Mount Sinai in the sight of all the people. **12** "You shall set bounds for the people all around, saying, 'Beware that you do not go up on the mountain or touch the border of it; whoever touches the mountain shall surely be put to death. **13** 'No hand shall touch him, but he shall surely be stoned or shot through; whether beast or man, he shall not live.' When the trumpet (horn) sounds a long blast, they shall come up to the mountain."*

Exodus 34:1 *Now the LORD said to Moses, "Cut out for yourself two stone tablets like the former ones, and I will write on the tablets the words that were on the former tablets which you shattered. **2** "So be ready by morning, and come up in the morning to Mount Sinai, and present yourself there to me on the top of the mountain. **3** "No man is to come up with you, nor let any man be seen anywhere on the mountain; even the flocks and the herds may not graze in front of that mountain.*

My friends, God is either completely vicious or he is warning them not to come up to the Mount because of potential exposure to radiation. Why would an animal or people die from going beyond a certain border? Why would God stone or have somebody shot through for going beyond a certain point or touching him? There were several reasons why God did not want them to come up to the mountain that we can be assure of.

The first one would be radiation exposure. He also wanted to conceal his identity and his vessel. He does not want to directly meet with the Egyptian slaves. He wants Moses and his brother to be the mouthpiece of the Lord. If we read the verses closely, you will see he is warning them about the potential radiation poisoning coming from his vessel leaking into the ground waters. That is why he spoke of not letting animals graze in front of the mountain. After all, we clearly discussed the Lord ate of their flocks in the burnt offering.

Therefore, he made this very important request. Radiation exposure is dangerous to every living being and animal. If exposed, they would have to be put to death. Radiation poisoning is a foul way to die and can be passed on through streams and ground yielding grasses and shrubs. It can be passed on from person to person if they are not scrubbed down properly. This would be a reason that God didn't want them to go beyond a certain boundary when grazing with their animals.

Now, we can highly understand why the God of Abraham said they would be "stoned or shot through". Because He mentioned, "surely, they will not live", we must interpret stoned or shot through as a humanitarian way of being euthanized.

There is a good sign from these verses from the bible, as well as my first-hand knowledge, that there was a nuclear reactor problem with this ship which had become damaged causing leakage to the core of the reactor and damaging other components. This would give us a sign that this is one of the vessels that was damaged when the spirit of the Archangel forced the dragon or serpent (Pharaoh) and the fallen Angels from the sky.

When the nuclear reactor becomes damaged from taking a direct hit in the battle of the heavens, the dragon spirit or Satan can no longer return into the heavens to conquer. The device they used to accelerate the nuclear reactor was severely damaged. This disabled the ship from traveling at speeds in which it needed to travel back into the heavens where cities of great treasure existed in the Orion's constellation. This also, will give much credence to those scientists or theorist who believe the pyramids were possibly used to manufacture nuclear energy at some point in time in their history. That is until Moses and his people stole the component for the nuclear reactor which was placed in the Ark of the Covenant to conceal and store its dangerous properties. This was the end of the Pharaoh's great rule in the heavens. As I mentioned before, we tried to start all over with nuclear power and we lost the war in heaven once again. Had you ever heard the phrase "insanity is doing the same thing and expecting different results"?

Moses had many conversations with the Lord in the biblical scripture. How does he avoid gazing into the Lord's face as requested? That is quite simple. Whenever the Lord comes down in the thick cloud of smoke and there are thundering and lightnings, he comes out in full cosmonaut gear protecting him from radiation exposure and concealing his identity. Concealing his identity was very important because he was among the Egyptians for a time. He did not want to be known as an Egyptian, he radiated the spiritual power of death. The Lord was of the elite order of magi, which is the order of the dead.

He did not like making eye contact with individuals because of demonic presences in which he became aware of long ago. The Lord of Mt. Sinai always ate alone away from Moses so that he would be very careful not to reveal his true Egyptian identity. Much like what Moses became, the Lord of Sinai was an incarnation, a spiritual master in the order of the magi, an archangel. This why Moses was frightened of the Lord. His spiritual father looked like Darth Vader from 'Star Wars' coming out of his descended vessel.

Exodus 19:14-25 *So Moses went down from the mountain to the people and consecrated the people, and they washed their garments.* **15** *He said to the people, "Be ready for the third day; do not go near a woman."* **16** *So it came about on the third day, when it was morning, that there were thunder and lightning flashes and a thick cloud upon the mountain and a very loud trumpet sound, so that all the people who were in the camp trembled* **17** *And Moses brought the people out of the camp to meet God, and they stood at the foot of the mountain.* **18** *Now, Mount Sinai was all in smoke because the LORD descended upon it in fire; and its smoke ascended like the smoke of a furnace, and the whole mountain quaked violently.* **19** *When the sound of the trumpet grew louder and louder, Moses spoke and God answered him by voice.* **20** *The LORD came down on Mount Sinai, to the top of the mountain; and the LORD called Moses to the top of the mountain, and Moses went up.* **21** *Then the LORD spoke to Moses, "Go down, warn the people, so that they do not break through to the LORD to gaze, and many of them perish.* **22** *"Also let the priests who come near to the LORD consecrate themselves, or else the LORD will break out against them."* **23** *Moses said to the LORD, "The people cannot come up to Mount Sinai, for You warned us, saying, 'Set bounds about the mountain and consecrate it."* **24** *Then the LORD said to him, "Go down and come up again, you and Aaron with you; but do not let the priests and the people break through to come up to the LORD, or He will break forth upon them."*

Moses cleans up his people, they wash their clothes and are sanctified by Moses and he tells them *"be ready against the third day, come not at your wives."* He's essentially telling them to be clean and not to defile themselves with sexual intercourse when the Lord comes down to meet Moses and Aaron to give them the word of God. Let us remember, the Pharaohs often killed other races when the population was out of control. The Lord on Mount Sinai seemed generally concerned about the people trying to break forth to meet the Lord when he descends from the heavens in His craft. The fact of the matter is, they were terrified. Moses started telling them that if they broke the boundaries that God had given, all kinds of consequences will be upon them. That was enough to keep them at bay when the Lord descended from the sky onto his people.

You'll notice in verses Exodus 19:16-20, the very specific descriptions about the voice of the trumpet being exceedingly loud so that everyone that was in the camp were terrified. Scripture tells us that Moses brought forth the people out of the camp to meet with God and they stood at the nether part of Mount Sinai as it was completely engulfed in smoke. The Lord descended upon the mountain with fire, and the smoke ascended as if from a furnace, and the mountain was shaking terribly as the trumpet became louder and louder.

I have watched the shuttle launch many times up close. I can attest this is an accurate and true depiction of exactly what they would have seen and heard. Again, this is describing the Lord descending from the heavens in a craft or ship capable of traveling in the universe when it is not damaged. Because if it is damaged, its limits are upon the earth itself. The exceedingly loud trumpet is a giant horn announcing to the inhabitants the angel's arrival. This is mentioned many times in scripture and described as the sounding of a trumpet.

This is the beginning of the law of God upon the inhabitants of earth and the Ten Commandments. This as well is the confrontation of God and the Egyptian Pharaoh using Moses as the vessel. God tried to warn Moses and his people of the great danger and educate them on why the Egyptian Pharaoh held his people in bondage. We can tell that the Lord of Mount Sinai had great spiritual power. When Moses came down from the mountain, his face shone with a brightness, so much that people were afraid to look at him.

There were two reasons Moses appeared differently when he descended from the mountain. He had become the incarnated angel of war (Michael) and was exposed to tiny amounts of radiation. Moses was fully aware of the risks he took for his people as much as the Lord of Mt. Sinai. This gives us a sign why the Lord of Mount Sinai did not want people to look directly into his eyes or face. The spiritual power that was radiating from him was omnipotent and hard to control.

The Lord of Mt. Sinai was dying of cancer and Moses was his replacement, the changing of the guard. Evidently, Moses handled the spiritual power very well and we must ask, why is that? Baby Moses, the prince of Egypt, who landed in the hands of the Pharaoh's daughter. Baby Moses, the one who also ran into the cosmonaut, God of Abraham, Isaac, and Jacob on top of Mount Sinai. Is Moses lucky or is it predetermined destiny?

God had to use Moses to keep order amongst the people when he came down to speak to Moses and his brother. After all, if you were a common man and saw something descending from the sky, would not your first thoughts be to see what it was? This is why God had to instruct these people through Moses. They respected Moses and they would listen to him. And although they respected him, they were people of very little patience and because of that Moses would become furious.

The Golden Calf *Exodus 32:1-3 When the people saw that Moses was taking so long in coming down from the mountain, they gathered around Aaron and said, "Come, make us God who will go before us. As for this fellow Moses who brought us up out of Egypt, we don't know what has happened to him." 2 Aaron answered them, "Take off the gold earrings that your wives, your sons and your daughters are wearing, and bring them to me." 3 So all the people took off their earrings and brought them to Aaron. 4 He took what they handed him and made it into an idol cast in the shape of a calf, fashioning it with a tool. Then they said, "These are your Gods, Israel, who brought you up out of Egypt."*

The Golden Calf *Exodus 32:27-29 This is what the Lord, the God of Israel, says: "Each man straps a sword to his side. Go back and forth through the camp from one end to the other, each killing his brother and friend and neighbor." 28 The Levites did as Moses commanded, and that day about three thousand of the people died. 29 Then Moses said, "You have been set apart to the Lord today, for you were against your own sons and brothers, and he has blessed you this day."*

Moses informed of Israel's sin *Exodus 32:7-8 Then the LORD spoke to Moses, "Go down at once, for your people, whom you brought up from the land of Egypt, have corrupted themselves. 8 "They have quickly turned aside from the way which I commanded them. They have made for themselves a molten calf, and have worshiped it and have sacrificed to it and said, 'This is your God, O Israel, who brought you up from the land of Egypt."*

Notice the content of these verses in Exodus 32:28. Moses breaks the law of the Ten Commandments by asking them to take up sword and kill their brothers, those worshipping the Golden Calf. Was Moses acting on his own anger like the day when he slayed an Egyptian man or was this the incarnation of the angel of war who rose against the people? Or could it have been he was taught violence as a kid in the Egyptian order and it only came natural. If we get this whole chapter and the conversations between the Lord and Moses, not once does he mention Moses committing any sin by ordering the extermination of 3,000 men after receiving the Ten Commandments. In addition to what Moses did to his people, with great sorrow, God released a plague upon those who sinned against him and Moses. This tells us the Lord of Sinai carried a heavy hand of Moses. We can tell from these biblical accounts that I have mentioned the God of the Old Testament and Moses are very different from Jesus and John the Baptist in the New Testament.

If you read the verses carefully, in the days of Adam, God punished Adam and Eve for being deceived into sexual immorality. How can this be the same God as in the day of Jesus and Moses? This is where we can start to ask ourselves if the Holy Spirit within God started to be more merciful to the bloodline of Adam. Nowadays, those who live the spirit, are starting to fully realize the deception that took place. As tragic and painful as it is, the spirit of the Father is trying to redeem the bloodline of Adam which had fallen to oppression by the highly sophisticated Egyptians. That serpent of the old who tempted Eve to eat of the forbidden fruit had changed the relationship between God, her, and eventually, Adam. After being escorted from the Garden, she became pregnant with two boys: Cain and Abel. God had to slaughter an animal to make them clothe to cover their nakedness.

The last thing I would like to cover in the Book of Exodus is the battle of Moses against the sorcerers and high priests of the Egyptian kingdom. There are so many things in the bible that we cannot take as literal. Clearly, these are symbolisms that are associated with spiritual vision.

Let us look at when God showed Moses how to turn his staff into a serpent. We know it appeared to be a serpent, but as he picked it back up it turned back into a staff or a rod. When Moses challenged the Pharaoh with a staff, this became a battle of sorcery. This was a challenge of the Pharaoh's high priests and sorcerers to see whose God had more power.

It did involve serpents and the casting down of staff's or their rods, not quite in the literal sense as it is translated. I will recommend anyone who believes that when Moses threw his staff down, it literally became a snake, to rethink this scenario. Just as when the Pharaoh, with the serpent crown, deceived Eve, and it was translated to read in a very vague way as to who and what the deceiver is. It gives us a false impression of those times and the powers in which it speaks of. Were there snakes present and battled each other? Yes, absolutely. This was merely a challenge against the Pharaoh and his spiritual power in a manner that the Egyptians would understand.

I do not wish to spend too much time on this because clearly Jesus Christ warns us of any type of sorcery of this nature. This is why when we see Jesus Christ in the New Testament, he does come with a staff in hand casting spells upon people.

The Egyptians did not wear the crown of gold with a serpent because it looked neat, they worshiped the serpents instead. Have you ever seen a movie or TV show where someone plays a flute mesmerizing the serpent as it pops its head in and out of a basket? These are the kind of people Moses was dealing with in those ages.

I would wish to settle the meaning of oppression and ignorance before my Lord put his final judgment on earth. When you keep people in poverty, in ignorance, or let them breed to epic proportion for your own greedy causes, know that I am watching. A great injustice was done to lower forms of humans, I will pay your debt for only so long. It is time to change the way we think. You, as my people, will give the natives back their lands. In return, I will restore your place in heaven and we will start over in a righteous way while there is time here on earth. This next verse explains to us when we speak about miracles. It also will explain my righteous anger.

Lazarus' Death John 11:1-4, *Now a man named Lazarus was sick. He was from Bethany, the village of Mary and her sister Martha.* **2** *(This Mary, whose brother Lazarus now lay sick, was the same one who poured perfume on the Lord and wiped his feet with her hair.)* **3** *So the sisters sent word to Jesus, "Lord, the one you love is sick."* **4** *When he heard this, Jesus said, "This sickness will not end in death. No, it is for God's glory so that God's Son may be glorified through it".*

Jesus Raises Lazarus from the Dead John 11:38-44 *Jesus, once more deeply moved, came to the tomb. It was a cave with a stone laid across the entrance.* **39** *"Take away the stone," he said. "But, Lord," said Martha, the sister of the dead man, "by this time there is a bad odor, for he has been there four days."* **40** *Then Jesus said, "Did I not tell you that if you believe, you will see the glory of God?"* **41** *So they took away the stone. Then Jesus looked up and said, "Father, I thank you that you have heard me.* **42** *I knew that you always hear me, but I said this for the benefit of the people standing here, that they may believe that you sent me."* **43** *When he had said this, Jesus called in a loud voice, "Lazarus,* *come out!"* **44** *The dead man came out, his hands and feet wrapped with strips of linen, and a cloth around his face. Jesus said to them, "Take off the grave clothes and let him go."*

As you can see, the translation of this is very crucial. Back in the days of Jesus, there was not a good clinical system. So that I may explain to you in greater detail about this miracle, I would have to enlighten you on certain things. The first question the reader would have to ask is how Jesus knows that this is a sickness that will not end in death.

To answer the question, we would have to ask where Jesus was in the missing years. We might also ask where John the Baptist was as well, the one who helped him become aware of the spiritual realm. I can answer this question for you if you're willing to accept the answer. He went off to study different illnesses and types of medicine with John the Baptist. He was well-studied in religion with different scholars because he traveled outside of Israel. Therefore, in the Revelation of John, the prophet discussed the seven churches of Asia. John the Baptist was the forerunner and it was time for him to hand over the reins to Jesus.

We, as humans, know today if oxygen is cut off to the human brain for over four minutes you would likely die. If you do not die, every minute thereafter can leave permanent damage to the brain. Not only that, soon after death occurs, your organs start to shut down and you go into post mortem. It is spiritually, scientifically, and physically impossible for the human organs and the brain to last four days into death and the human body be restored back to life.

There's a second alternative to this story when we look at it. When Jesus tells Martha is that the sickness will not end in death. Lazarus was not actually dead, but appeared to be dead to Martha. Let me give you some definitions that I think may help you in this scenario. I do not want people to be waiting for Jesus to come down from heaven to raise corpses from the dead.

In medicine, a coma is a state of unconsciousness lasting more than six hours in which a person: cannot be awakened, fails to respond normally due to painful stimuli, light, or sound; lacks a normal sleep-wake cycle. A coma can last from several days to several weeks. The closest thing we know in modern day to describe Lazarus was a coma. Many sources, besides head injuries, can cause comas including a stroke and diabetes. The actual miracle in this, is that Lazarus was in a coma and Jesus could wake him from that coma or suspended state of animation. He did this without any physical harm to Lazarus that is mentioned in John11:43-44.

I have come to give you truth and the truth I shall give. By no means do I wish to offend any by saying a lower race of being or lower forms of life when I give you my story of time. As we can see in this incident, there has been a huge gap in technology just as in the day of Adam and the Father God.

Jesus appeared to be much more intelligent than his own people if he knew Lazarus was not dead. Did they check for pulse? Listen to his heart and check for breathing? Did he appear to have discoloration or a foul odor? How sad, they stuck an undead man in a cave to die! Jesus's family, and people were not that smart or educated. He came to try to bridge that gap and they killed him just for that reason. This will show us the degree of intelligence between the angels and the common man just by Jesus's actions. This was some special baby boy that the angels put inside of Mary. Yes, Jesus is powerful and mighty in a spiritual way. For us to think that He could give a man a new set of organs, and a new brain by a single prayer might not be so correct. Jesus is following in the way of Adam's father, science, and medicine, Amen! We know science and medicine existed for the Lord, which helped Eve have her first child.

XVIII

MASTER'S SERVANT-PROPHECY

Master's Servant

I am the master of riddles, I am the master of rhyme
I am the master of seasons, I am the master of time
Not by mouth <u>but by yours</u>, in your heart was the open door
I am the master of puzzles, I am the master of games
I am the master of life, tell me, what is my name?
Call me as you will, many names I have heard
I hear you White Eagle, son of the earth
Listen in the silence, forever I'll call
Not by mouth, <u>but by yours</u>
In your heart was the open door

The whole nature of this book is very private, yet needs to be public. I think the whole book really speaks for itself. As I said it is not about me as a soldier, it is about the heavenly spirit who has ascended back to the throne. I guess it could be described much like this. Energy travels, in that respect, I as a very simple human became a vessel for advanced energy, not by choice. It is about our mighty lord of heaven who takes all forms and resurrects the dead. It is a message of his arrival. As a shell for such a great soul of wisdom I feel mighty, yet, I know just how fragile I really am in this world. I am as fragile as those before me.

The images you are about to view were sent by myself to family members with no response given. All the events that happened between John and I were witnessed by my longtime friend that I grew up with. My friend hand delivered these emails to my family and as well sent them to his family. If there is ever enough interest in my book, I am sure my friend and many witnesses will step forth to verify these facts to those who might be asking. I have erased email addresses in the book for privacy of my family and my own email accounts. In a day and age were hacking is rampant, I do not wish to go down that road. This would make me and my family the target of every hacker on earth. These prophetic images are only a verification in the accuracy of the return of the city of god, cosmic events approaching and inevitable climate change. They are worthless other than that, except, in the fact it shows the holy spirit is all consuming and powerful. I surely was not born this way.

I could care less if people think I am or my documents are a hoax, time shall be truly revealing. Glory is not with me and my flawed flesh, or my son who is now grown and is the same. He was a pure vessel that holy spirit needed to enter the world and be sacrificed for greater good and come to aid me in my spiritual battle. In heaven, this would be called an arch angel, one who fights against demonic powers. That which is willing to die or be sacrificed for the greater good of the Christ spirit. That is very different from alien powers who rule time itself. That is my most humble analogy of the spirit. If you keep your eyes on me it is a great mistake, I only bring you greater teachings from some-place else in time.

Glory is that which lifted the weak and made them strong. The spirit lifted the bloodline of Adam to almost the level of angelic creation, in doing so the bloodline of Adam prospered in spiritual teachings. I am the father, I am the son, I am the mother, brother and sister, I am who I am says the holy spirit. It is beyond our comprehension. I apologize for such poor grammar in the hurricane Matthew image. Sometimes late-night battles with sleep cause me to write very erratic. I am pretty sure you can cipher through it. Again, I am just a man, glory now sits in heaven, once more seated on the throne in the City of God.

Hurricane Gustav, August 25 to Sept 7th of 2008

To

Aug 6, 2008
in twenty days a sign will show ...in which way the winds will blow
big and strong yes she'll be..like the breathe of god in the sea..
and to all who still may doubt ...hurricane a blowin.. way down south
aint no doubt who holds _the keys..._ its just your lord of prophecy!

-----Original Message-----
From·
To:
Sent: Thu, Aug 7, 2008 9:34 am
Subject: Fwd: *is this the proof yu need*

i think this will settle once in for all your doubts of who i am...
in twenty days please when this takes place i never wanna hear
oh that was just luck..anyone could guess that ..
the rhyme and the letter ..it is very specific were and when it will start..

South Florida prediction-image...

Oklahoma tornado outbreak- April 30th 2017

4/30/2017   Fwd: tornado out break posted 4-26-2017

From: ·   @aol.com>
To: ,@aol.com>
Subject: Fwd: tornado out break posted 4-26-2017
Date: Sun, Apr 30, 2017 3:58 pm

At least 9 dead in 4 states as tornadoes and floods wreak havoc in parts of South, Midwest

By MICHAEL EDISON HAYDENDAVID CAPLAN
JOSHUA HOYOSDOMINICK PROTO
Apr 30, 2017, 2:03 PM ET

—Original Message—
From:
To:
Sent: Wed, Apr 26, 2017 11:48 am
Subject: tornado out break posted 4-26-2017

looking for heavy storm near Oklahoma,in the next 30 days, which is may 26 2017. violent tornado, news worthy event

Midwest prediction-image

Hurricane Matthew Sept 2016-October 10th

Greetings family-is that time agAI a timeN (2)

@aim.com

To

_@ca.rr.com :   @aol.com ,   @netzero.net

@embarqmail.com and 1 more...

Jul 31, 2014

Greetings and salutations family

I am writing this letter and I will follow up with a poem of prophecy that was written some time ago. Because I am engaged in finding out who I am and the reason I walk this earth I challenge myself with visions of the future. You will notice several things have come true already but what is in bold **print** has not quite. It was odd that I look back on it today to realize how accurate it is. I give you these letters so you as my family to make decisions based on the credibility of what I've given you. I've spoke of economic collapse and though this is a very slow process we all will suffer in some way because of it and I get no satisfaction from it. I myself suffer every day and somewhere mom thoughts that I told her that this would be so. Although I never understood exactly what it entailed a back injury was surely not what I had in mind. I do stay out of trouble and have plenty of time to think and do what I do best. A soldier of God. These are three specific things I have spoken of that to me are signs from God and though things are not always not pin down to an exact date you will notice I am pretty accurate. The first thing that I spoke of is that has not happened is the large earthquake on the west coast California in specific. I've been reading about the seven Seals prophecy each seal that is broken represents certain events that will happen on this earth. I believe all seven have been broken and Earth is about to repeat itself one more time. This by no means when these events happen that you do anything other than remember it was I who gave u this knowledge. The second thing we be the large hurricane where the eye centers somewhere around Daytona Beach. And the third in final event to watch for will be the Israel, I ran, conflict which more than likely US will be involved in the order in which I predict these things is as written to California to quake, the hurricane in Daytona, Israel Iran conflict. Everything that comes up when studying keeps telling me that a very large earthquake is going to occur soon my guess would be between August and December of this year. The rest will happen within the next three years. You must understand I do this to judge my accuracy and thought as well as any deception that might be coming my way. This will be a good indication to me that I have an advanced warning system in place. If none of these things occur it will actually be a relief to me because sometimes I do not understand what somebody is trying to tell me except that were headed for trouble! Is time short, is time not short, Will stars fall from the sky, or will we live to see another day. There is no doubt there is a flaw in biblical prophecy and that flaw is it's too generic, it gives no indication of what time these events take place. The one thing I am sure of is biblically Satan is bound on the chain by Michael the Archangel but that will not be for long been he will have unimpeded reign on earth without God being present.   That will be a bad day for sure!

Letter to family-image

Mexican mafia April 7ᵗʰ 2008

------Original Message------
From:
To:
Sent: Thu, Dec 24, 2015 3:38 pm
Subject: Fw: mexican mafia :)dated april 7th 2008

I found it. I hope you all have a Merry Christmas. God bless you!

blood is thicker than oil and money
or big ass lies that taste like honey
yachts and ships , diamonds and pearls
it talks so sweet ..to the fancy girls

blood is thicker than oil and money
or crack that kills all the junkies
*the caine that blows through columbias green
is gearing up like a war machine
Texas syndicate gonna claim its turf
mexican mafia gonna put the hurt*
as are money takes the fall
they will build the border walls
just a prophet of the pen
but god is mighty who lives within
the bombs of isreal will drop again
Obama takes the big win!!!!☺

peace my friends i know im an ass sometimes
but do you remeber that song by the who... i can see for miles and miles and miles

Obama wins presidency -image

On **August 25, 2008, <u>Hurricane Gustav</u>** formed in the Caribbean with storm bands extending all the way into the **Florida Keys**. Gustav was the second most destructive hurricane of the **<u>2008 Atlantic hurricane season</u>.** The poem accompanied with the prediction is very revealing since I live in the central Florida area.

On September 9, 2011, <u>Typhoon Roke</u> emerged and eventually turned it turned into a Category 4 system, Roke moved through the Philippines, over Okinawa and on into mainland Japan. There is just no way for a human to be this accurate without spiritual aid. These storms were accurately predicted almost 30 days in advance. I could not introduce the hurricane Roke image on the account it did meet the quality requirements of the publisher. This is one of many hurricanes I predicted in Asia, as well as the Caribbean, with extreme accuracy.

Neither storm was on radar at the time of the emails. The **East Texas Oklahoma tornado outbreak** was predicted 4 days before the tornado outbreak, weather patterns remerged 22 days later. These are very random events the spirit is forecasting with great accuracy. Random events that usually bring death. It is not a very comfortable feeling when you realize you have become the prophet of doom. It makes you very unpopular with family and friends.

May 17ᵗʰ headlines

At Least 2 Dead, Dozens Injured After Possible Tornadoes Hit Wisconsin, Oklahoma By Ada Carr and Pam Wright May 17 2017 07:15 AM EDT weather.com

Matthew was a Category 4 hurricane that grazed Florida coast almost making direct fall in **Daytona Beach Florida in 2016**. My family and I escaped severe damage 50 miles inland from the Florida's coast. I sent a letter almost three years in advance to family and friends on this hurricane in the Daytona area. This could not be just a lucky guess; it was a very rare Cat 5 storm that kissed Florida on the cheek, a strong warning of what was to come in the beautiful sunshine state. Previously my family thought I was tracking weather patterns like a meteorologist because of my accuracy. I had to point out that the previous hurricanes I predicted were 30 days prior. Not even the Doppler radar can be that accurate, the storms did not exist. I believe the tracking of Mathew almost 2.5 years in advance constitutes prophecy and spiritual accuracy. I gave them the proof they needed that many things come <u>spiritually</u> to us from another place and time. The spirit would tell you it is not the only spirit here on a mission. It no longer is a one-man show. When the spirit of Christ died he gave power to the seven angels to make them teachers of men. The spirit has multiplied, divided, and increased itself.

The hurricane near Daytona was one of three major signs given to me by the Holy Spirit announcing the rise of the anti-Christ spirit and the dragon. Prophets have never been treated well, nor Jesus Christ when coming to this earth. I am establishing accuracy for my family's protection and trust in my words. It is a very complicated matter, especially when they are living in Florida and on the San Andrea's fault line. As I see world events growing worse, it is highly disturbing.

The three events I mentioned to my family in the emails are listed as is below in their written order. <u>Much to my surprise the third event has not taken place,</u> gauging by accuracy on previous events. The atmosphere is very ripe for the third and final event to take place and fulfill this complete prediction. It is really in the best interest for the reader to hear the wisdom than put any focus on me as the author. Your glory is coming from heaven, not from any man on this earth alone that is for sure. By this you will know redemption is found through prayer and meditation in the Christ spirit, it not something I as man can give anyone or anyone else can give in this world. It is a constant walk in spirit.

1. Major earthquake in California:
   Northern California's Napa Valley Rocked By Strongest Earthquake in 25 Years **August 24, 2014** (40 days in advance, right on the money as far as my August and September prediction.

2. Large hurricane near Daytona Beach:
   Hurricane Matthew (2 years 3 months in advance, rare cat 5) **Sept 28 to Oct 9, 2016.**

3. Israel having conflict with Iran (incomplete, this is an event that could happen at any time)

We can see the first two of these three events happened already. The accuracy on Gustav as well as the tornadoes in east Texas should give some validation to the spirits accuracy. I as well prophesized hurricane Irma with great accuracy. On 8/23 I sent emails out calling for a category 4 in 20 days. Irma devastated the Caribbean islands and parts of Florida. I have several witnesses to verify that including my editor who I have no personal relationship with what so ever. I provided his email address in acknowledgements page. He personally received many of these emails with the addresses unconcealed to verify their authenticity. My family has not mentioned him, he must be convinced of their authenticity.

Prophecy is a tricky game, I do not base my life on it and only use it as a road map to help determine accuracy of important future events of humans. You really do not need a prophet to tell you we have great conflict in the middle east region and it could erupt at any time. It is more about trusting in all the words I have spoken about the city of god. As I have said to my friends and family, I am here to teach and enlighten or it is a very elaborate deception of my soul. I say that so humbly. I live day to day.

I can say this proudly and with great honesty, rarely have been wrong. Have I been wrong? Not really, I had some hiccups in the beginning. When you try to force prophecy by family emotion or self-emotion it never works. It should flow like butter from the hand to the paper so there is no mistaking who and what is the source. When I have approached it that way, I have never been wrong. I approach song writing or poems in the same way.

I really do not like to prove myself, it is very stressful on my soul. It is not something I really have any control over. Something is proving itself to me about being strong in my words and having faith in its message and very high rate of accuracy in events.

On the account Israel is the epicenter of biblical scripture, we must make sure they are never deceived by lies and false promises that have no merit in Gods kingdom. Israelis wanted a great military leader 2,000 years ago and they received him and rejected him. War is not always the answer when you're surrounded by hostile forces, that's is why Jesus laid his life down.

It was later after Michael the archangel and Christ had victory, where Britain, France, and America were formed. They gave Israel their great victory by supplying their people with advanced weapons and technologies. As well by great strategy from Israel's defense forces. This is one of the reasons radical Muslims do not like Americans, French, and Brits. This is the united alliance I spoke of in the sixth trumpet, a host of nations fighting under the colors of red white and blue. This was an act and gesture on behalf of the father and son of heaven who watched Israel suffer greatly. This was played out in a spiritual fashion and physical fashion in the resurrection. This shows us we must always be patient in God's word.

I will always be honest with you. All that I have is my word. Again, could I doctor and make this all up? Sure! I have saved several witnesses who are of credible stature. This is not about show boating or I am better than, it is about establishing trust with my people.

When we speak of Moses, hard time on this earth is for the crimes of murder. Moses was a very violent man and a lover of the ladies. A great soldier who the spirit used many times to fulfill prophecy and conquer. Undefeated in battle, he is an elite archangel of heaven.

Redemption is found through the Christ or Holy Spirit which descended upon man. Through time he redeems himself in a spiritual fashion. When there is countless blood on your hands as a high-ranking soldier, demonic battles become very heavy. This is why we have so many soldiers committing suicide after coming home from war.

That makes the spirit that was within Moses a great teacher of spiritual and physical prisons. The story of Paul, one of the great disciples, is similar in nature when we talk of finding redemption for violent actions.

A political address:

Mr. Obama, [during his term] President of the United States of America. It would be my rule usually never to engage with politicians for safety reasons, however, there is a time to break protocol even it costs me in the end. I have watched your speeches on climate change and gun control with great interest. I am a spiritual soldier and know very little of politics. This is a vision I wanted to share with you because your name is present in a prophecy and vision written April 7, 2008, which makes it very significant. It seems to have great meaning concerning events to follow your presidency.

I am honored and proud to call you the first African American President of the United States. I think you handled yourself in a way that should not be forgotten. Particularly in the way you held yourself as our leader under constant assault and your emotion and empathy for the people. Like long ago, many did not want leadership to exist that brings people together of different races, religion, and stature, so they simply block or opposed at every turn, spitefully.

It is sad when we still hate because of color of skin. Surely this much hate can't be all about policy. We have many failed policies in our short history as Americans. For someone to call Mrs. Obama, our first lady a gorilla in high heels, it is a sad day in politics. I deeply apologize for such ignorance. You have a very lovely wife and wonderful children!

I am not interested in the economics or the policies of your presidency, nor I am I hear to speak about health care or war. I am here to talk about scandal and honesty. No man or president has ever been perfect in politics. However, I believe in your character and integrity as a leader of humans. When the Holy Spirit chose me to be its voice long ago, it did not put terms or limits to my expression. Therefore, in my remaining days, your terms will always be_an expression of my voice. It is because your ideologies are much more equal to those in the city of God regarding violence issues, environment, and uniting humanity. Sometimes the <u>Dogs of War</u> must be set loose with great reason. I am very concerned on how ugly and divisive politics have become for the planet.

I have never asked any man or women for an autograph in times known existence. As crazy as it seems, it is your autograph I would like to have on my book and with a greater purpose in mind than my ego. To have it would mean a great deal to me. I believe it is one of the greatest historical accomplishments this earth has seen, no matter how people think you did as our commander and chief. Sometimes we are chosen by our roots to be a voice for the people. One thing you and I share are very old and deep roots. I know you love to read, so I hope a copy will make it to your desk one day or somehow when you leave office. I hope you will then reach out to me through my publisher. You are a voice of hope in my mind that is for sure. I believe history will claim you as a champion of civil rights. You don't need to be the president to be the champion of the people. You just need keep on caring and never give up. It no longer becomes just about politics. These sufferings soon become very personal. Know that heaven is watching closely and speaking on your behalf today.

As a spokesperson for heaven, you Mr. Barack Obama, and your wife have made into the hearts of many with a great message of peace, hope, and love. I like that much more than hate and division. There are many trying to kill that message and the dream upon. It is not the end; it is only the beginning. Please never silence your voice in the affairs of our earth. This is no longer just about Israel, for many humans have been violated who believe in Jesus Christ and Moses of long ago. I can never be a politician or shake your hand, however, your wisdom is something that heaven, as well as I, wish you to always extend to the masses on behalf of Jesus Christ and his holy spirit. It is important that the city of God has a person of political influence who might understand the message I am sending.

Our future depends on how we act this day forward as humans. I have a great spiritual war going on inside myself, I only wish to try to finish it with a little dignity and peace. Nobody wants a part of my suffering I assure you of that. I spend much time trying to master emotions and addictions. When you have a serious injury, these forces have more time to attack you over and over mentally, and thus, breaking you down. I feel so much compassion for the injured and those born with health issues. Many are a great inspiration to me when I feel like I'm on the pity pot and sometimes do not wish to go on. Someone wiser in law and ethics must be the voice of the people. <u>I am a solo act, a soldier of fortune</u>. I am and *will always be your pit-bull from heaven. I may not be a perfect person; however, I don't play when it comes to snuffing out that which has harmed my people and my son. This is something that is spiritual in nature. It's very ugly, and dirty business, I am lucky to be alive.*

In the end of the bible it says, "It has come time to destroy those who destroy the earth". The spirit is here to see that law is fulfilled, physically and spiritually, so says the Holy Spirit of our slaughtered king. The honor has been all mine to speak on behalf of a president who served with so very little scandal. See you at the cross roads, Mr. President.

I have never thought much of our neighbors in Canada, they are so quiet with very little drama. It is probably because I am so self-absorbed in my message for America. It was quite an honor to hear Justin Trudeau express his view on refugees and immigrants seeking safety from barbaric nations. I as well heard him say we have shed blood together for freedom and it will always be. I believe in Canada they are also very concerned about a clean stable environment just as many in America are. I acknowledge Justin Trudeau's words and actions, the actions of other nations, as well as those democrats and republicans who strongly and immediately denounced some pretty hateful actions against those who are in desperate need of help. Many who are also wise from various places on this globe acknowledge our weather patterns are changing drastically. I don't need to name everyone, you know in your heart I am addressing you.

I must take a moment to honor are American hero, John McCain. A man who after having his brain cancer removed, with very little recovery time, saw it in his heart to make a stand against what he saw as a flawed health care bill for the people. Under great duress he made a declaration for congress to come together for the people and to put all this political non-sense aside. God as my witness, the spirt in me was highly moved and leaped with joy. That is what God is looking for here on this earth. Just so everyone knows, God sees all, he hates phonies and fakes. Mr. McCain is the real deal. He knows what it's like to suffer and from that suffering I believe comes greater wisdom.

If all the Holy Spirit has spoken is true, we will one day not need nuclear energy being it is a very dangerous science. So, the many things we fight and have fears over will soon be eliminated in the return of our ancestors who live in the city of God. The timeline truly depends on us. Mr. Obama was very correct in what he said, there does come a day when it's too late and we have almost reached that day.

For those that confess the Holy Spirit and believe in the message, it's never too late. Heaven will give us great wisdom to rule over this earth eternally. As I have said it will take many women and men of great knowledge to change our course. No, not for money or for fame, for the sake of forever. Who wants to live in a barren waste land with no trees, poisoned streams and oceans? Not me or our beautiful children that's for sure.

These are the science's that caused our fall from grace many times. It's a repeating story with repeated offenses and consequences. These sciences are highly dangerous in a volatile world which soon is approaching. I have been down this road before. I am not a fan of the oil industry at all. For decades, it had it reasons. Now it has become the object of greed, pollution, and invasion of sovereign borders. This is old school technology; heaven is bringing the new. I am the only one who can fix it, so says the holy spirit of God. When you said these words as a politician you should be ready to answer to that statement. That is essentially putting yourself on a throne equal to Christ. I have yet to see that type of power an authority from any man on earth. <u>We on earth with Christ in our heart can fix it together.</u>

To me it is not a democrat or republican issue, left or right. There are too many good people on both sides. Somehow, we must end a divided country. I am a humanitarian who loves animals and a pristine environment. I will ask mercy for expressing my voice under a new administration. I am a man of low stature on this earth, when I return to heaven all that will change. I truly wish what is best for the people of earth, please know that. Surely, I would not like to be tortured or murdered for any information I may hold as men were long ago who had great wisdom. I have given all in my request for asylum in my return to North America. Like the film, *Hunt for Red October*, the holy spirit of the father and of the son, will soon surrender heavens great vessel and its technology. The City of God will be given to the people of the earth. This is the great promise of your king and lord. It will be your escape in very desperate times. The bibles description of hell is not even going to be close to mine. When the earth heats up as in the first and second judgment upon man, we will lose technology and the earth will be plunged into chaos. People will be scorched alive as it mentions in the bible. That is not to even mention spiritual hell or prisons.

Revelation 16:5 *You are just in these judgments, O Holy One, you who are and who were;* **6** *for they have shed the blood of your holy people and your prophets, and you have* *given them blood to drink as they deserve."* **7** *And I heard the altar respond:* <u>*"Yes, Lord*</u> <u>*God Almighty, true and just are your judgments."*</u> **8** *The fourth angel poured out his bowl* *on the sun, and the sun was allowed to scorch people with fire.* **9** *They were seared by the* *intense heat and they cursed the name of God, who had control over these plagues,* <u>*but they*</u> <u>*refused to repent and glorify him.*</u>

Heaven does not believe in approaching unannounced or unwelcomed. This is the nature of this very detailed book, protocol. Because Christ is love, those who occupy the city know they have a very high obligation to teach men and women who wish to leave this earth spiritually and physically. Never again will this ship and its great city mine planets, extract oil or harvest workers. It now has a greater purpose. I think soon people will start realizing the wisest of souls are men who have fallen and sworn their allegiance to heaven to find redemption within the Holy Spirit. "This is what I call GOD". A revolving wheel of souls that descend from heavens great city to evolve souls here on earth. It certainly is an honor and a pleasure to find redemption in my actions and come to you as a humble servant. What joy it is to know even those with a troubled past can become great warriors and teachers in the kingdom of highest.

Exxon Mobil Corp's pipeline in Montana ruptured

In 2011 a pipeline in Montana ruptured underneath the river. When all was said and done, 1,000 barrels of crude oil spilled into these pristine rivers costing the company about $135 million to clean up. There always are lasting impacts of these spills. *The Standing Rock tribes* protested in North Dakota over the pipeline that was to be built on sacred land has caught my attention. What a great victory for my Native American brothers! Do not give up! God bless those in power who heard their voice and shut it down.

We cannot continue this path of oil polluting our oceans and water ways. Have we not disrespected the Native American Indian enough? Would you like the army of Christ to conquer America and stick those who he thought were barbarians or dishonest on reservations or something even worse? I like the Indians just how they were long ago. Caretakers of the land who walked gently upon it. Many don't care about people unless money is being made or there is something to take. Those days will soon be a thing of the past. All they ask is to please do not build a pipeline through their sacred land.

We are playing a very dangerous game as time approaches with our rejection of climate issues. You surely will get all the warnings you need to see that the spirit is highly accurate in forecasting future events, please do not ignore them.

When President Obama was in tears talking about little children being mowed down in the streets by gun violence, people called him not sincere and a fraud. Why do people make fun of others who show emotion in tragedy? Many claimed he was planning to take America's 2nd amendment rights to have guns so that he could take control and hand America over to Muslims law. This is one of oldest tricks in the book: fear and paranoia. Please, what a joke. I never carry a fire arm. The fear of using a gun wrongly or in the wrong situation and facing life in prison is not even an option. I would rather die and meet you in heaven.

This is what is going to happen as guns continue to flood the streets. More life sentences, more killing, more dead children, police, and innocent civilians. We are not going to be carrying guns into the Holy City of the highest. We are not going to be saying *drill baby drill*. It would be wise when we see these unidentified vessels in heaven arriving that we soon come to an understanding about fire arms. Nobody will enter the City of God without the purest intentions, trust me on that.

I have forewarned all, you know not who or what you are dealing with. I raised my flag in surrender to heavens spiritual forces long ago, be wise inhabitants of earth, be wise. The spiritual realms of punishment are not something any man or women wants to face. Flat out, it is brutal. I speak from experience and not out of any judgment.

My president has asked in a very humble way for change. When the Lord's heavenly army arrives, they will not be as understanding as now former President Obama, you can be assured of that. If I were to show you the many pictures of dying animals in oil related spills it would wrench your heart. If it is heart wrenching too many of us, imagine how bad it hurts to those who had a hand in all creation. It makes me sad and angry all in the same breath.

Many must pay for these crimes, weather by change, repair and restoration or spiritual prisons that I assure will shake souls for countless ages. The consequences are played over and over in the countless ages you spend in your spiritual prison. It's no different than death row. This is where you meet the angel of death.

Many things had bonded us. The one thing that will bring us closer together as humans is the destruction of evil and putting an end to corruption. It is then we will return to the stars as rightful rulers of heaven.

Antichrists in this world can chose to be or choose not to be. When we see little children being killed by chemical weapons, choices become very hard because of very corrupt governments. I am not equipped to make such choices for humans in war, another reason I come in such a low position. With a federal investigation looming in the White House we do not understand all the consequences of this crazy season in politics just yet. It is fair to say that most people in politics have respect for General Mad Dog Mattis. We must feel secure with that choice no matter what happens politically in this scandalous season of politics. We need to feel protected by someone who is well respected. I hope our awesome power is always used for greater good since we seem to have had a series of failed wars. With all due respect, my physical father being a military man and in the defense industry, I salute my general, James "Mad Dog" Mattis, and the brave women and men of our armed services. My heart is always with you and I am thankful for my physical freedom at the loss of life.

I am not a man of bombs and guns, I am a man of souls. The power of the Lord is in how he deals with souls, the "risen dead". A prince of peace for all to see and hear. When it cannot be achieved, the destroyer of souls is set free. That comes in many forms. As I said in the early chapters, when peace cannot be made with blood thirsty rulers, I am then thankful for men like my physical father as well as the spiritual father who serve our military. The cost of war and death always has its price.

The antichrist spirit is the spirit of racism, hate, arrogance, and pride. I have shown you this with countless scripture of the plight of Jews under massive empires controlled by fallen angels. Since we conquered America, we have stopped immigrants Jews from coming in during war time, mistreated and put Indians on reservations, enslaved and beat the hell out of Africans. We now plan to deport major amounts of Mexican immigrants as well as deny refugees of the Middle East. In that respect, we are not talking a single man, this has happened through time. Even President Obama and his administration were guilty of deportation, however, I never felt it was with great malice. These are the problems we must solve together with Christianity in mind. There does need to be great attention to our borders, who's coming and going. Especially in arrival of the City of God.

This puts us in the category of a beast in the bible, as well by our currency. You cannot buy or sell without the number of the beast. Immigrants who do not have green cards or a social security card and state ID are subjected to deportation and imprisonment. They cannot buy or sell here in America without the number of the beast. That is the case in many countries nowadays and the reason the number of the beast expires with the roman empire, it is a spiritual law that cannot be fulfilled anymore by man and women. The ability to live off the land has been stripped from us in many places because of population. Desperate times will bring desperate measures. Over population has caused us to become a system of numbers rather than human beings.

By America being a great superpower of earth, it makes us the whole statue in the dream of Nebuchadnezzar. We are a portion of each super power in some way, yet, mightier than all previous beasts combined. Yes, safety for America and Americans is vital, with that said the great beast has it reason. I have lived a somewhat safe existence for many years with some ugly roads in between.

When humans breed at epic proportions like many did in the days of ancient empires we find in history they had population thinning. When the labor force or prisoners became too large in number, they slaughtered infants and children. They created settlements and prisons or sent people off to war as disposable heroes. It has been since time began and God warned many about sexual promiscuity and sexuality, among other reasons. It was not to be some ruthless dictator. I forewarn you again for the sake of your children and their children, change is coming.

These brutal actions I mentioned throughout this book are the types of behavior's that made Hitler, Nero, king Nebuchadnezzar and the pharaohs of Egypt anti-Christ's rise. Do they do it by choice or out of an ignorance? Is it out of an alliance with an evil so great they cannot stop their own actions and lies? Are they bought and sold on the day they were born like an Indian or African slave? <u>Bought and sold to the alliance of 666</u> and the greed of power and money. Just like Caesar Nero, the brutal blood thirsty roman dictator. When we see this number in any form coming up in political power, it is a great sign of caution. This is the work of the anti-Christ infiltrating the world to unsuspecting victims. Nero did not know he was an antichrist of scripture, we have only discovered that in modern day.

I do not believe you can love Christ's people, the environment and money all in the same breath. It just does not work that way. I only try to bring attention to these very clear and specific visions. I am the man who will keep it real. Money, power, and politics are a brutal game. I was a big fan of Mr. Trump's show *The apprentice* and his very lovely family. My family loves the *Trump's*. Being they are a Christian family, I hope they are aware of greater deceptions that may stray paths in the modern era.

We must take a moment to ponder why many see Mr. Trump as an anti-Christ figure in online propaganda. The masses treated Barack Obama in the very same way. When we see *Caesars palace* and New York's, fifth avenue 666 building, we must go back to revelation to consider if there could be spiritual or physical relation and meaning. How do these very luxurious properties even end up being hand in hand in the same family, like fate? 666, is widely known among biblical scholars and students to refer to Cesar Nero. I imagine some of the accusation could be based on mass deportations and the blocking of immigrants coming into the country. It probably does not help when your being investigated by a FBI special prosecutor for ties to a foreign country. Accidental or deliberate, by luck or chance, metaphysical or physical, these two buildings seem to be tribute to the rise of an emperor. Biblically, very little is spoke about the final beast and anti-Christ who tries to re-emerge and challenge Christ and his people. <u>Christ and his people, put an end to the spiritual reign of the dragon and his great beast.</u>

I want to thank president Trump and his family for committing to donate a million dollars to the hurricane Harvey disaster. This was a very kind gesture to those who are suffering. If one wants to be in the graces of heaven, this is how they should act when the world is in great calamity or very tuff times. Leaders need to have a little more compassion for their sick and poor. After all, in this twilight zone, sometimes you come back into this life in a different way. If you hated African American's, or suppressed them, you make come back as that which is suppressed or hated by many nations. Poor as that which eats dirt, plagued by mental health and injuries. Let me tell you from firsthand experience, you do not want that, it is pretty rough experience to have great wealth and be reduced in the next life. Especially, when God makes you painfully aware of it. Even so, come lord Jesus! This is how Jesus will act in our days of great turmoil. Because Jesus has so much to give, it is never a burden for the spirit to come share material wealth to those suffering. It is much harder to come to the earth and feed the world a message of love.

There are many secrets to be revealed when study Americas past. Yes, we are a great country, strong, master builders much like the Egyptians. I imagine that's why we have the Washington monument and the pyramid on the dollar bill, tributes to their great society and knowledge. Just as satanic bloodlines entered Egypt, they have entered into our country. With that said, so has the bloodline of the messiah. We know this because brutal slavery came to the United States just as it did to the Egyptian empire long ago. As well, I am very much alive, here to deliver this immense tale of men from long ago. Man went out and conquered lower races of men and women who had evolved very little in technology. They loaded their great ships, sailing off to the new world. The conquerors of men left many on islands to fend for themselves, pro-creating more slaves. That was only after they raped their women, leaving their evil seed in the belly of their womb's. Eventually, they would come back to retrieve them when the harvest was ripe.

If time is playing out a scenario in smaller scale of our offenses, it has repeated itself over and over, much like in time and space itself. Now are wings have been snipped, leaving us nowhere to migrate in time of distress. When you look at great kings or pharaohs of long ago, then picture an early Hebrew, native African or American, the level of evolution is not even close. We have discussed this in depth? This always brings us to the law that will be <u>enforced by heaven with fierceness</u>, human trafficking or grinding humans into forced labor by corrupt economics.

When we see all the hatred rise up around the solar eclipse that just passed over America, it is the final signs of the anti-Christ spirit trying to re-emerge. It's very astrological and time based, just as the seasons of the dragon. We do not have to buy into this deception that is plaguing our country and our world. We must also understand that when we see 666, or signs of an emperor like figure approaching in the political arena, the great temptation of Israel is also near.

As we see all the people gather to help out in the recent hurricane tragedies, what love is becoming is so much more apparent. Politics and religion, everything flies out the window when we see great suffering, for some at least. Let me say it now, I am so proud to be your fellow American during such times. What bravery and kindness from American rescue forces and every day citizens of the USA. Even those who wished to send a message of love from Mexico came and stood with us. I thank you. Heaven, surely thanks you for you sacrifice. This is what it's all about my friends. We should not always have to see tragedy to show this kind of love, for love is an infectious disease. To help others is a feeling that lasts so much longer than having fancy things. We cannot base this love on religion, race or economics. We are not divided, we are becoming united.

This is what it will take when the earth starts changing. A united force to save humans and animal life from great suffering. The almighty, he chooses us for this task, for we are well equipped emotionally and physically. We have proven ourselves so worthy of the task. <u>We are very unique in this aspect</u>, our great medical knowledge of earths vast species.

In the film, *The day the Earth stood still*, the main concept of the movie is that love can change our course. We do not have to go through the depths of hell to see heaven. Kindness and compassion will change our fate forever. Those that go against the grain and remain greedy little pigs, I can only pray that soon your eyes will be unsewn. Some times in this twilight zone you get more than you bargain for on the other side of time and space.

How long I have waited for the approaching day of heavens army cannot be fathomed. Heaven is standing by and watching every moment with great anticipation. It's never too late to love and forget how to hate. If the Israel, Iran prediction never comes into play, in this case I will be honored to have been wrong. When I see a large sale of weapons go to Saudi Arabia, I often wonder if this confrontation can be avoided. When we see a federal investigation into corrupt politicians, KKK neo Nazi behavior and Muslim caliphates, we soon know it will be choosing time.

When we see the heavenly warrior capture the beast it is a figurative. It is representative of God or the holy spirit taking back what is rightfully those in the heavens. It is by the love of the people, not their hate or their wars, that finally captures the beast and changes the fate of all nations. When we see thousands protesting racial hate, I know my job is near finished and I can I return back to my home that I miss very much. The victory is yours just as much as mine! You stood the test of time while I engaged very powerful demons to change our course. This is why the return of prophets and the messiah is so very rare, it's a heavy burden and task. Of course, the battle is not over, however, biblical prophecy declares the father and son will have their final victory. I will ask for your prayers and strength to strike the final blow to my spiritual adversaries.

The Heavenly Warrior Defeats the Beast <u>19</u> *Then I saw the beast {the rising anti-Christ} and the kings of the earth and their armies gathered together to wage war against the rider on the horse and his army.* <u>20</u> <u>*But the beast was captured, and with it the false*</u> <u>*prophet who had performed the signs on its behalf.*</u> *With these signs he had deluded those who had received the mark of the beast and worshiped its image. {money, currency, wealth, military power} The two of them were thrown alive into the fiery lake of burning sulfur.* <u>21</u> *The rest were killed with* <u>*the sword coming out of the mouth of the rider on the horse*</u> *{the word of God}, and all the birds gorged themselves on their flesh.*

There is no reason for me to talk down or hate. I advise many of the consequences of being disgustingly rich or just trying to be as in the days of the pharaohs. When the pharaoh lost his son to a strange plague in the kingdom of Egypt it made his heart very hard towards Moses and God. Why didn't the pharaoh just listen to Moses and let the people go or treat them with more respect or even step-down from the throne? What did the pharaoh's son do to deserve death? Probably nothing, for he was only a small child, the son of a monster who glorified women and treasures. Many died in the quest for the pharaoh's riches and deceptions.

Let us remember the pharaoh was almost like a father to Moses until the pharaoh found out he was different. He came from a bloodline of poverty, yet, he wore the crown of pharaohs. The pharaoh would soon realize, as well, the whole Egyptian dynasty, Moses was a man not to be taken lightly with his wisdom and powerful words. His father-figure racist ways boiled up in him. He could not accept the fact that his daughter had deceived the pharaoh into giving Moses, her spiritual son, the crown. A child of a Hebrew woman, the kind in which the pharaohs had ordered to be exterminated many times by throwing them to crocs in Nile. Excuse my forwardness, it is would have been like having an African American being the crowned prince of England. To say the least, it did not sit well with the pharaoh and his people. It made the pharaoh and his older son do something very foolish. This later cost them more than they could ever pay. A very long sentence in this time prison.

This made Moses sad for the pharaoh and his sons. Moses loved the sons. They were his brothers for a long time. He ate and drank of the same poisons that that his own family indulged in. This is a very significant tale in biblical scripture. It is also why I chose to give you a greater understanding of the verses.

Evil is no joke, it doesn't ask, it takes. It is a vicious poison that never stops.

Money and riches is not everything, my friends. It will be much less worthless when the City of God descends upon man. Even I have sipped from the cup of evils deception. That is why I must ask the question if the pharaoh and his prince were bought and sold to the number 666 when they were born. The pharaoh looked for every excuse to deny the reality in what Moses was telling him. The many privileged came from the bloodline of fallen angels who consumed all the lands with their beauty, knowledge, and corruption. Their love of money and neglect of other people's sorrows were quite concerning. Higher powers crushed their kingdom and everything in it, very swiftly. Let the ancient Egyptian empire be an example of hands even greater than Moses and his spiritual fathers, it is called time. You do not mess with "time" and its people without severe consequences, which is the power of death. Never does it cease to exist and it must be mastered for own corrections. This is the door that Jesus opened that no man can shut.

I believe in getting my people involved. In the following pages, there are many sets of clues to specific events. I believe I know what each means and a general time line. You really have to look at history, word clues, as well as dual meanings and underlined phrases. As time approaches, we all will enjoy this book's meanings and its teachings. I will post my deciphering of it in *Volume II, Master of Time.* For those that like puzzles and clues, much more is to come in the years ahead. Much like Nostradamus, this is the style I have adopted, poetic form. Poems that have deep meanings hidden within. I will tell you, I come as a servant and pay a heavy price. The order of magi has existed for many ages. One day we shall all have talents such as psychic and visions as many do but they abuse these powers where in some cases, for their own benefits.

As I mentioned, it is the age of prodigies.

Epilogue

The vision of the 8th Seal As I stood at the throne and watched the king receive his crown, the lamb with great sorrow took the final seal from the mighty being's hands. The mighty deity smiled upon his lamb who was slain from the foundation of the world to redeem all mankind. With a mighty voice the angel he roared <u>"People who live in glass houses shouldn't throw stones."</u> In an instant, they transformed in spirit. A white horse and a dark horse came forth upon plains of the earth. The rider of the white horse's eyes began to blaze like fire as he revealed the name written upon him which no man knows but only himself. The rider of the horse called "hades" called out to the demons of the abyss, hurt not the children with the seal upon their head.

The armies of the world began to march under one banner to destroy the wicked ones. Their speed was that of eagles descending upon their prey and the power of their army was that of a great thunder as they marched upon the earth. The rider of the dark horse dismounted amidst the chaos which reigned. The rider had in his hand an hour glass, saying "worship the lamb who was slaughtered, for the hour is late. Let us give glory to his name and peace to the brethren of this world."

The rider opened the sky and its contents revealing them to the kings of the earth. He showed them a vision of their future, those who oppose or did not believe the message of the slaughtered lamb, they chose war and hatred instead. They became stubborn in the eyes of the one who seated the lamb on the throne.

The rider gazed into the heavens as he held in his hand a crystal ball, he revealed many things in heaven to the kings of the earth in a great gesture of peace. As some of the kings of the east stood defiant, a ghost came forth from the dark horse breathe and the earth shook for the multitudes. As the armies of the east became enraged at the foundation the Christ spirit had laid, they prepared to march against his people. The rider showed them another vision in heaven. A mighty angel appeared with great golden wings in the sky and stepped forth with a stone in his hand, hurling it from the sky toward the earth. A great furnace erupted, the mountains started to shake and a great hole opened in the earth were the stone came from the sky. The sea blazed with fire, as the power of the dragon started consuming itself.

All the world watched in amazement at the power of the one who sat on upon the dark horse, whose voice was one with the great creature who had hurled the stone. As the creature *in heaven prepared to hurl another stone, the rider on the white horse called "faithful and true," noticed the fire in his eyes began to dissipate. "He said wait!" And the inhabitants fell and gave glory and said "save us from the hour at hand and the rider who sits on the dark horse. We give glory to the one seated on the throne." And a new day began for all mankind, and a silence of peace followed in heaven. The mighty being said to me seal up these books, there shall be no more. It is finished, I am the alpha omega the begging in the end. He said, "Take these keys to death and hades and release them into the lake of fire. Now we shall reign forever."*

There is always an easy way and a hard way. We control how much force heaven will use, if any, in the days to come. No matter any nations majority religious faith, threatening peaceful nations and peaceful people will bring terrible karma to nations that choose to act like bullies. Causing asteroid impacts or just allowing them to happen can be devastating to the earth. It would be the weapon of choice in heaven, it is nontoxic. We are under protection by the heavens at this very moment. The near asteroid approaches should be a great warning. As well, Russia getting hit by a meteorite in 2013, the Chelyabinsk meteor. It is a sign of the times. I cast down my golden crown of the serpent long ago to serve the holy spirit of Christ. Now, it is you who have the story of the father and son and servants to the highest order. I walked the earth many ages for the son of God who is loved by all creatures in heaven. The greatest of sinners can become the greatest of saints. I plead with the earth to hear this message as well as the consequences of not hearing this message. Don't keep your eyes on me, look up to the stars. Amen.

Today, I'm not what I use to be. I am the common man telling the story of time and the power of heaven. I have been dethroned by the fall. I'm honored I was used as a vessel and a soldier in the war of ages upon earth. All wisdom and honor belongs to the one whose spirit was slaughtered as a young man and he never got to live life to its fullest at my expense. His spirit now sits upon the throne in the City of God. The time of your king approaches and there is not one thing this world can do to stop it. He has been handed great authority at victory over death. I have taken his place spiritually. This is so this message might be received and preserved, that was his mercy at my expense. Because I hold sensitive and crucial information he gave up his life to save yours, twice.

This kind of information can be crippling if it comes too fast for the human mind. Steps were taken to ensure the safety of our chosen son, a spiritual transition. Because I have told you both the son and the father come from the Egyptian dynasty, you will know that men and women chose peace over hatred long ago and made way for change in oppressive empires. The Holy Spirit tells me the people of America are forgiving and they will forgive me for my wrongs of long ago, they will understand my wisdom and thus, you will have my very important information about the seeking of asylum for the great City of God and the message of the Christ. It is not that he needs permission, I am using the appropriate channels for the safety of all. I fear any place else in this world I might be killed for this message. I am about to become a ghost in this ghost writer's tale.

I, guilty of having slaves long ago and indulging in life's treasures. We were the magi, the highest order. This is why Christ was born into a lower-class family, similar to the days of Moses. The angels did not want wealth to influence their king in the matter of law. However, emergency plans came into action to deceive the reigning pharaoh. Vanity and wealth became the fall of countless souls.

You will soon recognize the hand of the universe is so very heavy. My sentence was long and hard even though I helped my spiritual son have victory. I'm the Lord of Mt. Sinai, fighter, and protector of the King of heaven. A one-time friend to the pharaoh and prince who were part of Moses family. We can all leave this world holding hands in peace singing "kumbya", or many are going to become organic fertilizer in this future *Body Farm*. Everything grows much better with a little decomposing flesh and guts. I say that with much love and respect for all. You will be recycled in more than one fashion.

Do not let the demons of this world hand you a sentence you might regret by putting so much emphasis on this life and the material world. Even though I saw my errors, I still have to pay for those mistakes. I saw the truth and began to help the less fortunate. To hold humans as slaves or oppress them is a crime that is serious. The Son of God is giving out lessons free of charge these days.

I have given you some very solid proof spiritual beings exist and can foresee many events. I have used the power of the magi to explain many things. This will be the last time in this season. In your world, you fight wars with weapons dangerous to our existence. In my world which is time infinite, I fight my enemies in a much unique way and time.

I swear by the heavens it is not going to be good if some other nation comes and tries to destroy our country. Our country is a humanitarian nation that adopts kids from poverty-stricken counties, protects wild life refuges, and heals the sick in third world countries. We aid in natural disaster and refugee crisis. We feed the world and hand out money to prop nations up or aid them in disaster. We will deal with the corruption as we are doing now. We will march the streets peacefully in the masses till we are heard. God help those that would like to strike them down, for they are your own people and they will cast judgment on you as martyrs in heaven.

Not everybody can be so holy as to cover their skin every minute of the day in public. As I have said "I will always respect this act, knowing what is holy and what is not. However, many in America would save a child from hunger or abuse, animals from being tortured and living in their own feces. We are a different breed than most. America was built on a different principle than devout devotion formed from ancient laws. We are enforcers of new law, the laws of Christ. Laws concerning sex with children, sex with animals, human trafficking, satanic worshiping, and sacrifices. Long ago many did not have control of their desires, monsters of society. Not even the hijab could save women from such deviates. When we look at America we have a high rate of deranged people. Societies that flourish attend to attract predators. It is easier to fit in, slip in unnoticed and perpetrate evil.

The world has changed, some for a greater good, some for much more deviate purposes. We have come a long way from the book of Enoch were giants devoured each other and drank the blood of their victims. Let us always remember are roots and the glory of holy spirit your master and teacher.

We are the elite, the first resurrection, here to challenge the ideologies of the great beasts of the earth. When we gather as one, are voice will be strong. Now that man knows who Jesus Christ is and they know his great city exists in the sky, the only fear they should have is selling their soul to a demon on the throne.

The final message of our son is this. When we pray, we say that Christ or God is a part of us. It is a little different than that. It is the pain and suffering that humans have endured and the lessons that have come through these sufferings that the Christ spirit has taken to the grave. His pain was to be equal to those who have suffered by men who came from the heavens. Jesus wanted to fulfill punishment for our fallen state and the fall of his Father. With that respect, Christ came to give the worst of the worst a final chance at eternal life rather than meet the angel of death. It is only because He knows how much you will suffer. If that is not love we will have to rewrite the definition. Many have died much worse deaths than the cross. To be rejected by your own people, have spit in your face, be whipped, and your mother and significant other crying while you bleed out roasting in the hot sun. Calling out to his father who could no longer help him when he set foot on the earth as a baby infant. That's heinous and ugly. He had no friends to be found with a good word. The devil was laughing within in his soul saying, "I told you they would reject you". Let us say it was a horrific death.

All teachings of Christ are the fruits of greater thought in women and men which have walked this earth and spoke against or experienced great injustices. Those thoughts have been preserved to determine law and punishment. All these things we experience are so that spiritual beings can aid us in our time of spiritual need and sorrows. That is how God and his elite are in every place, everywhere, all the time, by power of resurrection. This was the nature of our first death and resurrection. So, it is not Christ that is part of us, WE ARE A PART OF HIM. We are forever preserved in his spiritual conscious.

Those that would choose his way of life and serve others have attained eternal resurrection. This is why it has taken so long and so many walks in life to learn about humans. The spirit of Christ or Jesus was not human; however, it loves to walk among us and see that times have changed and the fruition of its work. When many think of Jesus with long flowing beautiful hair and clean white robes, you are only buying into deception. He was a homeless man who wandered around the Mediterranean with tremendous anguish in his soul.

His mother was rejected to give birth to him in an Inn because they were poor and unkempt and what people considered dirty. It was late November when Christ was born and it was some of the coldest weather the region had ever seen. What proof do I have, none, other than I know the birthdate of our child king. Jesus was born in freezing cold weather while animals and the Shepard's gathered around him and tried to keep him warm and alive. He cried out in the cold of the night, even a deadly winter could not stop this baby's cry. The Shepard's and Mary just kept praying for their little baby Jesus to live. These are the ones in whom I will love. They did not have gold and silver and precious oils, they had love in their heart and a promise of hope in their tiny little vulnerable messiah. Though they did not know the great glory of their king, so soon they will. He brings his reward with him, the great city of God. No child should ever go hungry or freeze to death because they are what some consider a lower class. Next time someone sees a mother and child hurting and they are of good character, please remember my teachings. I am sorry, when you treat people badly there is price to pay for snobby, snootiness. Jesus' mother was desperate and she was rejected just as Jesus. Let us remember that when we turn mothers away to go back to desperate conditions and slaughter.

Many will offer you their version of religion and science, it so filled with holes and gaps. I have come to give you the son Jesus Christ in the most open honest fashion that I possibly can. Never will it be or could it ever be replicated again. I am the *master's servant*

The Sheep and the Goats *Matthew 25:31-46* *"When the Son of Man comes in his glory, and all the angels with him, he will sit on his glorious throne. 32 All the nations will be gathered before him, and he will separate the people one from another as a shepherd separates the sheep from the goats. 33 He will put the sheep on his right and the goats on his left. 34 "Then the King will say to those on his right, "Come, you who are blessed by my Father; take your inheritance, the kingdom prepared for you since the creation of the world. 35 For I was hungry and you gave me something to eat, I was thirsty and you gave me something to drink, I was a stranger and you invited me in, 36 I needed clothes and you clothed me, I was sick and you looked after me, I was in prison and you came to visit me." 37 Then the righteous will answer him, "Lord, when did we see you hungry and feed you, or thirsty and give you something to drink? 38 When did we see you a stranger and invite you in, or needing clothes and clothe you? 39 When did we see you sick or in prison and go to visit you?" 40 The King will reply, "Truly I tell you, whatever you did for one of the least of these brothers and sisters of mine, you did for me." 41 Then he will say to those on his left, "Depart from me, you who are cursed, into the eternal fire prepared for the devil and his angels. 42 For I was hungry and you gave me nothing to eat, I was thirsty and you gave me nothing to drink, 43 I was a stranger and you did not invite me in, I needed clothes and you did not clothe me, I was sick and in prison and you did not look after me." 44 They also will answer, "Lord, when did we see you hungry or thirsty or a stranger or needing clothes or sick or in prison, and did not help you?" 45 He will reply, "Truly I tell you, whatever you did not do for one of the least of these, you did not do for me." 46 "Then they will go away to eternal punishment, but the righteous to eternal life."*

Closing out this book, I would like to talk about wild life. The day there are no birds in the sky and squirrels and little fuzzy animals running all over, that would kill me inside. The change at Sea World with the orca whales tells me humans are choosing a new path. Caging animals for our pleasure is very wrong unless they become wounded and need our aid. It is very displeasing to my soul. I applaud the writers and producers of *Blackfish* for bringing attention to this matter. I as well want to bring attention to the *Sea Sheppard* who tirelessly attempt to protect beautiful endangered whales which are still being hunted in modern times. I am sure it a very expensive venture. Know that by my acknowledging your purpose it has only just begun. It is weighed and measured as a very purposeful need on this earth. When God gives you eternity and the tools needed, many creatures we will save.

We must choose to live among these beautiful animals and creatures with a much softer approach. I am an animal lover and nothing gets to me more than the capture, caging, slaughtering of animals. Especially just for skins, tusks, aphrodisiacs, and such. I realize poverty is a factor in many cases in which people illegally hunt or capture animals. It is for financial reasons and food. When the Lord descends on our planet a new day will come for those who choose our mighty king. Even when the world is on the brink of a catastrophe, many will come to save as many creatures as possible. Why? Because it is the will of the highest.

I would much rather you be part of the City of God and preserve these animals than slaughter them into extinction. They tell me their pay is large for those who will be care takers and protectors of the future wildlife sanctuary that Jesus has claimed. We have come to realize animals are huge therapy for the sick, emotionally distressed, handicapped, and little children with deformities. The Lord has such a great purpose for all, if only if we could make it happen much quicker.

Veterinarians, doctors, therapists, dentists, are what the Lord has brought you forth as well as many others here on earth for a greater future cause. You are prisoners of a different kind. Caught up in the mix of fallen angels, I believe you will come to love to be part of the children of Christ and his creations. You will love your job as I have come to love mine. Wealth is not always coin and paper. What is pleasing to the Lord makes him want to do good things for the people of this earth.

This comes in many forms and fashions. It may come as a huge vessel descending from the sky with a massive medical facility searching for a qualified staff. A staff to fill its medical team and facilities before departure on a mission to preserve all human kind and its wild life. It may come in the form of being introduced to new planets, new medicines, and new way of life. A way of life where we serve out of love for life rather than financial paychecks. I see many doctors and nurses who work in third world countries as volunteers in time of epidemic or tragedies. What bravery to stand on those front lines.

This was the will of my father's fathers before they fell from great heights and so it will be. Remember, how we treat this kingdom and life on it is how God will place us in the next life. Know that is not easy to conquer evil in our world. If there were not innocent people among us, the world would be grinded into submission quickly. Therefore, my brothers and sisters, let us rejoice with the Lord and His son, Jesus long with the holy spirit as they are one. Let's embrace ourselves as we will never know the day when the return of Christ so that we can be with Him at peace forever. With that said, just know that...

Our journey to the new world awaits us!

OUTRO

In any great symphony or orchestra there is a climax or crescendo, even in a symphony of destruction. *Symphony of Destruction* is a popular song by a legendary heavy metal band called *Mega Death*. No matter what you think of heavy metal music, this song and its powerful lyrics strike to the core. Music is such a powerful tool to move masses, a battle of good and evil entirely itself. Some music soft and simple, some deep and very hard core. I feel the climax running through my veins like a freight train. <u>All the elements are coming together for the orchestrator to come and take his final bow.</u>

Sands of Time 1990

Like flightless birds stranded in the winter
Like the tears of snow white children
These are the sands of time

Its dark outside is anyone home?
I'll turn on the lights so you can see someone
Welcome to my spheres of sand and stone
Time is a dream, I've walked alone
Sands of the hour's glass, oh great children of the fall
Why must I repeat this, every time my son does call?

It's cold outside, is anyone home?
I'll turn out the light, Demons will fight
Just take a piece of your soul
Oh why, oh why must it be?
The riddles inside of you and me
When I found that time was more than fistfuls of treasure
The hell inside me was extinguished forever
Oh, son of God, you're more than just clever

Your love conquers worlds that soon last forever
Our walls in this prison became something much better
When your love was the law, so I preserved it forever
So, sit on my throne and watch from the sky
Your archangel has risen; I fight fire with fire

Purple House 1990

This is not a test, this is not a dream, this is reality
This is not a test, this is not a dream, this is not reality
This is not, this is not, this is not
When I wake up in the purple house, with walls of green
When the windows are smiling back at me, back at me,
I'm on fire, I'm on fire

Where the trees are made of yellow
And the insides are so hollow
You can hear the echoes of the leaves, leaves, leaves
Falling to the ground in a circular motion round
I wonder, I wonder, when it is going to happen to me
When I wake up in the purple house, with walls of green
Warsaw, I see you now, the Warsaw fires I see you now
I'm on fire, you're on fire, were all burning up
Burn it up, burn it all up
In the purple house with walls of green

When will I wake up, when you wake up?
When will I wake up, when you wake up?
When I wake up in the purple house with walls of green
I'm on fire, I'm on fire

Opium Winter 1992

I'll be the fires that turns flesh into ashes
While you steal the thoughts of the sleeping masses
We'll keep all our slaves in the fields of the thought factory
In opium winter, there is blood on the seed
All tied up and wired are their social classes
So that the thought rarely passes
All those standing in line for the great milk machine
In opium winter, there is blood on the seed

Eruption 2014

I'm like a volcanic eruption, I live in conjunction
I shake with the world that's my primary function
So, let me do something, rather than nothing
I'll tell you the tale of rail roads and junctions
Yes. I said something, spoke the son from a cloud

There's big ones and little ones and some in between
I'm not talking about that girl, it's about prophesy
When it slides between her legs, the land, and the sea
She'll climax so good, then start to scream
My hands on your ocean, yes, I hear her BODY breathe
I'm going down deep into your sea
I'm caught in the waves of explosion and ecstasy

I'm not talking about that girl, it's about a prophesy
So, fall to your knees and do what you please
I think I feel weak when you start to tease

I'm like a volcanic eruption, I live in conjunction
I'll rock your world, it's my primary function

So, let me do something, rather than nothing
I'll tell you the tale of rail roads and junctions
Yes. I said something, spoke my son from a cloud

Is it Love (?) 2014

I fight for a dream my father had
I fight for the children that never have
I laugh at the rain she's my friend
I dance in the sky like the winds

I ask for forgiveness everyday
For time and its mistakes
I ask for a leader who can tame the lands
Who will show great mercy to the common man!
I sing of earth the beast and trees
I sing of angels and their heavenly decrees
I laugh with family when times are tuff
Tell me father is it love?

I dance in stars with heavenly hosts
I fly by wings coast to coast
You see I have family and they are mine
Couldn't ever leave them if I tried
Every day I try to walk away
Wings come running to heal my pain

Tell me father is it love
All I see under the sun?
I asked your name and you replied
"A soul as you, trapped in time"
I bowed before, "rise" you said
I have raised you up from the dead

Your eyes shall see
Your chains will break
Your heart will grow
Toward time and space
Until at last we are one
We had a dream and yes, its love

Darkness to nowhere-Lord of Flies 2017

Listen to the tale few live to tell
Tales of strange powers in place called hell
Down in the molten pits far down below
Yellow eyes sink deep into the flesh of this world
I smell it in the streets, I see it everywhere
Faces oh so empty, it's rude so don't you stare
The power grows hungry, Darkness to nowhere

When the seventh winter comes to pass
He'll meet you down by the old railroad tracks
Bring your pleasure, your treasures and material trash

He's foul as the blood of old nicks goat
He's the Lord of the flies, he's knows what you don't
He'll prey on your fears, he'll prey on your soul
Is it power or our weakness, for whom the bell tolls?

He'll keep you all so busy killing each other off
All in the name of your money, dope, religion, and God
So, my greedy little pigs sleep well tonight
When tomorrow comes, he'll feed your belly heart to the flies

Count Down Zero 2017

Will you drop bombs on my ghettos just like Aleppo?
Creatures of heaven hear a stir in their echo
Their certainly sad in the lands of the gecko!
They wanted to say "halo", so I said "hello"!
Now I feel so alone, they want to get me back to my home

Seems like a thousand years gone by
I watched the calendar of the sky
Did you ever wonder why?
Dragon hunters are born to die!
I'm the Suicide knight dressed in white
Robes dipped in blood, I'm ready to fight
So, let me get a shout out, for me and the crew
Slaying the dragon in your red, white, and blue

Will you drop bombs on our ghettos just like Aleppo?
While women are sleeping with babies and children
They wanted to say "halo", so I said "hello"!
We will bring your wings on "countdown zero"

Oil and War 2017

They tell me a man can't profit the soul
Until he lay down his heart and cry to the Lord
They tell me a man will prophet no more
When he cherishes the things like oil and war

Moses on mountain, Elijah with wings
Jesus of Nazareth, John followed him
Moses and pharaoh, prophets with dreams

They cried for the glory of the son and their king
Oh yeah, oh yeah

They tell me a man can't prophet the soul
Unless he lay down his life and cry to the Lord
They tell me a man will prophet no more
When they cherish the things like diamonds and gold
Moses on mountain, Elijah with wings
Jesus of Nazareth, John followed him
Moses and pharaoh, prophets with dreams
They cried for the glory of the son and their king
Oh yeah, oh yeah

Jesus, I love you, Jesus I love you!
Jesus, I love you more than this life
Take me on wings, let's burn out the night
Jesus, I love you,
take me far from this life
Take me away so high in the sky
Oh yeah, oh yeah!
<u>I AM THE ALPHA and OMEGA</u>
<u>THE BEGGINING and THE END</u>

"Hunger knows no fear of time, hunger eats itself alive,
death in the candy store."

Printed in the United States
By Bookmasters